THE TOPIC OF CANCER

THE TOPIC OF CANCER
New Perspectives on the
Emotional Experience of Cancer

Edited by
Jonathan Burke

Foreword by Brett Kahr

KARNAC

First published in 2013 by
Karnac Books Ltd
118 Finchley Road
London NW3 5HT

British Library Cataloguing in Publication Data

A C.I.P. for this book is available from the British Library

ISBN-13: 978-1-78049-113-4

Typeset by V Publishing Solutions Pvt Ltd., Chennai, India

Printed in Great Britain

www.karnacbooks.com

To all whose lives are touched by cancer

Gracious words are a honeycomb,
sweet to the soul and healing to the bones.

—Proverbs 16:24

CONTENTS

ACKNOWLEDGEMENTS

I owe a huge debt of gratitude to colleagues and friends who inspired and encouraged the "Topic of Cancer" series of talks that has led to this publication.

To Sally Griffin, fellow of the London Centre for Psychotherapy (now part of a new organisation: the British Psychotherapy Foundation), whose guidance and enriching advice helped bring not only the series but this book into being, I owe a very special thanks.

I would also like to record my gratitude to Rachel Adema and Helen Zane for their steadfast support of the "Topic of Cancer" project and for their insights and suggestions as the book took shape.

Thanks are due also to the following:

Carcanet Press for permission to reproduce "The Broken Bowl" by James Merrill;

Shoestring Press for permission to reproduce "Missing Things" by Vernon Scannell;

Bloodaxe Press for permission to reproduce poems from *Stitching the Dark: New & Selected Poems* (2005) by Carole Satyamurti;

HarperCollins Publishers and Jonathan Cape Publishers for permission to reproduce "Beach Roses" by Mark Doty.

The response received to the "Topic of Cancer" initiative has been generous, profound, and creative and for this I am deeply grateful to all the contributors.

The series would not have come into being without the help of Dorothy Judd, Anne Lanceley, and Martin Schmidt who stood by the project, nurturing its development from its inception, and for this I am extremely grateful.

That leaves me to express above all my sincere thanks to all the patients and families referred to anonymously in the pages that follow who allowed their own stories to be shared.

ABOUT THE EDITOR AND CONTRIBUTORS

Jonathan Burke first trained in social work and health care, and later became a health planning consultant to UK hospitals and ministries of health abroad. Author of the *Enfield Cancer Directory*, funded by Macmillan Cancer Relief (now Macmillan Cancer Support), he managed the *CancerLIFE Project* at Enfield Disability Action before training as a psychoanalytic psychotherapist. He has facilitated a range of seminars on cancer-related issues, most recently helping develop the *Topic of Cancer* Seminar Series at the London Centre for Psychotherapy (now part of a new organisation: the British Psychotherapy Foundation). He now works as a psychotherapist in private practice.

Jane Eades is a clinical nurse specialist and manager of the day therapy unit at the Marie Curie Hospice, Hampstead. She has extensive experience working in nurse-led outpatient clinics, day therapy and in-patient specialist palliative care services. She recently served as the project lead when her unit was accepted as one of the test communities for the NHS Cancer Survivorship Initiative.

Jane Elfer started her working life as a social worker in a child and adolescent mental health services team and then in fostering and adoption where her interest in psychotherapy began. She trained as a counsellor and worked with the National Society for the Prevention of Cruelty to Children in their child protection team. She trained at the Tavistock Clinic and now works at University College London Hospital as a principal child and adolescent psychotherapist. She is currently studying for her clinical doctorate, researching the emotional impact on sibling bone marrow donors.

Faye Gishen is a Consultant Physician in Palliative Medicine at the Marie Curie Hospice, Hampstead. She is an Honorary Senior Lecturer at University College London Medical School, where she leads for one of the vertical spines in the undergraduate course. Her areas of interest include cancer survivorship and rehabilitation, self-care for medical professionals, and medical education. She has introduced into her unit regular clinical supervision for the multi-professional team, and is a trained coach and mentor. She has spoken at local and national conferences on cancer survivorship.

Dorothy Judd first trained as an art therapist, then, at the Tavistock Clinic, as a child and adolescent psychotherapist, and later as an adult psychotherapist and marital psychotherapist. She was principal child psychotherapist at University College Hospital and Middlesex Hospital, on the adolescent oncology unit and the paediatric ward. She is the author of *Give Sorrow Words: Working with a Dying Child* and, with Aleda Erskine, co-edited *The Imaginative Body: Psychodynamic Approaches to Health Care*. She has written chapters and papers over a number of years on working with children with physical disability, and illness including terminal illness. She has worked at the Tavistock Marital Studies Institute, and taught infant observation on various courses, including in Dublin. She was a psychotherapist for fifteen years at University College School, London, and is in private practice.

Anne Karpf is a writer, sociologist, and award-winning journalist. For seven years she was radio critic of *The Guardian*, where more recently she wrote a column on the family. She writes regularly on social, political, and cultural issues for *The Guardian* and the *Independent on Sunday* among other publications, and broadcasts regularly for BBC Radio 3 and Radio 4. She is the author of three books, including *Doctoring The*

Media: The Reporting of Health And Medicine (Routledge) and *The War After: Living With the Holocaust* (Faber Finds); and co-edited *A Time to Speak Out: Independent Jewish Voices on Israel, Zionism and Jewish Identity* (Verso). She is reader in professional writing and cultural inquiry at London Metropolitan University.

Anne Lanceley is Senior Lecturer in Women's Cancer at University College London's Elizabeth Garrett Anderson Institute for Women's Health. Anne undertook her nurse training at St. Bartholomew's and the Royal Marsden Hospitals, London. Her research and academic training includes degrees in English Literature and Research, and a PhD in Nursing from King's College, University of London. Anne currently combines the roles of Honorary Clinical Nurse Specialist at University College London Hospital and clinical supervisor with research leadership in the Department of Women's Cancer at University College London. Anne leads a research programme in symptom management, recovery after treatment, quality of life and innovative psychological therapies—their implementation and evaluation in the clinical setting.

Anthony Lee was formerly a senior research fellow in the field of developmental psychopathology, during which time he obtained his PhD at University College London. He undertook his clinical training at the Tavistock Clinic. He is now a consultant child and adolescent psychotherapist and lead of the child psychotherapy discipline at University College London Hospital. He is also a senior research fellow and founding member of the Observational and Psycho-Analytic Studies of the Child: Family, community, educational and clinical settings (OΨ-ASC) at the University of Geneva.

Judy Parkinson trained in general, intensive care, and mental health nursing, before she trained as a psychodynamic counsellor and psychoanalytic psychotherapist at Westminster Pastoral Foundation (WPF), where she later worked for the Seriously Physically Ill Counselling Service. For ten years she served part-time as a clinical nurse specialist in psychological care at the Royal Marsden Hospital. Judy works in private practice and is a supervisor to trainee psychotherapists at WPF and to trained volunteers at Sutton Counselling, Surrey. She has also developed a particular interest in working with people who want to talk about spirituality and faith as part of their work in therapy.

Carole Satyamurti is a poet, and a sociologist with a particular interest in psychoanalytic ideas and the application of these ideas to an understanding of social processes and to the stories that people tell about themselves. She contributed to, and co-edited with Hamish Canham, *Acquainted with the Night: Psychoanalysis and the Poetic Imagination*, a collection of essays on the connections between poetry and psychoanalysis. She has taught at the Tavistock Clinic, and at the University of East London, on a variety of MA and PhD programmes. An award-winning poet, Carole has published several volumes of poetry, with Oxford University Press and Bloodaxe Books, and is currently working on a verse version of the Indian epic, the *Mahabharata*.

Martin Schmidt is a Jungian analyst, psychologist, and professional member of the Society of Analytical Psychology in private practice in London. He lectures widely both in the UK and abroad. His paper *'Psychic skin: psychotic defences, borderline process and delusions'* in the Journal of Analytical Psychology won the Fordham prize for best clinical paper of 2012 and has also been shortlisted for the Gradiva Award in New York in October 2013 by the National Association for the Advancement of Psychoanalysis. He was, for seven years, a visiting supervisor/lecturer for the International Association of Analytical Psychology (IAAP) in Russia and is currently the IAAP liaison for Serbia.

Adrian Tookman is a Consultant Physician in Palliative Medicine. He is Medical Director of the Marie Curie Hospice, Hampstead and Clinical Director for Marie Curie Cancer Care. He has recently held previous positions in senior clinical management at the Royal Free London NHS Foundation Trust that include Medical Director and trust lead for cancer and public health. He is an Honorary Senior Lecturer, University College Medical School, and Clinical Advisor to the Marie Curie Palliative Care Research Unit, University College London. He has a large palliative care practice and specialist interests in rehabilitation in palliative care, survivorship and long-term use of opioids in chronic pain.

Robert Twycross, Emeritus Clinical Reader in Palliative Medicine, Oxford University, is one of the founders of modern palliative medicine. In the early 1970s he worked with Cicely Saunders at St. Christopher's Hospice in London as research fellow in therapeutics. He was then appointed consultant in palliative medicine at Sir Michael Sobell House in Oxford, subsequently becoming Macmillan clinical reader in palliative medicine at Oxford University. He retired as a clinician eleven years ago, but continues to contribute as co-editor-in-chief of the Palliative Care Formulary. He has received numerous lifetime achievement awards from organisations across the world, and has written nearly 300 articles, chapters, and editorials, and also several highly regarded textbooks.

Jonathan Wittenberg is rabbi of the New North London Synagogue and senior rabbi of the Masorti Movement which fosters traditional, non-fundamentalist Judaism. Author of *The Three Pillars of Judaism*, *The Eternal Journey: Meditations on the Jewish Year*, and most recently, *The Silence of Dark Water: An Inner Journey*, Rabbi Wittenberg is a sought-after speaker and an advocate of interfaith dialogue. Joining with Christian and Muslim religious leaders he strives to promote understanding and co-operation between different faiths. Rabbi Wittenberg has worked in multi-faith hospital and hospice settings. He writes and broadcasts about the Jewish faith, moral issues, his love of nature, the spiritual search, human responsibility, and the transience of life.

John Woods is a principal psychotherapist at the Tavistock and Portman NHS Trust. He is also in private practice working with both children and adults and runs workshops and training events. He is the author of *The End of Abuse: A Playreading in Three Parts* (2004), *Boys who have Abused: Psychoanalytic Psychotherapy with Victims/Perpetrators of Sexual Abuse* (2003), *Compromise: A Play About Psychotherapy* (2007) and, with Andrew Williams, is the editor of *Forensic Group Psychotherapy: The Portman Clinic Approach*.

FOREWORD

"If you could hear, at every jolt, the blood
Come gargling from the froth-corrupted lungs,
Obscene as cancer, bitter as the cud"

—Wilfred Owen, *Dulce et Decorum Est*
(Written between October 1917 and March 1918)

I do not generally take notes on dinner parties. But after one particularly memorable and troubling supper, more than thirty years ago, I seem to have done so.

Dr. X, a distinguished psychologist, and one of my former teachers in the mental health field, rang me with the sad news that he had developed a malignant tumour in one of his vital organs, and then explained that he would have to undergo an immediate surgical procedure. An elderly widower whose children lived overseas, Dr. X had invited me and three other former students to spend the evening with him prior to his operation. No doubt he wanted some company, but in view of the fact that he had requested that his one-time students should come for what could be a "last supper", I suspected that he also hoped that we would be able to carry on his work and edit his papers for publication should he die on the operating table. Dr. X, a talented chef in his own right, instructed me to come for what he hoped would be a "happy meal", and he underscored that under no circumstances must we talk about cancer. In view of his impending ordeal, he wanted this dinner party to be completely pleasant.

As I had to see a patient at 6.30 p.m., I arrived at Dr. X's house some-what later than the other former students—all of whom I knew—two of whom had trained in psychiatry, and one in psychoanalysis. By the time I sat down on Dr. X's sofa, the assembled company had already become deeply embroiled in a very spirited discussion about the theatre.

Although we all immersed ourselves in a most interesting chat about the plays in London that season, I found myself quite disturbed by our dialogue; and after the dinner party had ended, I returned to my home, and recorded what I could remember in a diary, which I only recently rediscovered. Hence, I can report the actual dialogue as I had recalled it, practically verbatim, on the night of the supper:

PSYCHIATRIST 1:   "Did you see the new Tom Stoppard play? It was bloody brilliant, but it closed before its time".

PSYCHOANALYST: "Yeah, it's those bloody critics. They can really put a stop to a show if they want to with all their power. It's their own murderousness, and they project it outwards, onto the author of the play".

DR. X: "Yes, and the actors project all of their own power into the critics. The critics really can cut things short. But if the critic is good, you know, then that's a different story. Take Kenneth Tynan, for instance. He said some bloody brilliant things; and when he gave a good review, a play could run and run forever. I hope I can find the time to read his essays".

PSYCHIATRIST 2:   "Yes, Tynan wrote some great *obituaries* … I mean, he wrote some great reviews, didn't he?"

Perhaps having arrived late, fresh from my consulting room, I still had my psychotherapeutic ears primed to listen for unconscious communication; and not having participated in the dinner party musings from the outset, I could perhaps hear it from a somewhat different stance. Although superficially a conversation about theatre, I knew that we had really orchestrated an unconscious conversation about death and cancer, with frequent references to the word "bloody", and with comments about critics having all the power to cut the run of a play short, rather like an incompetent surgeon, or, indeed, cancer itself. And of course, the shocking parapraxis (slip of the tongue) of the young psychiatrist, substituting the word "obituaries" for "reviews" crowned the evening in an all too chilling way. Would one of us soon be writing an obituary notice for our beloved teacher?

Of course, Dr. X had put us all in a difficult position by having told us beforehand that we must not speak about cancer or death. After all, he had hoped that we would have a "happy" dinner. Nevertheless, in spite of Dr. X's injunction, the spectre of cancer infiltrated even a seemingly innocent supper party discussion about the theatre.

The two psychiatrists and the psychoanalyst have all progressed to distinguished careers in mental health, and Dr. X, who did survive the surgery, managed to produce several more books before he died. But even these highly experienced and well-trained people could not bear to face the agonising realities of cancer—at least not easily. Perhaps I did no better. But after I had arrived back at my home following the dinner party, I jotted down these chilling fragments of the conversation, wondering, "If five mental health professionals cannot manage to have a straightforward conversation about cancer and about the fear of dying, what chance does the rest of the population have?"

In the decades which have followed, we have all become more adept at speaking about cancer and in thinking about cancer, whether we come from the world of psychotherapy, or whether we have had no mental health training whatsoever. As one in three of us will succumb to cancer nowadays, we have no choice but to grapple with its cruel complexities.

Fortunately, the authors in Jonathan Burke's truly outstanding and moving book have managed to speak about cancer in a direct, compassionate, non-defensive, and non-catastrophising way; and thus, have managed infinitely better than my young colleagues and I had done at that dinner party of long ago. An experienced clinician who has worked in the psycho-oncological field for many years, Jonathan Burke, along with psychotherapeutic colleague Sally Griffin, had organised a highly successful lecture series in 2011 on psychotherapy and cancer, sponsored by the London Centre for Psychotherapy, now part of the British Psychotherapy Foundation. Happily, Burke managed to persuade the contributors to write up their talks in chapter form so that those of us not fortunate enough to have attended the original presentations can now share in this rich, moving, and edifying experience.

In order to help readers to understand the emotional needs of the cancer patient and his or her family in greater depth, Burke has assembled a dream team of expert contributors from a multitude of backgrounds, ranging from art therapy, marital psychotherapy, child and adolescent psychotherapy, psychiatric nursing, Jungian analysis, adult psychotherapy, counselling, and social work; to general medical practice, oncology, palliative care; as well as poetry, playwriting, broadcasting, and the rabbinate. Perhaps we really do need to have a veritable village of professionals on call who can provide a broad diversity of perspectives, forming a sturdy team to help tackle that which often cannot be tackled.

In thinking about the interface between psychotherapy and cancer, none of the authors offers magical solutions or quick fixes. Most of the writers present their work in a slow and careful manner, sharing in clearly written detail how they interact with cancer patients, how they speak with cancer patients, and above all, how they care for cancer patients as people with unique lives, profound histories, and varying levels of ego strength and family support. Most of the authors do not practise a special technique of psychological intervention; most work in a classical psychotherapeutic mode, engaged in the art of ordinary psychotherapy, or what I have sometimes come to think of as "advanced conversation", helping patients to unburden themselves, to share their fears, to put their oppressive secrets into words, and to enjoy the relief that someone else has agreed to accompany them on this journey. Dr. Dorothy Judd, a psychotherapist who worked for many years on paediatric oncology wards, has written in her chapter that the clinician endeavours to provide "conversations" or "journeys" for the patient, "which do not have a strict agenda", but which could, nevertheless, produce "surprising rewards". Dr. Judd's chapter, and those of her fellow contributors, offer beautiful, privileged glimpses into some of these private conversations and journeys between patients and their professional caretakers.

The chapter writers describe themselves, variously, as "impotent", "overwhelmed", or full of "inadequacy", in their efforts to help patients with cancer. One can certainly understand why, because, as child psychotherapists Dr. Anthony Lee and Ms. Jane Elfer have observed, cancer can turn our world "upside down", transforming a life of "certainty and order" into one of "uncertainty and disorder". And yet, in spite of the enormity of the challenge, these sturdy and sensitive specialists have found ways of helping their patients to feel less isolated in what may be their final struggles, often facilitating patients to create a new sense of how they might think about their lives. As the pioneering palliative care physician Dr. Robert Twycross has observed sagely in his contribution, professionals can definitely help to improve the quality of a cancer patient's life, if not the quantity.

Shortly before I began to write this brief "Foreword", I received a telephone call informing me that one of my own psychotherapy patients—a person who had suffered from a metastasising cancer of the kidneys, liver, and lungs—had just entered a hospice. All attempts at chemotherapy and radiotherapy had proved unsuccessful, and the patient now needed deeply specialised medical and nursing coverage during this final stage. The patient had asked to see me in order to say goodbye, and of course, I went to the hospice for what I knew would be, in all likelihood, our final visit.

The prospect of seeing my patient hooked up to a morphine drip and looking skeletal from massive weight loss filled me with profound sadness. But having only recently finished reading the moving chapters in Jonathan Burke's expertly edited book, I knew that many other professional colleagues had had far more challenging experiences over far longer periods of time; and I experienced great comfort in knowing that cancer can be engaged with, however painful it may be for the person who might be dying, and for those who will survive.

As I walked into the serenely calm hospice, the nursing staff greeted me in a warm and friendly fashion, speaking in quiet and soothing tones, mindful that not only will the patients need a peaceful ambience, but so too will their visitors. Sadly, by the time I had arrived, the patient had lapsed into a coma, but the nurse in charge felt quite certain that my patient might still be able to hear me. And so, I sat at the bedside, and spoke some final words.

This patient had come to psychotherapy rather late in the day—only six months previously—and yet, during this time, we had managed to review the patient's life, and, I believe, to put some family ghosts to rest. The patient harboured, however, a fantasy that the psychotherapy might cure the cancer, in spite of the fact that the most sophisticated oncological treatments had not done so. I tried—being both frank, but also diplomatic—to question this idea, but the patient, desperate to live, clung to the hope that through free association and through verbalisation of deep-seated anger, the cancer might, perhaps, disappear. Certainly, I respected my patient's defences and resistances, ever aware that in similar circumstances, I might cling to exactly the same wish.

Although the case histories, clinical vignettes, and examples of professional work described in these chapters often bring tears to one's eyes, they also provide a great sense of relief to the reader. With deep sincerity and, dare I suggest, with true love for the people with whom they work, the contributors to this book have provided a roadmap for psychological survival in the face of what might often feel like the most horrible and never-ending of mental torments. As a reader and as a learner, one feels fortified and much less isolated in one's own attempt to deal with cancer in one's patients, in one's family members, and perhaps, one day, in oneself.

The Topic of Cancer: New Perspectives on the Emotional Experience of Cancer deserves a crucial place not on our bookshelves, but rather, more immediately, on our bedside tables. The editor and authors have created a tome designed for use and enlightenment, and not simply for storage alongside our other unread books. I thank Jonathan Burke and his comrades for having produced a truly seminal and memorable work which might help us all learn how to have more honest, more meaningful, and more therapeutic conversations about one of the greatest scourges of humanity.

Professor Brett Kahr

PREFACE

I have always been fascinated by the senses, by instinct, and the expressions we use in everyday life to recapture our sensual or instinctual experience: "He has an eye for this", "It feels to me", "You could smell her fear", "I could taste his displeasure", "the mind's eye". For me the most alive memory of my parents is the memory of their smell: the box of scented handkerchiefs that lay on my mother's bedside table, the smell of my father's pipe that he was always at odds to clean.

I became interested in cancer for no intellectual reason but because of a sense—a sense that I have known it all my life. It was always around, akin to the "unthought known" of which psychoanalyst Christopher Bollas speaks: I instinctively knew I was acquainted with this grim stranger.

So when three years ago the topic of cancer came up in conversation with my colleague Sally Griffin at the London Centre for Psychotherapy (now part of a new organisation: the British Psychotherapy Foundation), I immediately agreed to help "organise something", the exact contents of which I was as yet unsure. It should be straightforward enough, or so I thought at the time. I had, after all, been involved, already, before my psychotherapy career began, in setting up and, for some seven years, running a self-help project for people living with cancer, their families and friends.

Before long, however, I began to feel that on this occasion "the topic" was anything but straightforward. Asking colleagues and friends for their inputs brought an unusual mix of responses—sincere, modest, curious yet at the same time reluctant: "I really don't know very much about this", "I don't have a great deal of experience in this area", "Sounds interesting—quite an undertaking. I wish you luck!" Carrying around this strange bag called "cancer", I was beginning to feel like the worthy enough suitor whom everyone knew but no one wished to embrace.

Finally, a paper entitled "Psychoanalytic therapy with cancer patients: Some speculations" by Harold Searles (In J. G. Goldberg (Ed.) (1981). *Psychotherapeutic Treatment of Cancer Patients*, pp. 163–177) brought home the problem. Searles, arguably one of the most original and gifted psychoanalytic thinkers of his day, begins by talking about his immediate reaction to the invitation he had received in 1978 to write his paper:

> My initial naïve response to the invitation … was based less on any realistic lack of relevancy of this subject in my life and work than upon my unconscious reaction to it as being all too relevant. In addition to my attempt to maintain under repression my long-time fear of death from cancer, there are additional determinants of my denial-based, subjective naïveté …

As for me, the very word "cancer" had been absent in my childhood, while "malignant" or "benign", spoken in hushed tones, were simply beyond my ken. By the time I had reached my twenties, with some close family members having already died of cancer and my mother also facing a life-depleting illness, I had somehow managed unconsciously to repress my own feelings of fear by defensively converting them into an omnipotent phantasy that I could somehow stand above them. Was my instinctual desire some fifteen years ago to take on the optimistically coined *CancerLIFE* project reflective of an Oedipal desire to join the adults in their "conspiracy" around talking about cancer or was I determined to overcome my fear; or were there other unconscious motivations? In agreeing now to help organise what emerged as the "Topic of Cancer" seminar series, was I really getting any closer to the subject or, with an unconscious sleight-of-hand, was I still remaining at one remove from it?

In the early months of planning the series, it was becoming increasingly clear that I was not alone in my experience. For so many of my contemporaries, including those of us engaged in the *talking cure*, silence around cancer had been the norm in their formative years. As for today, with family and friends directly struck by the disease, the very issue of such a series was decidedly charged. At the same time, the very fact of its increasing universality both as a disease and as the subject of our defences surely pointed to the need to explore and reflect on the emotional experience of cancer.

With this in mind, and after having met with colleagues, some of whom were in remission from their cancer and others whose partners were experiencing a relapse, it was decided to approach the topic of cancer from a variety of perspectives, starting with medical and moving to psychoanalytic and creative—with the overall focus to lie in our experience of the person with cancer, their conscious anxieties and unconscious phantasies.

The starting point: the "Topic of Cancer" seminars

A panel of general practitioners from London: Dr. Robin Cartwright, Dr. Jackie Ketley, and Dr. Eleanor Hitchman—each at a different stage of their careers and one with experience of her own cancer, were invited to start the "Topic of Cancer" series. Referring to their primary role in teasing out from a range of presenting symptoms those requiring further investigation, these family doctors spoke sensitively about the care needed to investigate without, to the extent possible, causing undue anxiety.

Of their encounters with couples in which a partner has been diagnosed with cancer, the GPs remarked on how, at times, each appears to hear totally different things from the same encounter. In an unconscious sharing and containing of emotional burdens "one partner seemed to be holding hope, while the other, despair".

Of emotions often held in abeyance by patients protective of themselves and those close to them, our family doctors reflected on the struggle commonly experienced once cancer treatment has ended—an inner conflict expressed so powerfully by one patient who said: "Do I really want to tell my husband or my children that I really feel rubbish when everyone is expecting me to feel brilliant because I've survived? In fact, I've been through the mill!" The persistent sense of being alone with one's cancer and one's treatments no matter how successful, of being uprooted from everyday life and thrown into a different world, very much formed the backdrop to the seminars that followed, as they do to the chapters ahead.

The importance and the challenges of a relationship, this time of patient and oncologist, were the subjects of the second seminar: "An Oncologist's Perspective". After offering an overview of today's increasingly complex treatments, the range of medical skills required, and the consequent need for a multi-disciplinary approach to care, Dr. Anna Cassoni, consultant clinical oncologist at University College London Hospital, moved on to consider this crucial relationship.

She stressed the advanced communications skills required of oncologists if they are to gain the trust of patients facing uncertainty; and the importance of allowing patients an outlet to express often unbearable feelings, whilst offering themselves as oncologists to become, at times, the objects of their patients' fury.

The series then moved from a consideration of the medical to thinking in greater depth about the affects of cancer, how shocking and bewildering the experience of cancer is, and how small and vulnerable we all can feel when confronted by it.

Some of the seminars lent themselves to adaptation into chapters for this book, such as Dr. Robert Twycross' consideration of the growth of the palliative care movement and its importance in developing a focus on the patients' and their families' emotional and practical experience of living out life with cancer; and Dorothy Judd's presentation of her clinical work with cancer sufferers. This included consideration of, amongst other things, how the patient and the therapist manage hope alongside anxiety.

Further seminars in the series were in the form of conversations, such as that between psychotherapists John Woods and Helen Bender on the "Psychotherapist with Cancer". Here a variety of issues were explored including ethical questions around what, if anything, to tell patients, how the therapist's clinical practice is going to be affected by their cancer diagnosis, and considerations around the therapist taking on any new commitments. Some months after the seminars ended John revisited the issue of what a cancer may reveal and wrote about one of his experiences that came in the wake of his own diagnosis (Chapter Four).

A panel discussion entitled "On Being with People with Cancer" brought together psychotherapists Mary Pat Campbell, Praxoulla Charalambous, Florangel Lambor, Macmillan oncology counsellor Caroline Armstrong, and Dr. Anne Lanceley from the University College London Institute for Women's Health in a conversation led by Jungian analyst, Martin Schmidt. Both Martin and Anne agreed to contribute chapters to the book which was by this time beginning to form in our minds.

Themes of isolation and powerlessness arose repeatedly in the seminars, feelings experienced both by the patient and their carers, be they family members, doctors, specialist nurses, counsellors or therapists. One patient was quoted as saying that she needed "to align herself with those people she felt carried life inside them and were not tainted by death".

But how are psychotherapists and fellow professionals to serve as "carriers of life" when, in the face of cancer, we all feel so impotent? Our audiences contributed very actively in furthering and deepening an understanding of this dilemma. There was evident relief that a topic which demanded attention was now receiving it. Florangel Lambor, a psychotherapist whose husband had died of cancer, described struggling with the impact of having a patient with cancer. She remarked on how unsettled she had felt from the moment her patient told her about her tumour:

> I felt very anxious in the sessions, I couldn't think clearly, I felt unable to be with her. I started to feel very angry but not understanding why, only sure that it was not against her, until in one session a thought came to my mind: "She's receiving something that my husband didn't have when he had cancer".

Drawing on analytic supervision and personal analysis allowed Florangel to reflect further on this, ultimately enabling her to work with her patient and "accompany her on her journey" without feeling herself powerless.

The seminar series was brought to a conclusion by the poet and sociologist Carole Satyamurti, who focused first on what psychoanalysis has to offer to an understanding of the creative process and then on issues that arise when trying to give expression to the experience of having cancer: how, and why, one might turn to poetry as a suitable container for this experience.

Indeed, for the author and psychotherapist Bernardine Bishop (interviewed on the BBC's *The Culture Show* (episode twenty-four) about her new novel *Unexpected Lessons in Love*) the relationship with her creative self had provided an imaginary "friend" needed to lift her out of the depths of despair when facing her own terminal cancer. Though few of us are poets or novelists, Carole's poetry, Bernadine's novel, and similar works all bear testimony to the containing and potentially sustaining power of engagement with the creative in ourselves.

Looking back over the series, I was left with many impressions and a range of questions, perhaps foremost of which being: Why now? Why has cancer, so long the "whispered" disease, become the stuff of daily discourse? No doubt the internet era and advances in scientific research, including the rapidly growing field of cancer genomics, where mutations in the so-called "cancer genes" are being mapped, have today sparked not only interest but, without doubt, a degree of hope.

In an eloquent and incisive summary of the nature of cancer and the complexities of developing treatments, Professor Michael Stratton, Director of the Wellcome Trust Sanger Institute, has spoken of a "constant *wrestling match* between the scientists who are continually trying to find ways to kill the cancer and a cancer which is continually trying to evolve itself in resistance to those new drugs" (*Frontiers*, BBC Radio 4, 5 December 2012).

Meanwhile, a related but clearly very different struggle continues for patients today working internally to protect and continue to develop their sense of personhood in the face of a cancer diagnosis. Participation in the seminar series and the desire of professionals in and outside the psychotherapy world to contribute to the "The Topic of Cancer" book attests to the enormous interest in looking at this pernicious disease and the emotional impact that it continues to have on us all.

Jonathan Burke

INTRODUCTION

Jonathan Burke

The Topic of Cancer focuses on our emotional responses to cancer, the disease that physician, researcher, and writer, Siddhartha Mukherjee, citing a nineteenth century surgeon, called "the emperor of all maladies".

The Topic of Cancer is divided into two parts broadly titled "Bearing the Unbearable" and "Containment and Creativity".

A subject that so many of us may want never to have to consider, the prevalence of cancer locates it never far from our conscious awareness. This book aims to open the topic up for reflection by offering a range of perspectives on cancer: psychoanalytic, medical, spiritual/religious, and literary.

Psychoanalytic publications traditionally introduce their theme by referring back to the works of Freud in much the same way as we might draw on the inspiration of our parents or the sayings of our ancestors. *The Topic of Cancer* being largely, albeit not entirely, a psychoanalytic publication, also begins by drawing on Freud, but from a different, deeply personal perspective: a Freud we barely know.

In the opening chapter, "Freud's cancer", Martin Schmidt shows us Freud not only as a pioneer possessed of extraordinary, original thought and imagination but also as a man dogged by anxieties and fears, preoccupied with thoughts of his own death. The Oedipal drama of Freud's own life is sensitively followed, his experience of friends with cancer examined, and then the almost unbearable news of his daughter Sophie, his "Sunday child", dying of pneumonia, age twenty-six.

It is in the light of these and other personal losses, and against the political backdrop of the rise of Nazism and the invasion of Austria, that Freud's experience of his own cancer is explored. His extraordinary output of path-breaking, creative ideas during years of turbulence in both his external world and internal life are reflected upon. The context in which Freud's seminal work *The Ego and the Id*, was first published (1923 being the year his cancer was discovered) is considered, as are so many other of his writings including, ultimately, *Moses and Monotheism* in which Freud applies the findings of psychoanalysis and his experience of living with cancer to, amongst other things, morality and religion.

In Chapter Two, "Understanding the patient with cancer", Dorothy Judd focuses on the inner world of meanings held unconsciously and consciously by her patients with cancer, and how a particular type of attention to these meanings may offer a profound comfort in the face of terminal cancer and indeed in the face of illness of any kind.

After powerfully conveying her intense experience of learning with her adult patient to bear what seems impossible to bear, Dorothy then provides an example of a young adolescent's oscillation between knowing and not knowing, a reaction that may be present in any of us when faced with the stark reality of cancer that can feel so overwhelming. Finally, she sensitively describes her clinical work with another ill adolescent patient who, not being able to put her meanings into words, painted her meanings instead.

What then of children with cancer? In Chapter Three Anthony (Tony) Lee and Jane Elfer reflect on the painful experiences to which they bear witness in their daily work with children and their parents at University College London Hospital. They describe something of the devastation and pervasive terror around a world turned upside down by a cancer diagnosis and the psychic disturbance that is wrought. Drawing on experiences portrayed by the children themselves, their close observations and countertransference, Tony and Jane write of their work "to retain a thoughtful presence in the face of the trauma" they witness in a way that can best support both child and family.

In the two chapters that follow, our focus moves to the dilemmas and challenges faced by today's psychotherapist experiencing his or her own cancer. The picture here, though perhaps different in nature, is also complex, and is taken up first by John Woods and then by Judy Parkinson. John focuses on his experience of a patient who had been in analytic treatment with him for some three years when, in the year that John was undergoing chemotherapy, the patient recovered memories of child sexual abuse. John reflects on what happened at that phase of treatment, and discusses the delicate interplay between transference and countertransference feelings.

Judy then considers, amongst other things, the history of attitudes and thinking around disclosure of a personal health condition by the analytic psychotherapist. She explores circumstances for the thoughtful use of self-disclosure, and then offers us a sense of her own work as "the wounded healer", the archetypal dynamic described by Jung.

Perspectives on the work of the nurse specialist, whether in a clinical setting or in the cancer patient's home, have not previously received attention in the cancer literature. Anne Lanceley begins to redress the issue in Chapter Six by offering her observations of the emotional life of cancer patients and nurses on the wards and clinics where she has worked. Anne's first-hand account gives us a powerful flavour of what this work is all about, including the enormous pressure so often felt "to do something". She writes of "the sheer sensual bodiliness" of nursing care and the "powerful unconscious knowing" that lies at the heart of this care. Highlighting the anxieties experienced by nurses when their own professional, and indeed very human, desire to repair is frustrated, Anne considers the meaning of these experiences and the functions they can serve along "the cancer journey".

As cancer incidence rises and mortality falls, the number of people living with this disease continues to grow significantly, with as many as one in six adults over the age of sixty-five seen by a GP likely to be a survivor of cancer, especially of breast, colorectal, or prostate cancer (*British Journal of General Practice, 61*(*584*): 197–199). Today half of survivors have unmet needs relating to ongoing health conditions including the secondary effects of the disease and its treatment, the risk of secondary cancers, and the attendant emotional affects such as depression and anxiety. In Chapter Seven, Dr. Adrian Tookman and colleagues Dr. Faye Gishen and Jane Eades focus on the ongoing struggle experienced by cancer survivors, the changing perceptions and behaviours of patients hoping to return to normality after treatment, but finding themselves in a different state of mind, feeling cheated of a healthy future, defeated by the burden of treatment and uncertain about the future. The importance of understanding "change behaviour" and ways of helping different patients to manage at this stage are among the issues underlined in this chapter.

Dr. Robert Twycross, a founding father of palliative medicine, then describes the tragedy of depersonalisation evidenced when patients see out their lives in an alien environment, isolated from the spiritual support of others (Chapter Eight). His impassioned call for a "patient-centred", as distinct from "cancer-centred", approach has become the hallmark of work in hospices throughout the world. For those involved in palliative care, healing has a broad, holistic meaning involving, amongst other things, restoring relationships with self and with others through reconciliation and forgiveness.

It is this that Jonathan Wittenberg, as a rabbinic leader and former hospice chaplain, has witnessed, and about which he writes, but from a different perspective, in Chapter Nine. With a sense of awe he describes, amongst other things, his experience of people in states of extreme vulnerability finding new depths of spirit and discovering "profound resources of love and courage" in the face of cancer. He writes not only of the spiritual experience in addressing psychological need but also of the importance of religious tradition and ritual in providing a containing structure in which human anguish can be negotiated.

Part II of *The Topic of Cancer* continues with the idea of containment, this time explored by the poet and sociologist Carole Satyamurti in "Finding creative expression". Here Carole links the idea of art as reparation with the idea of containment—"the way that the infant's unbearable and chaotic feelings can, in normally good circumstances, be projected into the mother who is able to tolerate and digest the infant's distress and, through the way she talks to and touches him or her, transform the painful feelings into something manageable". It is such an experience—one that touches us, that resonates with us—that we seek in our relationships generally and, more specifically, when we want to express our feelings, including our fears in the face of cancer or grief.

Carole draws a fascinating parallel between the development of the poem and the development of psychic structures, the work required of the poet and the challenges faced by analyst and patient. The psychotherapist's attention to the particular words that the patient uses, she suggests, is unlike anything else except, perhaps, the work of the poet. She then offers a sample of poetry, including her own around her experience of cancer, for us to read and explore.

Where are we today with the topic of cancer? Once felt best "suppressed", akin to a taboo, the topic has more than gained public attention. It has demanded it. Cancer's "profile" has been raised as a result of advances in medical care but, as sociologist and social commentator Anne Karpf has argued, also in response to a growing consumer approach to the doctor-patient relationship. In "The cancer memoir: in search of a writing cure?", the concluding chapter of *The Topic of Cancer*, Anne provides a wide-ranging exposé on the growth of the so-called cancer "pathography", the ways in which these memoirs, whether in books, newspaper columns, or online through cancer blogs "make visible the lived experience of the person with cancer".

Though there have been improvements in treatments and increases in survival rates, and though cancer has arguably become a topic more open to consideration and discussion, a cancer diagnosis remains traumatic, and we all struggle with hope and fear, whether sufferers ourselves or a member of family or a friend. Treatments, benign as their intention is, still evoke fears of being attacked, with the objects of invasion and intrusion that they signal in our minds serving a malign kind. While medical research into cancer continues its careful but determined pace, the emotional experience of cancer also demands continual attention and care, and with this in mind it is hoped that this book might start, or continue, a conversation that, at least for now, it seems we are all bound to have.

PART I

BEARING THE UNBEARABLE

CHAPTER ONE

Freud's cancer

Martin Schmidt

> Anyone turning biographer commits himself to lies, to concealment, to hypocrisy, to flattery, and even to hiding his own lack of understanding, for biographical truth is not to be had, and even if it were it couldn't be used. Truth is unobtainable; humanity does not deserve it...
>
> —*Freud to Zweig*, 31 May 1936, in *Freud, E. L.*, 1961, p. 430.

Hardly words of encouragement. So it is with some trepidation that I attempt a biographical account of the influence of cancer on the pioneering father of psychoanalysis and his theories.

One of his closest friends and colleagues, Ernest Jones, identified two features which exemplify the last twenty years of Freud's illustrious life. The first was "the truly astonishing fresh outburst of original ideas" which "effected a revolution in both the theory and the practice of psycho-analysis". The second was the "dauntless fortitude with which he endured the political and financial dangers that threatened to engulf both him and his work, the loss of several of those dear to him, and above all the cruel tortures of the many years of suffering from the devouring cancer that ultimately killed him" (Jones, 1957, p. 1).

A heavy smoker, with a penchant for cigars, Freud's addiction staved off recurrent depressive episodes. Without cigars, he couldn't think. His twenty-a-day habit was one of his greatest pleasures. He tried to give up many times: "I have given up smoking completely, after it has served me for exactly fifty years as sword and buckler in the battle of life. Thus I am now better than I was, but not happier" (Freud to Salome, 8 May 1930, in Pfeiffer, 1963, p. 187). His abstinences were short-lived and he returned to his cigars. In his excellent biography of Freud, Peter Gay (2006) reminds us that in German, food (the stuff of life) is *Lebensmittel* and that Freud contrived a neologism for his own cigars—*Arbeitsmittel* (p. 384), the stuff of work. They became the stuff of death.

Freud the man

One of the greatest minds of modern times, he lived for his work: "I cannot face with comfort the idea of life without work; work and the free play of the imagination are for me the same thing, I take no pleasure in anything else" (Freud to Pfister, 6 March 1910, in Freud, E. L. & Meng, 1963, p. 35).

On a typical day, he was up and dressed by seven, ready for breakfast. Patients arrived from eight to noon. At one o'clock, lunch was shared with whichever family members were available. His wife, Martha, sat at the opposite head of the table whilst the maid administered the soup tureen. Then he would take a walk before further consultations from three until nine. After the family supper, there would be either a game of cards, or another walk, before reading and writing until lights out at one.

Rather than a doctor "in the proper sense", Freud preferred to see himself as a pioneering research scientist or conquistador. Indeed, he concluded that the wish to practice medicine is an attempt to compensate for unconscious sadism: "I have no knowledge of having had any craving in my early childhood to help suffering humanity. My innate sadistic disposition was not a very strong one, so that I had no need to develop this one of its derivatives" (1926a, p. 253).

Aware of his own genius, he expected the Nobel Prize (which didn't come): "…modesty—I would be enough of a friend of the truth or, let us rather say: objectivity, to dismiss this virtue" (Freud to Ferenczi, 8 April 1915, in Falzeder & Brabant 1996, p. 55). Paradoxically, he was often scathing of his own work, dismissing it as worthless, childish, and feeble, but I get the sense that he didn't really believe his own bad press, rather that this mock censure was a type of obsessive superstitious ritual to counter the danger of narcissistic inflation and to "get in first" on his own hypercritical superego.

Whilst rigorous and intolerant of forays into wild analysis by his disciples, he was less severe on his own breaching of boundaries. On occasion, patients were fed, fees waived, and analyses conducted during evening strolls in the park. Some patients were allowed to be privy to intimate information about his personal life and one, Horace Frink, who was also a psychoanalyst, was encouraged by Freud to divorce his wife in order to marry one of his patients. We know that he analysed his daughter and befriended a number of his favourite patients including Princess Marie Bonaparte. It was Marie who, perhaps as an expression of the inevitable ambivalence that this evoked, enabled him to escape the Nazis but also kept him supplied with his precious cigars. Freud was not the supreme practitioner of his art, Ferenczi complained bitterly about his own analysis with the master, and others, such as Alix Strachey and Melanie Klein, found Karl Abraham a much sounder analyst (Gay, 2006, p. 461).

In the words of Max Schur, his physician for over twenty years, Freud "... was always a deeply human and noble man ... I saw him face dying and death as nobly as he had faced living ... I saw him suffer pain and sorrow. I saw him show scorn and contempt for brutality and stupidity as well as tender love and concern for those close to him" (Schur, 1972, p. 2).

Gay suggests that he was prone to explosive outbursts: "His life, it appears over and over, was a struggle for self-discipline, for control over his speculative impulses and his rage—rage at his enemies and, even harder to manage, at those among his adherents he found wanting or disloyal" (2006, p. 316). However, this fury was not evident at home. Contrary to the sometimes wretched portrayal of himself that he furnishes us with in his correspondence, with his family he was: "even tempered, optimistic, and even gay" (Anna Freud to Jones, 16 June 1954, (in Jones, 1954)). Although he suffered at times from a cheerless Weltanschauung, he considered himself neither depressed nor pessimistic but a realist, subscribing to the view that a pessimist is nothing more than a well-informed optimist.

Generous by nature, he enjoyed providing financial support (when he had the money) not only to his extended family but also to colleagues and patients. He felt that he had to keep working to make enough to maintain his standard of living but was far from avaricious. The *Chicago Tribune* tempted him with 25,000 dollars to go to the United States to psychoanalyse two killers in a high profile murder case, and Samuel Goldwyn offered him 100,000 dollars to participate in the making of a series of films about the great love stories of history (beginning with Anthony and Cleopatra). Freud declined all such offers.

He was a loving, but not demonstrative father, rarely kissing his children, but more likely to be physically affectionate towards his daughters. The demands of his work meant that most of the domestic and childrearing duties were left to Martha. She was a model *Hausfrau*, diligent, meticulous, and devoted, but did not share his passion for psychoanalysis. In fact, Minna, his sister-in-law, was more of a confidante in this regard. Sigmund and Minna sometimes visited Swiss resorts or Italian cities alone. Jung suspected that they were lovers, and claimed that Freud had indeed confessed this to him (Billinsky, 1969). In later life, as his passion for both Martha and Minna dimmed, it was his daughter, Anna, who became the object of his deepest affection and his closest companion.

Although he did love his wife, children, and grandchildren, he preferred the company of men, cultivating a series of very close passionate friendships: "In my life, as you know, woman has never replaced the comrade, the friend" (Freud to Fliess, 7 August 1901, in Masson, 1985, p. 447). With predictable candour, he alluded to this being a feminine quality, a sublimation of "androphile" tendencies or, simply put, his latent homosexuality.

Todesangst *and hypochondria*

Throughout his life, Freud had been obsessed with death and plagued by attacks of *todesangst* (dread of dying). Though beset by bouts of hypochondria, his health was generally good. He did intermittently suffer from attacks of tachycardia, arrhythmia, dyspnoea, chest pain, fainting fits, migraines, gastro-intestinal complaints, and abdominal problems, but they didn't prevent him from working.

Nevertheless, long before his cancer was diagnosed, he was convinced that he would die prematurely. Surprisingly, for a man renowned for his antagonism to unscientific magical thinking, he subscribed to a peculiar superstitious preoccupation with prospective dates of his own demise. He was impressed by his beloved friend Fliess' (1897) theory of "vital periodicity" which predicted critical periods and dates in an individual's life. Indeed, Freud idealised Fliess and was so influenced by his tenuous hypotheses, including reflex nasal neuroses, that he even referred some of his patients to him for treatment of their neurosis by nasal surgery.

He also applied Fliess' permutations to himself and accordingly expected to die at the ages of forty, then forty-two, forty-three, fifty-one, sixty-two, and eighty-one and a half. After an "absurd dream", Freud became persuaded that the age of fifty-one had special significance: "fifty-one is the age which seems to be a particularly dangerous one to men: I have known colleagues who have died suddenly at that age" (1900a, p. 438). Here, he is referring to the death of the physicist Kundt who actually died at the age of fifty-four not fifty-one.

Fliess provoked his fears by arguing that all vital processes are developed in a cycle lasting twenty-three days in men and twenty-eight days in women. He predicted that the age of fifty-one years (twenty-eight plus twenty-three) would either be the year of Freud's death or at least a critical period for him. As luck would have it (or perhaps synchronicity), the year in question was 1907 in which he was first to meet Jung, Abraham, and Ferenczi. He survived his fifty-first year, but then anticipated the next promised date of his own death, in February 1918, with both terror and yearning: "I have worked hard, am worn out, and am beginning to find the world repulsively disgusting. The superstition that has limited my life to around February 1918 seems downright friendly to me" (Freud to Ferenczi, 20 November 1917, in Masson, 1985, p. 249).

Even reaching this milestone offered Freud little relief: "So I have really reached sixty two … My prevailing mood is powerless embitterment, or embitterment at my powerlessness" (Freud to Abraham, 29 May 1918, in Falzeder, 2002, p. 378).

This was most peculiar, as nineteen years earlier he had already predicted his own retirement to be at the age of sixty-seven. In the writing of *The Interpretation of Dreams* (1900a), he refers to "2,467 mistakes— which I shall leave in it" (Freud to Fliess, 27 August 1899, in Masson, 1985, p. 368). Two years later, in the *Psychopathology of Everyday Life* (1901b), Freud tried to explain why he picked this seemingly random number from the ether. He remembered that in 1899, at the age of forty-three, he had been wondering about when he would retire. Perhaps this wish to know evoked his unconscious to provide him with the answer of another twenty-four years' work which would take him to the venerable age of sixty-seven (2467)? Curiously, it was in 1923, at the age of sixty-seven, that he became ill but did not retire! To add to this uncanny coincidence, it was also in 1899 that Freud first referred to himself as a cancer: "… I have turned completely into a carcinoma. The neoplasm in its most recent stages of development likes to drink wine. Today I am supposed to go to the theatre; but this is ridiculous—like an attempt to graft onto the carcinoma. Nothing can adhere to it, so from now on the duration of my life span is that of the neoplasm [a tumour]" (Freud to Fliess, 19 February 1899, in Masson, 1985, p. 345).

Georg Groddeck, one of the founders of psychosomatic medicine, heard about this story and became convinced that Freud's own unconscious had produced the malignancy. He held that unconscious thoughts evoked somatic processes including cancers and invited Freud to his private hospital for treatment. Freud refused but nevertheless admired and encouraged Groddeck (1923) who coined the term "id" which Freud later adopted in his structural model of the psyche.

So why was such an advocate of rational science so superstitious and preoccupied with his own death? Could we consider his fatalistic and morbid musings the expression of an unconscious death wish?

Superstition

Freud proposed that superstition derives from repressed hostile and murderous impulses which can be most clearly recognised in obsessional neurotics, people of often high intelligence: "Superstition is in large part the expectation of trouble; and a person who has harboured frequent evil wishes against others, but has been brought up to be good and has therefore repressed such wishes into the unconscious, will be especially ready to expect punishment for his unconscious wickedness in the form of trouble threatening him from without" (1901b, p. 260).

However, at first, he was reluctant to apply this reasoning to himself. Instead, his self-analysis revealed that his own superstition "… has its roots in suppressed ambition (immortality) and in my case takes the place of that anxiety about death which springs from the normal uncertainty of life …" (1901b, p. 260, n. 3). Here he accepts that his superstitious preoccupation with death is abnormal, but felt that those, like himself, who had experienced the death of loved ones at an early age were predestined to such a fixation. We must remember that Freud lived through the First World War, with death as a constant companion, and lived in fear of his sons being killed (his eldest, Martin, was captured by the Italian Army).

Guilt

Freud considered his addiction to nicotine as a derivative of the primary addiction of masturbation which he described as the original sin. Did he imagine that he was being punished for this sin? As Max Schur (1972, p. 194) opined, he did not develop cancer as a result of guilt, but did punish himself by persisting in smoking. He was aware that smoking was potentially dangerous, but would only abstain during his most severe cardiac episodes.

At the tender age of eighteen months, Sigmund was displaced from the breast by the birth of his brother Julius. This led to prototypical guilt when Julius seemed to surrender to Sigmund's hatred by dying within a year. He said that he had welcomed this brother with "adverse wishes and genuine childhood jealousy ... and his death left the germ of (self-) reproaches in me" (Freud to Fliess, 3 October 1897, Masson, 1985, p. 268). Freud believed that his guilt and preoccupation with death could be traced back to the death of this baby brother.

He also suffered from remorse in relation to the death of Ernst Fleischl, a brilliant physiologist and beloved friend, who lent him money when he was destitute. Sigmund treated him for morphine addiction by administering cocaine orally. The results were at first miraculous but he then deteriorated drastically with symptoms worse than before. This resulted in harrowing nightly vigils comforting his friend until his death in 1891. His contrition was amplified by the memory of envious death wishes he entertained towards Fleischl who had a career which Freud, mistakenly, felt he could never hope to match.

Rudnytsky (1987, p. 20) argues that Freud must have also believed that his patricidal wishes had caused his father's death as well as that of Julius. In Totem and Taboo (1912–13), Freud describes the murderous wish to kill the father as primal sin. Sometimes, however, he forecast that these violent fantasies are projected out, for example when he imagined that he was the father suffering from the death wishes of the son, Jung, his heir apparent.

Through further self-analysis, Freud came to recognise that his fear of death was caused by feelings of guilt expressed as aggression directed towards himself. Behind every fear is an unconscious wish. His obsessive superstitious fear of death was a reaction to the guilt he experienced in harbouring murderous fantasies in relation to those he hated, including his father, his brother Julius, his sister Anna, Fliess, Fleischl, and Jung. In *The Ego and the Id* (1923b) this was reframed, when he argued that if the ego is threatened by a persecutory superego then the fear of death, like the fear of conscience, could be seen as a development of the fear of castration.

Freud wavered between a dread of death and a longing for it. Could this simply be an expression of the fear of father and the desire for reunion with mother? Whatever the answer, it is impressive how determined Freud was to try to understand his own obsessive superstitions, treating his own neuroses as scientific problems to be solved.

Freud's own Oedipal complex

It is no surprise that the Oedipal complex is central to Freudian theory as his own personal family history was an Oedipal drama. His father Jakob, a wool merchant of limited means, was only seventeen years old when he married Sally Kanner in 1832. She bore him two sons, Philip and Emmanuel.

Following Sally's death twenty years later, Jakob married Rebecca who also died. Then, in 1855, at the age of thirty-nine, Jakob married for a third and final time. This new bride, the beautiful Amalia Nathanson, just nineteen years old, bore him a further eight children.

Sigismund Schlomo Freud was the first, and most cherished, of Amalia's children. Born on 6 May 1856, in Freiberg, he excelled academically and was given special treatment by his mother. "Golden Sigi" not only experienced guilt at having won his mother's love, at the expense of his father and other siblings, but also reaped the benefits: "… if a man has been his mother's undisputed darling he retains throughout life the triumphant feeling, the confidence in success, which not seldom brings actual success along with it" (Freud, 1917, p. 156).

The family set-up must have been very confusing for young Sigismund. After all, his half brothers Emmanuel, at eighteen years of age, and Philip, a few years older, would have seemed far better suited to Amalia than the relatively old man, Jakob, with whom she slept.

Sigmund adored his beautiful mother and became aware of wishing he could have her to himself. Later, he adopted Jung's use of the term *"complex"* (Jung, 1904–7, p. 72n.), to describe this Oedipal conflict. Jung, in turn, expanded the theory by introducing the concept of the *"Electra complex"* (1913, p. 154) to portray the difficulties girls experience in relation to the mother in competition for the father.

Later, after Jakob's death, Freud's guilt towards his father was to be compounded when he only furnished him with a modest funeral. Following Julius came the arrival of his sister Anna when Sigmund was two. He also showed this newcomer great hostility and she remained the least liked of his sisters.

This unresolved Oedipal legacy seems to have been handed down to his youngest daughter to whom he gave the same name as his sister, Anna. He was unable to help her resolve her father complex. She remained his favourite "little only daughter" (despite the fact that he had two others), who sacrificed the possibility of a family of her own to take care of her father to the end. He even referred to her as his Antigone (Oedipus's favourite daughter who was guide to her blind father). To make matters worse, Freud took her into analysis secretly, interpreted her dreams, and interfered with her budding courtships (on one occasion warning Ernest Jones off "the most gifted and accomplished of my children") (Freud to Jones, 22 July 1914, in Paskauskas, 1993, p. 294). He admitted to Lou Andreas-Salome that if Anna were to leave home he would feel as impoverished as he would if he had to give up smoking! In due course, she became further enmeshed in her father's world as his secretary, confidante, colleague (she became a renowned analyst in her own right), and nurse. She was far more intimate and physically involved in her father's care than was his own wife.

In those early heady days of psychoanalysis, boundaries were lines in the sand and many pioneers fell prone to incestuous enactments and Oedipal dramas. Jung had tried to analyse his wife and slept with at least two of his patients. Ferenczi kissed his analysands and wanted to marry one of them. Anna Freud analysed her nephews, Klein her own children, and Freud his daughter plus close colleagues including Ferenczi.

The cancer of friends

Some may consider Freud fortunate to have lived a full life of nearly three score years and ten before the onset of his illness. However, the bitter claws of cancer had clasped his soul long before his own diagnosis. In 1912, his friend Binswanger underwent surgery for a highly malignant tumour. Freud became his pillar at this time. Providence smiled, as Binswanger was to survive another fifty years.

Less fortunate was Anton von Freund, one of Freud's closest allies and an ex-patient, who succumbed to the same cancer. He entered analysis with Freud in 1918 for a severe neurosis following an operation for sarcoma, but sadly his cancer returned. Bitter war years had wiped out Freud's savings. The family subsisted on hand-outs and food packages from friends. He had to borrow money to survive and relied on Ernest Jones to refer him wealthy English and American patients just to make ends meet. 1917 found him at a particularly low ebb. After the defection of Jung, Stekel, and Adler, there were few he could trust to further his work in the way he envisioned. It was von Freund who came to his rescue by making a very generous donation towards the founding of the private publishing house of psychoanalytic work, the *Internationaler Psychoanalytischer Verlag* in 1918. He became a dear friend and was to become a member of Freud's inner circle, the private Committee, before falling ill to the cancer. Just as he had done before with Fleischl, Freud visited his dying friend every day and did all he could to comfort him throughout his decline. His death, on 20 January 1920, was a mighty personal blow and a significant factor in Freud's ageing.

A couple of weeks later Jones's father died, also from a malignancy, prompting Freud to write: "So your father had not to hold out until he got devoured piecemeal by his cancer as poor Freund was ... I was about your age when my father died and it revolutioned [sic.] my soul. Can you remember a time so full of death as this present one?" (Freud to Jones, 12 February, 1920, in Masson, 1985, pp. 369–370).

Freud's "Sunday child"

On the same day that von Freund was buried, came a bolt from the blue—the news that his pregnant daughter Sophie was critically ill with pneumonia. She was Freud's "Sunday child", only twenty-six years old, with two young children. Train lines were down, which meant that it was impossible to visit her. Within two days she was dead. The dreadful news, coming so soon after von Freund's death, was almost too much for her father to bear. There was nowhere to deflect his own bereaved fury: "... since I am profoundly unbelieving, I have no one to blame, and I know there is no place where one can lodge a complaint … Very deep within I perceive the feeling of a deep, insurmountable narcissistic insult" (Freud to Ferenczi, 4 February 1920, in Falzeder & Brabant, 2000, pp. 6–7).

The cancer

To understand the impact on Freud of his own battle with cancer, we have to see it not only in the context of the personal losses he had already suffered but also of the political situation at that time. During the sixteen years of his struggle with the illness, he witnessed the rise of Nazism, the invasion of Austria (which made him a refugee), and the start of World War II.

There were cancer scares in 1914 (requiring a rectoscopy) and 1917 when he noticed painful swellings in his mouth. He seemed to know that something was up and in 1921 was moved to write: "On March 13 of this year I very suddenly took a step toward really getting old. Since then, the thought of death no longer leaves me at all, and sometimes I have the feeling that seven organs are vying with one another for the honour of being allowed to make an end to my life" (Freud to Ferenczi, 8 May 1921, in Falzeder & Brabant, 2000, p. 56).

Two years later, in February 1923, at the age of sixty-seven, he detected a leucoplastic growth on the right side of his palate and jaw (a precancerous condition consisting of small thickened white patches inside the oral cavity associated with smoking) but chose to ignore it for a couple of months, telling no one. Then in April, he showed his friend Felix Deutsch, who at once recognised the malignancy but kept the truth from Freud. Perhaps he was alarmed to hear Freud ask for help to "disappear from the world with decency" (cited in Jones, 1957, p. 95) if he was destined to die in agony? Whatever his thinking, Deutsch continued the deception stating that there was merely a simple leucoplakia which needed excision. Freud was later to be furious with Deutsch when he discovered that he had misled him by underplaying how serious his condition was. Although he didn't know it, Freud's self diagnosis of buccal cancer, a squamous cell carcinoma of the palate or malignant epithelioma, was correct.

In April, he consulted an old friend, Hajek, a leading rhinologist, to perform the operation. He attended Hajek's clinic for day surgery without informing the family. Anna and Martha were therefore shocked to receive a call asking them to come quickly. The operation had not gone well. Freud had lost so much blood that it wasn't safe for him to return home. In the absence of a free room, he had to share with another patient, a dwarf. There, Freud had an attack of profuse bleeding but couldn't speak or call for help. He tried to ring the emergency bell but it was out of order. His roommate saved his life by raising the alarm. Eventually, his bleeding was arrested and he was stabilised. On discovering this disturbing state of affairs, Anna refused to leave her father's side, staying with him all night. He was weak from loss of blood and in great pain, unable to swallow. Hajek had been dangerously cavalier in his methods, failing to take the necessary precautions to prevent shrinking of the scar, which caused a restriction in the opening of the mouth and numerous associated problems thereafter.

From this day forth, Freud refused any other nurse than Anna. She willingly complied with his wishes and even agreed to care for him with a degree of emotional detachment to protect both from their feelings. For the next sixteen years, he was to endure an agonising ordeal of another thirty-three surgical procedures at the hands of otolaryngologists, maxillofacial surgeons, prosthodontists, and general surgeons.

One of Freud's former analytic patients, Holzknecht, performed two X-ray therapies which were then followed by radium capsule treatments. The doses were extremely high, causing him serious side-effects. Four months later, he reported that he had not had an hour free from pain since the procedure. Sadly, like so many pioneering radiologists, Holzknecht also developed cancer (of the skin) eight years later. Successive amputations of his fingers, hand, and arm failed to halt its proliferation. Freud visited the dying doctor, both men poignantly aware of their fate, and told him: "You are to be admired for the way you bear your lot" to which Holzknecht replied: "You know that I have only you to thank for this" (cited in Schur, 1972, p. 427).

Later that year, on 26 September, Pichler and Hajek found a malignant ulcer in the hard palate which had invaded the neighbouring tissues including the upper part of the lower jaw and cheek. A radical operation was now needed performed in two stages, on 4 and 11 October. The first consisted of the ligature of the external carotid artery and the removal of the submaxillary glands. The second involved the dissection of the lip and cheek to allow the removal of the entire upper jaw and palate which left the nasal cavity and mouth with nothing to separate them. Both procedures were performed under local anaesthetic! Freud was unable to speak for a number of days and was fed by nasal tube.

For the rest of his life, Freud was now encumbered with the imposition of a succession of crude prostheses (a type of denture) designed to separate the mouth from the nasal cavity which grievously affected his capacity to eat, drink, sleep, and talk. The prosthesis was monstrous, extremely difficult, and painful to put in. On one occasion he and Anna failed to insert it after thirty minutes' struggle. It produced constant sores and he developed the habit of holding it in place with his thumb. He permitted himself to continue to smoke but in order to indulge in a cigar he had to use a clothes peg to force open his bite. Damage to the Eustachian tube left him almost entirely deaf on his right side requiring the position of his consulting room couch and chair to be reversed.

The rest of the year comprised almost daily visits to his surgeon, Pichler, more X-ray treatments, and constant modifications to the "monster" in the hope of making it more comfortable and possible for Freud to speak. One of the more unusual interventions was a "Steinach vasoligature" in November. This operation consisted of a ligature tying off the *vas deferens* on both sides. It was believed that this would help "reactivate" male patients, increasing sexual potency and recovery time. Unfortunately, Freud did not experience any benefits as a result of the procedure.

He was unable to see any patients until the New Year and earned nothing for six months. On 2 January 1924 he resumed psychoanalysis with six patients but was exhausted by the exertion prompting him to write "The right thing to do would be to give up work and obligations and wait in a quiet corner for the natural end. But the temptation— nay the necessity—to go on earning something as long as one spends so much is strong" (Freud to Eitingon, 22 March 1924, in Jones, 1957, p. 107). Before the diagnosis, he had already started to reduce his workload to eight patients a day and he promised his Swiss colleague Pfister that he would never see nine patients a day again. Despite the cancer, he remained stoic and continued to see at least four a day until he was seventy-five when he dropped temporarily, to three. In Easter 1924, he took his first weekend holiday in thirty-eight years!

By August 1925, Freud was able to enjoy the best week of health since his first operation. However, remission was short-lived as he had to contend with the inevitable degenerative progression from leucoplakia, proliferation, and precancerous papillomata to carcinoma.

Multiple operations ensued which included skin grafts, excisions, cauterizations, and radium treatments. Freud refused sedatives up to the very end and had only occasionally taken an aspirin or Pyramidon for migraine but, as his sores became more painful, it was necessary to take stronger pain relief. Ironically, the analgesic of choice was Ortho-form, a member of the novocain group, a fillip from his own early work on cocaine. By 1929, it was necessary to appoint a regular medical attendant, Dr Max Schur, to attend to Freud on a daily basis. Freud was the model patient, gracious, polite, and able to endure considerable pain without grumbling. They agreed a "contract". Schur should never withhold the truth from Freud and, when the time came, would help relieve him from an extended pointless agonising existence: "I can stand a great deal of pain and I hate sedatives, but I trust you will not let me suffer unnecessarily" (cited in Jones, 1957, p. 154). The fellow physicians shook on it.

The cancer had been kept at bay by removing precancerous tissue, but the malignancy returned for good in 1936.

Further setbacks

This painful litany of loss did not abate. Shortly after Freud had contracted cancer, Sophie's son and his favourite grandchild, Heinerle (Heinz Rudolf) died of tuberculosis in June 1923, aged four. It was the only occasion in his life that Freud was known to have shed tears. This dreadful event affected him more profoundly than any of the others he had suffered. Other losses had brought agony whereas this one had killed something in him for good. Freud adored Heinz Rudolf, the most intelligent child he had ever encountered: "He was indeed an enchanting little fellow, and I myself was aware of never having loved a human being, certainly never a child, so much … I find this loss very hard to bear. I don't think I have ever experienced such grief, perhaps my own sickness contributes to the shock. I worked out of sheer necessity; fundamentally everything has lost its meaning for me" (Freud to K. and L. Levy, 11 June 1923, in Freud, E. L., 1961, p. 344).

This elicited something he described as the first depression in his life, which is odd as we know that he had long suffered from recurrent depressive episodes. For three years there was little amelioration; he feared that he would not be able to enjoy life or love anyone ever again.

Cancer claimed another victim in 1925. One of his unfaltering allies, Karl Abraham, fell to bronchogenic carcinoma. Although stricken by grief by these relentless blows, his gravest fear was not realised as he preserved his capacity to love. Not all bereavements were traumas. Surprisingly, he reported no feelings of grief at the death of his mother in 1930, only a sense of freedom and relief that she was delivered from further suffering.

The work

Freud's cancer did not stem the flow of his prodigious output. On the contrary, he was teeming with ideas and wrote profusely. After all, the conditions were favourable for his writing as he felt that a "modicum of misery" is "essential for intensive work" (Freud to Fliess, 16 April 1896, in Freud, E. L., 1961, p. 181).

A number of articles were published in 1923 but most had been written the year before Freud's diagnosis, including *The Ego and the Id*, "Remarks on the theory and practice of dream-interpretation" and "A seventeenth-century demonological neurosis". The most important paper that he wrote that year was "The infantile genital organization of the libido" in February when his cancer was first detected.

There was a surprising outburst of creativity in 1924 with the publication of five papers. Two were expansions of ideas expounded in *The Ego and the Id*: "Neurosis and psychosis" and "The loss of reality in neurosis and psychosis" written during his convalescence in 1923. A very significant paper, "The economic problem of masochism", along with "The dissolution of the Oedipus Complex" was also published that year.

Owing to his impaired speech, Anna now addressed the public on his behalf and read his new paper "Some psychological consequences of the anatomical distinction between the sexes" at the Congress of 1925. As well as this paper, 1925 saw the publication of his *An Autobiographical Study* and clinical papers on "Negation" as well as the establishment of the Institute of Psycho-Analysis in London.

All in all, from the detection of his illness until his death, he remained prolific, publishing over forty significant papers and major works including *The Ego and the Id* (1923b), *Inhibitions, Symptoms and Anxiety* (1926d), *The Future of an Illusion* (1927c), *Civilization and its Discontents* (1930), and *Moses and Monotheism* (1939). In addition to this phenomenal bibliography, he wrote countless letters, prefaces, tributes and obituaries. He continued to write into his dotage with "Analysis terminable and interminable" (1937) and "Constructions in analysis" (1937a) both produced when he was over eighty. The former moved Jones to write, "It is for the practising psycho-analyst possibly the most valuable contribution Freud ever wrote". (1957, p. 269).

Change in theoretical thinking

The terrible loss of his friends, daughter, and beloved grandson, together with the relentless onslaught of his own cancer, had a huge impact not only on his mood but also on his writing. This change in direction reflected a darker, sombre tone in his prose. He now used the language of death and destructiveness rather than pleasure seeking to explain the aetiology of anxiety, aggression, and guilt.

However, the groundbreaking *Beyond the Pleasure Principle* (1920g), where he propounded the hypothesis of the conflict between life and death instincts, was written before Sophie's death and the onset of his cancer. Nevertheless, the term "death instinct" first appeared shortly after she died and I find it hard to imagine that Freud's intimate involvement with Anton von Freund's prolonged battle with cancer, together with presentiments about his own malignancy, did not influence his writing of it.

Life and death drives

Before this monumental work, he considered psychological health to pivot upon the axis of hunger and love. He envisaged a dualistic system where love, expressed in the sexual instincts, serves the survival of the species and pleasure seeking. These sexual drives, he argued, were at odds with hunger, expressed in the ego drives, which serve self-preservation and reality. To his consternation, he couldn't satisfactorily explain sadism, masochism, and repetition compulsion (the need to repeat traumatic experience) in terms of a conflict between the pleasure principle and reality. In *Beyond the Pleasure Principle* (1920g), he dramatically revised his theory. Now the libido, instead of being at variance with the life instinct (Eros), is considered a core part of it and represents its sexual dynamic. Here, he adopts a position that Jung (1913) had long argued, namely that there is a life force, not only sexual in nature, which pervades all psychic life. The counterpart to Eros is the death instinct, Thanatos, the psychological equivalent of the organism's physiological need to return to its prior inorganic state (ashes to ashes, dust to dust). The idea of a death drive was originally proposed by the Russian analyst Sabina Spielrein in her seminal paper "Destruction as the cause of becoming" (1912). The psychical manifestation of the death instinct Freud described as a longing to return to a state of no pain. Put simply, the aim of all life is death. Freud's formulation reads like the billing for an epic prize fight: "... the mute but powerful death instincts ... desire to put Eros, the mischief-maker, to rest" (1923b, p. 57).

In the year his cancer was discovered, he published his colossus *The Ego and the Id* (1923b) and bequeathed us his structural model of the psyche with its division of the mind into ego, superego, and id. This in turn led to a restructuring of two of the pillars of his thinking—anxiety and aggression—in *Inhibitions, Symptoms and Anxiety* (1926d).

Originally, he considered aggression as a self-preservative ego instinct triggered by frustration, but now argued that an innate destructive drive was present from the very beginning. In other words, rather than frustration causing aggression, aggression is inherent. It finds expression when the death instinct is deflected outwards towards an object. This, in part, happens because the individual feels threatened by his own potentially self-destructive death instinct.

In this way, Freud configured the conflict between the life instinct (sexuality and survival) and death instinct (self-destruction and aggression) at the centre of his psychology. This struggle was now seen as the main cause of anxiety and guilt. Before 1920, he saw guilt as the product of infantile sexuality. Now, he saw aggression as its prime source.

In his paper, "The economic problem of masochism" he states: "The libido has the task of making the destroying instinct innocuous, and it fulfills the task by diverting that instinct to a great extent outwards ... towards objects in the outside world. The instinct is then called the destructive instinct, the instinct for mastery, or the will to power. A portion of the instinct is placed directly in the service of the sexual function, where it has an important part to play. This is sadism proper" (1924c, p. 163).

This was revolutionary. These concepts of the life and death drives, together with his new ideas on the dynamics of aggression, reshaped Freud's contribution to psychoanalysis.

Anxiety

Similarly, his views on anxiety, the bedrock of psychoanalytic thinking, changed. Originally, he understood anxiety to be the result of repression of sexual impulses but now he reversed the formula—anxiety causes repression. So what now evokes anxiety? He explored this question in depth in *Inhibitions, Symptoms and Anxiety* (1926d), three years and four operations after his initial diagnosis of cancer. As well as "reality fear"—the natural response to external danger, he identified four internal causes of anxiety arising at different libidinal phases: the loss of the object (separation from the protecting mother); castration fear, superego anxiety (or fear of conscience); and the loss of the love of the object (also referred to as fear of death).

Revenge on God the father

After the onset of his cancer, Freud took on God with a vengeance. Earlier, in *Totem and Taboo* (1912–13), he exposed religion's role in promulgating the denial of death either by promising an afterlife in heaven or by reincarnation. Here, he also posited an evolutionary hierarchy of thought in man, from primitive animistic/mythological ruminations through religious musings to that which he saw as the ultimate achievement, scientific thinking.

Now he focused on the role of religion in civilisation, producing three notable works in this vein: *The Future of an Illusion* (1927c), *Civilization and its Discontents* (1930), and, ultimately, *Moses and Monotheism* (1939). Here was the culmination of a lifetime's work, the application of the exacting study of individuals to the development of human history (Freud supported Haeckel's maxim that ontogeny recapitulates phylogeny). Now, he felt he was ready to apply the findings of psychoanalysis (and the experience of living with death and a Godless cancer) to politics, cultural development, morality, and religion.

He proposed that the principle purpose of civilisation is to defend us against nature—its elements, disease and death. Religious doctrines are designed to falsely protect us from these realities. Man makes a divinity of his father. The belief in a holy patriarch, who exacts retribution on those who defy him and promises life everlasting to those who obey, is a projection of the superego and expresses man's omnipotent wish to avoid death. God and religion are neurotic consolations, illusions used to refute the inevitability of death. He ventured that neurosis is an individual religion whereas religion is a universal obsessional neurosis.

His pessimistic vision of the future of civilisation was underpinned by his conviction that men are a barbaric horde destined to be forever unsatisfied with the unhappy compromise that is society. He confesses: "In the depths of my being I remain convinced that my dear fellow creatures—with few exceptions—are a wretched lot ..." (Freud to Salome, 28 July 1929, in Freud, E. L., 1961, p. 182). Stirrings of this are evident in 1914, where he refers to the inevitable destructive nature of mankind as demonstrated in the Great War: with regard to civilisation, mankind is "organically unfitted for it. We have to abdicate, and the great Unknown, He or It, lurking behind Fate, will some day repeat this experiment with another race". (Freud to Salome, 25 November 1914, in Freud, E. L., 1961, p. 20). Here, in Freud's nihilistic vision, God is replaced with a "great Unknown" who is vivisectionist to the lab rat that is man.

Is Freud offering us psychoanalysis as an alternative religion? He would protest strongly that what separates his science from religion is that science is open to examination. However, when approached by Rosenzweig, who wished to conduct experimental research to test the validity and efficacy of psychoanalysis, Freud felt it unnecessary "because the wealth of dependable observations" upon which psychoanalytic theories are based "makes them independent of experimental verification" (Freud to Rosenzweig, 28 February 1934, in Shakow & Rapaport, 1964, p. 129). Sadly, it is the legacy of this kind of isolationist thinking which fostered the notion of psychoanalysis as a cult and opened the door for cognitive behavioural therapy, and other evidence-based therapies, to win favour within the scientific community.

Exodus

Hitler came to power in January 1933 and by May was burning Freud's books. Ironically, it was only the year before that Freud's name (along with that of Bertrand Russell and others) was removed from the British Broadcasting Corporation's blacklist of "dangerously immoral persons". Fervent and ubiquitous anti-Semitism provoked Freud to examine the "special character of the Jew" in *Moses and Monotheism* (1939).

In spite of everything, he was able to see five patients again and enjoy life in 1935 at the age of seventy-nine. He didn't lose his sense of humour. When Elisabeth Rotten came to call and asked how he felt he replied: "How a man of eighty feels is not a topic for conversation" (cited in Jones, 1957, p. 220).

1938 brought the *Anschluss* and Hitler's reign of terror to Austria. Stores, homes, and synagogues were looted, with widespread persecution of Jews by angry mobs. When Anna was arrested by the Gestapo, Freud knew it was time to leave. His money was confiscated by the Nazis but he had savings in gold secreted abroad. There was a concerted effort by Princess Marie Bonaparte, Ernest Jones, and other friends to help him leave. Even Mussolini and President Roosevelt pulled strings to facilitate his emigration.

They were able to secure a safe passage for him and his immediate family but reluctantly he had to leave behind four elderly sisters (who later perished in concentration camps). He arrived in London, via Paris, on 6 June 1938 and rented a house at 39 Elsworthy Road near Regent's Park. Freud was delighted to receive a very warm welcome which prompted this emotional portrayal of his new homeland: "…a blessed, a happy country inhabited by well-meaning, hospitable people…" (Freud to Alexander Freud, 22 June 1938, in Shakow & Rapaport, 1964, p. 447). Within two weeks he had resumed work on Moses and by July was drafting his *An Outline of Psychoanalysis* (1940a). This new lease on life was curtailed by the enlargement of the tumour. On 8 September, he had what proved to be his final operation as he was now deemed too frail to endure more.

At the end of the month, the antiquities, books, and his couch, which he had managed to ransom from the Nazis, arrived in London. These were accommodated in his new home, a comfortable spacious house with a magnificent garden at 20 Maresfield Gardens (now the Freud Museum). Although weak, exhausted, and eighty-two, he somehow managed to see three analytic patients and continued writing.

The final year

In February 1939, a biopsy indicated that the now inoperable malignancy was spreading. Palliative care consisted of Roentgen ray treatments with Freud now dependent on painkillers. He had already started to say goodbye and entertained some distinguished guests including

H. G. Wells, Arthur Koestler, Salvador Dali, and Virginia Woolf. For a number of years, he had exchanged correspondence with Thomas Mann and Albert Einstein.

Thrilled to see *Moses and Monotheism* (1939) published, it was nevertheless an act of defiance. It attacked envious anti-Semites, Christianity as a delusion, and robbed the Jews of Moses (claiming that he was not a Jew but an Egyptian). It is worth noting that here he also performed a volte-face. Having always disputed Jung's notion of a collective unconscious, he now went even further than Jung and adopted the Lamarckian idea of the inheritance of acquired characteristics. This took the form of "inherited tradition" and the "survival of memory traces in the archaic heritage" where "men have always known that they once possessed a primal father and killed him" (1939, p. 99). In his theory of the archetypes, Jung (1938/1954, p. 79) argued that archetypes are inherited forms without content whereas here Freud is arguing that primal fantasies (i.e., actual memories) are inherited. Freud also couldn't resist adding, as a footnote, his long-held and rather spurious conviction that the true author of Shakespeare's plays was really the Earl of Oxford, Edward de Vere.

In July, there was further deterioration with ulceration of the cancerous tissue. He had lost a lot of weight, spent most of the day sleeping, but still conducted occasional analytic consultations when the pain receded. It wasn't until 1 August that he finally closed his medical practice. By 3 September, Britain was again at war with Germany and Freud's bed was moved to a safer room in the house following an air raid alarm.

He had had enough. Necrosis of the skin and bone produced a powerful foetor. His favourite chow couldn't bear the smell, refused to approach her master and instead cowered in the corner. Freud understood all too well what this meant as he "looked at his pet with a tragic and knowing sadness" (Schur, 1972, p. 526). His skin became gangrenous whilst the odour grew worse. A mosquito net kept at bay the flies attracted by the smell.

Despite sleepless nights, he refused sedation, spending his last days downstairs looking at the garden and reading. Balzac's *La Peau de Chagrin* (1831) was the last book he read. On 21 September, he reminded his physician of their old agreement: "My dear Schur, you certainly remember our first talk. You promised me then not to forsake me when my time comes. Now it's nothing but torture and makes no sense any more". When Schur let him know that he had not forgotten, Freud said, "I thank you" and then "Tell Anna about this" (Schur, 1972, p. 529). She wanted to delay the inevitable, but Schur convinced her that it was pointless. Later that day, he injected the old man with three centigrams of morphine (two centigrams was the usual dose for sedation). He fell into a peaceful sleep. When he became agitated, his doctor repeated the dose and gave a final injection the next day. Freud slipped into a coma and died at 3.00 am on 23 September 1939 aged eighty-three years.

Three days later, he was cremated at Golders Green Crematorium. His ashes rest in an ancient Greek urn, a gift from Marie Bonaparte, which he had treasured and kept in his study in Vienna for many years. When Martha died in 1951, her ashes were mixed with his.

Life's special and enhanced charm

Cancer helped him to overcome his lifelong fear of death. He loved life and, despite his torment, was grateful for the heightened sense of being alive that cancer gave him. His state of mind vacillated between "... a little island of pain floating on a sea of indifference" (Freud to Bonaparte, 16 June 1939, cited in Jones, 1957, p. 258) and a sense of what he called life's "special and enhanced charm" (Freud to Binswanger, 14 April 1912, in Freud, E. L., 1961, p. 286) which comes with knowing that one is going to die. When he became convinced that he had cancer, he was more able to appreciate the wonder of springtime which prompted him to write ruefully: "What a pity that one has to become old and sick to make this discovery" (Freud to Bonaparte, 27 April 1926, cited in Jones, 1957, p. 129). He felt that it was the eternal transitory nature of life which makes it so beautiful. These lines from *Frühlingsglaube* (Faith in Spring) by Johann Uhland (1815), which he could recite from memory, reflected his sentiments:

> The world grows lovelier each day
> We do not know what still may come;
> The flowering will not end,
> The farthest deepest valley is abloom,
> Now, dear heart, forget your torment,
> Now everything must change

References

Balzac, H. de (1831). *La Peau de Chagrin*. Paris: Gallimard (1966).

Billinsky, J. M. (1969). *Jung and Freud (the End of a Romance)*. Andover Newton Quarterly, X: 39–43.

Falzeder, E. (Ed.) (2002). *The Complete Correspondence of Sigmund Freud and Karl Abraham 1907–1925*. London: Karnac.

Falzeder, E. & Brabant, E. (Eds.) (1996). *The Correspondence of Sigmund Freud and Sandor Ferenczi Volume 2. 1914–1919*. Cambridge, MA: The Belknap Press of Harvard University Press.

Falzeder, E. & Brabant, E. (Eds.) (2000). *The Correspondence of Sigmund Freud and Sándor Ferenczi. Volume 3, 1920–1933*. Cambridge, MA: The Belknap Press of Harvard University Press.

Fliess, W. (1897). *Beziehungen zwischen Nase und weiblichen Geschlectsorganen*. Leipzig. Vienna: Deuticke.

Freud, E. L. (Ed.) (1961). *Letters of Sigmund Freud 1873–1939*. London: Hogarth.

Freud, E. L. & Meng, H. (Eds.) (1963). *Psychoanalysis and Faith: The Letters of Sigmund Freud and Oskar Pfister*. London: The Hogarth Press and the Institute of Psycho-Analysis.

Freud, S. (1900a). *The Interpretation of Dreams. S. E., 4 & 5*. London: Hogarth.

Freud, S. (1901b). *The Psychopathology of Everyday Life. S. E., 6*. London: Hogarth.

Freud, S. (1912–13). *Totem and Taboo. S. E., 13*. London: Hogarth.

Freud, S. (1917). A childhood recollection from *Dichtung und Wahrheit. S. E., 17*. London: Hogarth.

Freud, S. (1920g). *Beyond the* Pleasure *Principle. S. E., 18*. London: Hogarth.

Freud, S. (1923b). *The Ego and the Id. S. E., 19*. London: Hogarth.

Freud, S. (1923c). Remarks on the theory and practice of fream interpretation. *S. E., 19*. London: Hogarth.

Freud, S. (1923d). A seventeenth century demonological neurosis. *S. E., 19*. London: Hogarth.

Freud, S. (1923e). The infantile genital organization of the libido. *S. E., 19*. London: Hogarth.

Freud, S. (1924). Neurosis and psychosis. *S. E., 19*. London: Hogarth.

Freud, S. (1924a). The loss of reality in neurosis and psychosis. *S. E., 19*. London: Hogarth.

Freud, S. (1924c). The economic problem of masochism. *S. E., 19*. London: Hogarth.

Freud, S. (1924d). The dissolution of the Oedipus complex. *S. E., 19*. London: Hogarth.

Freud, S. (1925). Some psychological consequences of the anatomical distinction between the sexes. *S. E., 19*. London: Hogarth.

Freud, S. (1925a). Negation. *S. E., 19*. London: Hogarth.

Freud, S. (1925d). *An Autobiographical study. S. E., 20*. London: Hogarth.

Freud, S. (1926a). *The Question of Lay Analysis. S. E., 20*. London: Hogarth.

Freud, S. (1926d). *Inhibitions, Symptoms and Anxiety. S. E., 20*. London: Hogarth.

Freud, S. (1927c). *The Future of an Illusion. S. E., 21*. London: Hogarth.

Freud, S. (1930). *Civilization and its Discontents. S. E., 21*. London: Hogarth.

Freud, S. (1937). Analysis terminable and interminable. *S. E., 23*. London: Hogarth.

Freud, S. (1937a). Constructions in analysis. *S. E., 23*. London: Hogarth.

Freud, S. (1939). *Moses and Monotheism. S. E., 23*. London: Hogarth.

Freud, S. (1940a). *An Outline of Psycho-Analysis. S. E., 23*. London: Hogarth.

Gay, P. (2006). *Freud: A Life for Our Time*. New York: W. W. Norton and Company.

Groddeck, G. (1923). *The book of the It*. New York: International Universities Press, 1976.

Jones, E. (1954). *Jones' papers*. Anna Freud letter to Jones, June 16, 1954 Archives of British Psycho-Analytical Society, London.

Jones, E. (1957). *Sigmund Freud Life and Work, Volume Three, The Last Phase 1919–1939*. London: Hogarth.

Jung, C. G. (1904–7). *Studies in Word Association*. CW2. London: Routledge.

Jung, C. G. (1913). *The Theory of Psychoanalysis*. CW4. London: Routledge.

Jung, C. G. (1938/54). *Psychological Aspects of the Mother Archetype*. CW9i. London: Routledge.

Masson, J. M. (Ed.) (1985). *The complete letters of Sigmund Freud to Wilhelm Fliess, 1887–1904*. Cambridge, MA: Harvard University Press.

Paskauskas, R. A. (Ed.) (1993). *The Complete Correspondence of Sigmund Freud and Ernest Jones 1908–1939*. Cambridge, MA: The Belknap Press of Harvard University Press.

Pfeiffer, E. (Ed.) (1963). *Sigmund Freud and Lou Andreas-Salomé Letters*. London: The Hogarth Press and the Institute of Psycho-Analysis.

Rudnytsky, P. L. (1987). *Freud and Oedipus*. New York: Columbia University Press.

Schur, M. (1972). *Freud Living and Dying*. London: Hogarth.

Shakow, D. & Rapaport, D. (1964). *The Influence of Freud on American Psychology*. New York: International Universities Press.

Spielrein, S. (1912). Destruction as the cause of becoming. *Jahrbuch fur psychoanalytische und psychopatologische Forschungen, IV*: 465–503.

Uhland, J. L. (1815). *Vaterländische Gedichte*. Paris: Baudry.

CHAPTER TWO

Understanding the patient with cancer*

Dorothy Judd

I am often struck by how many basic psychoanalytic concepts describing states of mind are magnified by those facing a life-threatening illness. As human beings we may grapple with these conditions, ordinarily, but having cancer can give us a heightened awareness of them, exemplified in Freud's (1916) description: "Transience value is scarcity value in time".

Some of the states of mind which a life-threatening illness may illuminate, or make starker, include:

Uncertainty
Nameless dread
Falling forever
Catastrophic change
A sense of "going-on-being"
Existential questions about life and death, and spirituality
Guilt

---

*This paper was first presented at the London Centre for Psychotherapy (now part of a new organisation: the British Psychotherapy Foundation) on 29 October 2011.

A need to make reparation, or a failure of reparation

The passing of time as a fact of life, which involves an awareness of mortality

Creativity, that is to say, the lack of, or failed, or stimulation of creative potential

Gratitude

Loneliness

Fragmentation

Emptiness and bleakness

Containment, or failures of containment

Mourning: the loss of the hoped-for future, mourning of past losses reactivated.

In this paper I will touch on some of these.

I will begin with "container/contained", Bion's original concept of the mother's role in the developmental trajectory of the infant: the way the infant projects his or her distress into the mother who, if all goes well, processes the distress and returns it to the infant as something more manageable. The emotional experience of having cancer can feel too overwhelming for one's internalised container, even if we are generally coping with life. Cancer, as we know, carries widespread associations with something aggressive and deadly inside oneself. We are familiar with the ubiquitous phrase "fighting cancer", and what can feel like a state of war between the cancer and the treatment. If the initial diagnosis and some of the treatments are traumatic in the true meaning of the word (i.e., breaching the psychic protective apparatus—from "trauma", in Greek, meaning "wound"), then the working through, the transforming of the trauma into something that can be thought about and reflected upon in order to find resilience would depend on what Fonagy (1994) and others call "reflective self function". This gives the capacity to lend meaning to one's experiences.

Isabel Menzies Lyth (1989) writes about "pre-disaster resources": what we have made of previous trauma influences the way we react to subsequent traumata.

Emily came to see me one March, a few years ago. Other than holiday breaks and breaks when she was unwell, I saw her weekly until her death nine months later, in December. I have changed many details to preserve confidentiality.

I knew from the referral that this fifty-four-year-old woman had a recurrence of breast cancer and metastases. Later I learnt that this recurrence had been diagnosed ten months earlier: a six centimetre mass in her breast, which had spread to her spine. She then had six months of chemotherapy, and surgery—all before I met her.

She was slim, attractive, well dressed, with something decisive and masculine about her. She was extremely articulate, and her voice had a gritty quality. I found her likeable, but potentially intimidating, as if she would be quick to find me inadequate. She was married, had two teenage children, and was the eldest of three children (with a brother and a sister) in her family of origin. Early on she described herself as "managerial" and bossy as a child, and extremely self-sufficient. She said her father, an air force man, was mild, and her mother had had a breakdown when Emily was about eight, which must have been when her younger sister was about two. She had gone to boarding school, and then to Cambridge, and had always been expected to be clever. She had had a Jungian analysis years previously.

In the first session I gathered that she held a very high managerial position in a well-known worldwide organisation. She had been part of a team which planned for change, and she herself had received huge accolades. She had recently retired, but had not yet had the special event to mark her retirement. She had thoughts about returning to the same organisation to work part-time, adding, "to prove that I'm wanted, good enough". I felt that this was immediately projected into me, for I had fears about my inadequacy in really understanding her. She acknowledged what she called "separation anxiety" about leaving the organisation. She was aware that in spite of her success she had an insatiable need to prove herself. In fact, she said, the two problems that she wished us to work on were this need for affirmation, and her relationship with her mother. She added that she was very "goal orientated". I must confess that my heart sank at this, realising that this feisty and thrusting woman would probably be disappointed by the kind of explorations I might offer. I did not know what her "pre-disaster resources" were, before the cancer, and how much of her drive was a defence against the uncertainties of her illness. I suspected that the illness came as a shocking interruption to her hardworking life. Indeed, she asked for "tools" to help her with her goals. I said something about not being sure that I could offer her such specific direction, and said that we might have conversations, in which we might meander, … and perhaps find greater understanding. She didn't like the word "meander". (By the way, it is not a word I usually use. I think it was my attempt to slow her down, and to suggest that conversations, or journeys, which do not have a strict agenda, can bring surprising rewards.)

She fought back tears as she said something about actually wanting to see me, she *did* want to make a commitment, knowing she was choosing a psychoanalytic approach. I thought about her hunger for containment which, probably, she had not experienced before but knew from her unconscious preconceptions (Bion, 1962) of its existence. I said that she seemed ashamed of her tears right now. "Oh yes", she replied, "and I have a phobia about vomiting". Both her parents, she said, found her physical self unbearable, hating vomit and tears. She mocked herself for crying now.

I learnt that as a child she had a fear of wolves and wild animals prowling around if she cried. This showed me how persecutory and helpless it was not to be contained, and to be at the mercy of unmodulated feelings, including rage at the failure of containment.

She said she had nearly been late today because she was helping her brother with a presentation. Next week would be the last week of her radiotherapy, she said; she would see the oncologist in a few weeks. Other than that, there was no mention of the cancer, and very little about her husband.

When someone brings such a range of issues (all being legitimate reasons to commence psychotherapy) while at the same time I know that a serious, possibly fatal cancer is also in the room, and that the treatment may therefore need to be time-limited and fit around medical treatments and conditions, does it affect the way that I work? In short, the answer is no. I do not see it as my job to comfort, reassure, or avoid what she and I knew about a possibly imminent death. Just as with any other patient, I am interested in the analytic process, which is really about the patient's unconscious, and how it manifests in the present. Generally it is up to the patient to find her wish to tackle her more frightened feelings, once some trust in me and in the therapeutic relationship has been established. However, although I say that, when up against another's powerful defences and projections, I often fall short of that approach, and the reader will see when and how in this paper.

At this early stage I was struck by Emily's urgency in what she brought, and the volume of it—rather like a huge vomit at times— but sensed that the pre-cancer Emily was probably like this. I knew I would have to slow her down at times in order to hear, understand, and process. I did not know at this early stage if her apparent lack of regard for my capacity to take in everything was because she did not hope for much processing, or if she was testing my capacity, or if she assumed I was as frenzied as she was. I also wondered if she was projecting the part of her that was afraid of being found wanting.

With a full nine months of therapy to survey, all I will focus on here, in an abbreviated form, are the ways in which Emily used the therapy, her particular responses to her illness, as well as my approach. I will convey this under date headings, chronologically, which perhaps illustrates the relentlessness of Time and of the Illness. My notes, made after the sessions, were often not very detailed. I recorded dreams in detail, as I usually do, but otherwise just the general drift, as well as some striking phrases:

> **11th March**—2nd session: Emily has sleep problems; wakes every two hours. "Fear of fear", she surmises. "And fear of stopping treatment", she adds. I begin to recognise her capacity for succinct aphorism.
>
> She brings a dream of a garden where primroses grow, only she can't see them at first. She associated this with a positive memory of digging up primroses as a child. I interpret something spring-like and beautiful in her—growth—which she can't see. She is sceptical about my comment. Later I realised that I did not interpret the deadly implications in the dream: digging up something alive, which would then die (if not replanted.)
>
> She is very excited about a plan of hers to offer career coaching in the future.
>
> **18th March**: Markedly different. Emily takes off a wrist brace she is wearing. Many moments of silence, and there is a darkness about her. Eventually she talks about hating her "blobbism" as she calls it, adding, "You know, 'lumpen'". She says she is either highly charged on adrenalin, needing one or two people around her, or she becomes blobby. She is fearful, she says, of these sessions leading to something she doesn't want to find. She acknowledges that she has spent most of her life "in front of the lights", and knows it's a facade.
>
> She brings several dreams, mostly about food, and one about her father on crutches. She adds that she has been ravenous this week. One dream has a broken wooden rocking horse in it, with no rockers.

Most of this session can be understood as a vivid representation of what Bick (1967) called a "second skin" phenomenon: the use of second skin muscularity in order to compensate for the failure of real containment, or internal good objects. Bick writes about disturbance in the primal skin function that "can lead to a 'second skin' formation through which dependence on the object is replaced by a pseudo-independence, by the inappropriate use of certain mental functions … for the purpose of creating a substitute for this skin container function". Emily does not believe there will be any help in managing the feelings arising from this experience of having cancer, presumably like the feelings with which she was left at boarding school. The wooden horse in her dream cannot hold her and gives rise to fears of falling.

She talks about her husband's overwhelming fears about her cancer. I say, "It seems that there's no space for yours yet", letting her think about the implications of what I say regarding a space here.

4th April: Very moving. She breaks down and cries. It is, it seems, over a sense of a lack of a "source", as she calls it. What a good description of the lack of a containing mother, I think.

She brings a dream of her sewing machine being burnt in a fire, and the machine's tension for the thread not being right. This was her mother's sewing machine, and she says something about a lack of a good connection with her mother. She loved the machine in the dream, but it is unrepairable. This refers to the lack of belief that her container can be rehabilitated. She needs to mourn its loss, in order then to repair it.

Emily brings another dream of a place of disrepair, tatty curtains, her father in nappies, rough ground outside. I wondered if this was a representation of the lack of support she felt from her weak father.

Yet, I cannot touch on all that yet, and clearly share my thoughts, for she zooms on to her job of making a "to-do" list, wanting to use time in a good way, yet feeling guilty, she says, for making time for herself. I think the "to do" lists are forms of "second skin holding", to keep moving, because if she does not she will become "lumpen" or "blobby".

(Later I wonder if, by not interpreting much, I am letting down the part of her that has come to me for analysis, not life coaching. However, she is at least allowing me to see her poor inner state.)

8th April: She is a quarter of an hour late, and brings three very full dreams. One is about falling into quicksand, another about trying unsuccessfully to stop factory workers doing pointless mechanical work. Again this shows second skin falling into non-holding quicksand, and the pointless mechanical work being second skin "doing". And yet, we could say that, by dreaming this, her unconscious is giving her a picture of the problem, even if, in the dream, she fails in stopping the pointless work.

Emily says she has been tackling her "to-do" list. She says she is aware that, arising from some of our conversations, she is not allowing unstructured time, what she calls "transitional time", which could include chaos.

She cries over her son being moved—not Emily being moved—by Emily's attempts to change. So she can feel moved to tears by someone else's feelings for her.

She feels that the ending of the session is very abrupt and asks for an extra session this week, to which I agree.

11th April: It is clear how much Emily needs to be superlative. I find myself wanting to be special for her. I ask myself how much this is because of the sword of Damocles hanging over us, and how much it is a last chance for her to repair her connection to her internal mother via the transference.

She tells me that as an eleven year old she overheard her mother saying, "I can't wait for Emily to go to boarding school". Nowadays she sends emails to her parents about her illness. Mother's reaction is, "Oh no, not now", or, "I thought something like this would happen". Yet somehow she begins to feel more forgiving towards her mother's emotional "thinness".

15th April: She talks about not wanting to be "ordinary". I take up her possible disappointment with me. She says she does find something special here, through *her* creative endeavours. I think she means her bringing dreams, her gradual lessening of her defences.

But I am not sure what part I, as a separate other, play in this. Something, however, was percolating through to her, in her increasing capacity to *feel* (at times) and her indirect but implicit ways of approaching death: death as the ultimate deadline. "To-do" lists can be a second skin "holding", as I have said, but they also convey an awareness of finiteness. She is then protected from "nameless dread" (Bion; Judd, 1995), in other words, unnamed and uncontained fears of dying. "To-do" lists can be like building a rampart of sand on a beach, to keep out the encroaching tide.

With someone as powerfully defended as Emily, I had to provide a broad thinking base, and tolerate my feelings of helplessness at times, for her to make discoveries in her own somewhat omnipotent way. I began to see that she was projecting into me her helplessness and fear of failure, which I had to contain.

The speediness of her delivery and manner made it very hard to pause and try to explore some of these feelings. I had to hold them in an active processing way, and be patient. Emily would have to come to making real links in her own time, if at all.

As in all work with dying patients, one has to ask oneself where at times are one's own fears of death, of looking death in the eye; and so from time to time I would ask myself if my "patience" was in fact cowardice.

Emily says she is not really ill yet, but shares painful thoughts about what she will be leaving others with when she dies: the "legacy", as she calls it.

Again she feels full of the trivia of life, which stops her working on "the big project", her version of which is: "What to do with my life".

22nd April: She cries terribly, about dying. Later, she says that it's alright to cry so much here, because she pays me. This shows how she cannot believe I would be willing to contain her unless I was paid to do it, that I would be like her mother who says, "Oh no, not now".

How tired she is, she says, of so much caring for others. She quotes an article in *The Guardian* on cancer, which describes a two to four year prognosis for metastatic cancer. "How to face death, and *live*?" she asks.

She talks about her bad indigestion and nausea. I find it hard to know when to make, at least tentatively, an interpretation of the indigestible thoughts, the "nameless dread", when there may be a physical cause of her symptoms.

Again she wants an extra session later this week, to which I agree.

25th April: She is worried about becoming dependent on me. She feels better today, says something about the fears of death being "absorbed". This, I think, has a nuance of containment, that is, another's capacity to absorb, receive, process, and metabolise her distress. She says she should be looking at death again, and that I would feel she should!

She feels very relieved about a helpful discussion with her son and husband last night, a discussion which she initiated.

Then Emily says she had thought of making plans as follows: if she is alive in two years' time, if in ten years, if in fifteen.

29th April: I see this session as one of several turning points.

Emily brings a dream that she got the wound (site of her mastectomy) wet, and the dressing came off, but the wound looked healthy and had healed.

She tells me about her fear of the unknown when she had her son, her firstborn. She had no instinct to call upon. This again reflects the psychological disaster of the lack of a containing mother, and references a baby-in-nappies-father from an earlier dream.

Then she talks about her feeling that she has now come off a roller coaster. She can hardly remember the ride, but then she says, "Oh yes I can remember, of course I can. But I am not on it any longer".

She takes pleasure in talking with cancer patients, in a group she attends, and does not feel depleted. She says it's her way of passing on her good experience, honing her understanding.

She wants me to find a therapist for her son to see.

She looks duller today. I feel she does need to shine.

She expresses fears about symptoms in her right hand and their function. I think of the profound meaning of that, but do not say anything.

6th May: A dream of cancer in every cell. Then another very long confusing dream which includes something about a sculpture which she describes. The image leads me to interpret it as being about her finding her combined internal parents. She herself understands the dream as her search for her authentic self, that doesn't need external affirmation.

Today I had forgotten to put water out for her, and then I had a bad coughing and choking fit in the session. How concrete was the projection of the lack of a digestive capacity!

She will be away on a Group Relations event for ten days.

3rd June: Emily seems lighter, perhaps more in control, full of projects and plans for her work. She reports hosting a successful tea party for everyone who has helped her.

10th June: Very controlled and bright, yet somehow thoughtful. She fears appearing "stupid" if she has to cancel some work for her previous organisation. She says that "things have to go according to plan".

Eventually she cries over the pressure she feels to conform and to be the dutiful daughter. She says, "Even though I may be dying, I can't feel free to make my own choices". I say, "But perhaps this is a golden opportunity".

(Later, I think about Emily's super-ego, and how it may be what Bion (1962) calls a "super" ego. Like the usual psychoanalytic meaning of superego, it is a superior object asserting its pre-eminence by finding fault with everything. The most significant aspect of this "super" ego, however, is "its hatred of any new development in the personality, as if the new development were a rival to be destroyed". Her mother was envious of Emily's new kitchen, and generally of her successful career, I gathered. In the following session, she grapples with that very problem.)

17th June: She quotes JK Rowling as saying: "It's important to fail in life, to allow for failure, as part of life." I acknowledge what she is saying, and talk about humility.

She then acknowledges that she is bad at failing, and laughs, "I'll die failing to fail!"

She begins to think about telling her father, but not her mother, about significant scan results due tomorrow.

She had a panic attack in Dublin over the previous weekend, with thoughts of dying horribly, letting her daughter down, and appearing stupid. (The panic signals "minus container/contained" (Bion).)

24th June: Scan results are good; she plans to live in three-month bursts. But somehow she conveys that the good results make her more anxious about death. Though I cannot remember how we understood that, I later wondered if the relief and space afforded by good results, and some sense of my containing capacity, grant her more mental space, to feel fear, and to be able to name it.

1st July: Dream of playing charades, and she has to mime "Life on the brink". No one guesses her mime. I cannot remember if I interpreted this in the transference by saying that she feels I am not picking up her feeling of being on the brink of life and death, especially after her telling me last time that having good results made her more anxious.

Lack of space now, in this paper, means I can't bring the July, August, and September sessions in much detail, although I was away for five weeks during the summer months, with fairly brief email contact. Yet perhaps my brief notes here reflect Emily's lack of time, her need to condense her last weeks and months into something meaningful. I am aware that my account sounds clipped at times, and think that this is partly due to scant notes, but, perhaps, also reflects the abbreviated contact we had in her truncated life.

In August, Emily has a recurrence of fluid around the brain affecting the optic nerve, leading to vision problems. As not much is known about treatment and protocols, she tells me that she is doing research herself, and making decisions.

She now feels she does not have to do so much, to achieve every day; she wants people to spare her.

At the end of one session she seems to fall out of the room—unconsciously and concretely letting me know about a collapsing part of her.

2nd September: I mention that fall in the following session. She cries silently. Then, "Yes," she says, "it's about not knowing if the exhaustion is the disease, or the treatment, or is emotional." She then adds, "And the doctors probably don't know".

9th September: A dream of a close friend at a concert, singing, "In Dublin's fair city … Alive, alive-o". She says she manages her envy in the dream, and appreciates the friend's singing. Perhaps, given her panic in Dublin recently, this dream seems quite a hopeful dream, in the sense of finding something beautiful, that lives on.

18th October: While in hospital with raised intra-cranial pressure she writes me an email: "I am having difficulty finding any kind of silver lining in this particular storm of clouds, and suspect I would benefit from a short email exchange with you". At the end of the email she writes, "As ever, support from friends and family has been overwhelming. I thought you'd also like to know that plans for my leaving 'do' are falling well into place—all I now have to do is try to be fit enough to be there!"

Over the next several sessions she is in touch with what she won't achieve, and feels cheated over missed opportunities. She envies those in their eighties.

She has an attack of neurological symptoms during a few sessions, that is, spasm, pain, numbness. It all feels too much for her, and, privately, for me too at times. So it is not surprising that on occasion she returns to a powerful determination to keep feelings out, that she talks about doing some coaching professionally, and that she refuses to call herself "retired".

Markedly thinner each week.

Dream of her mother being there. Emily can hear her, but can't see her. This seems to convey a mother who is present, but cannot really take things in, or contain.

A hole in the head operation brings relief. More chemo, for symptom control. When she looks at difficult things, she tells me, she literally gets a pain in her head. To my relief she is now brought by her brother, instead of driving herself to her sessions.

2nd December: Much calmer. She tells me she was twice moved to tears in the past week, to her surprise. The first time was when visiting her Jewish friend Rachel's house, where they were sitting *shivah* for Rachel's father who had recently died; and how pleased they were that Emily had visited. The other tearful experience related to a note her father wrote about Emily's achievements.

She then describes how undermining and bitter her mother is of her father. But then, Emily says, "My mother didn't receive kindness as a child, so has none to give".

I feel very moved by her insight, and her own struggle to be kind to herself.

9th December: This is the last time I see her in the consulting room. She is in pain, and is extremely thin. She tries to be what she calls "normal". But unbidden thoughts and figures appear, such as her seeing Jessica (her daughter) on my left shoulder. She is perturbed by these occurrences. I say that I wonder why Jessica comes to her mind now. She is quite agitated. I attempt to talk about her mind being feverish, that we don't know how much the disease is affecting her mind, making it hard for her to think. I add that perhaps she feels that her fears of dying cannot be understood.

She half hears me. She says she would rather deal with practical things now.

Then anxiously she says, "It's a state of fragmentation, because of a transition from my old self to the new".

I think about huge uncertainty, listen, and nod. There is a silence. She seems upset.

I ask her if she wants to say more about what she has just said. She looks down, at her hands.

I think about the catastrophic change that she is going through, and how fearful she is, and say, "When you say 'new' you will, of course, have aspects of your old self". She smiles with relief.

I realise that I did not allow Emily to name the uncertainty, to be able, in a way, to be curious about it. I used the phrase "old self" because I could not contain the uncertainty and unknown "new".

She asks if it's worth it, the transformation?

I say, "Well, you have a way of, in a way, embracing things, even if they are hard".

She agrees emphatically.

Then she is very preoccupied with her son's Cambridge interview this week, and hopes to go away in late December.

Afterthoughts on this session: In our brief, rather elliptical conversation, constrained by her physical symptoms, I realise that I reassure her that she would still have some aspects of her old self, but I do not stay with the *not knowing*. She seemed so anxious about this change. Yet reassurance is not what I am here for, and I did not contain the uncertainty.

Later I wonder if by "transformation" she meant a transition from her task-orientated driven state to one that was more accepting now, accepting of her physical symptoms and of her imminent death over which she has no control? Did this mean that she could now *think* more, in the transformative way about which Bion (1967) writes? Her long-held fantasy is that action (i.e., "to-do" lists, clear plans for the future, a potent professional identity, all of which represent "second skin" phenomena) is required to rid herself of painful thoughts, or, perhaps, not to allow those thoughts in the first place. Did she feel fragmented in the process of change, some transformation of disparate paranoid-schizoid elements into something closer to the depressive position, even a sense of a "new" self who risked not knowing, having now gained a taste of a containing mother through her experience with me?

Yet her next sentence was about wanting to help her son with the Cambridge interview, and then to make plans for a holiday next month. So perhaps it was all the more understandable for her to revert to making plans, and to practical things, given that I had not stayed with the uncertainty.

I was phoned by her husband five days later. Emily was in hospital, dying. He asked if I would like to visit her. I said Yes, I would go the next morning. He asked if there was anything he needed to know, to help Emily now? After a moment's hesitation, I said that I thought that she would like it very much if her mother visited her, if possible.

I remember the deep snow on the way to the hospital, my anxiety that the bus would not get through. But then the warmth and calm and order of the hospital, with its formal flowers and deep blue carpets. Her husband met me and told me that Emily's mother had spent hours at the hospital the previous night, with Emily, and they had had some close contact.

Her brother, sister, children, and husband left the room, in order to grant me a few minutes alone with her. She was in a calm, semi-conscious state. I said goodbye to her. Her eyes flickered.

She died that night.

From the foregoing account, the reader can see how I had to put aside many of my preconceptions, to try to work with Emily in the ways she wanted. I did find her accelerated understanding of her struggle impressive, particularly because for Emily it went so against the grain. This is no easy task for most of us. As Freud wrote (1929), about looking at the unconscious: "So if someone tries to turn our awareness inward, in effect twisting its neck round, then our whole organisation resists, just as, for example, the oesophagus and the urethra resist any attempt to reverse their normal direction of passage".

So we often need to put up defences against a truth—that of a life-threatening or fatal illness—that is too painful, especially if our internal resources are limited and we find it hard to use another's mind.

In 1624 John Donne wrote: "A sick bed is a grave … Here the head lies as low as the foot … miserable and … inhuman posture … I cannot rise out of my bed till the physician enable me … I do nothing, I know nothing, of myself".

It is easy to see how serious illness can feel like being forced into helplessness, and into infancy. One of Emily's greatest difficulties was this helplessness and its associations with being a child—and an adult— without a containing mother. This is the essence of a lack of pre-disaster resources. For others it can be an almost welcome opportunity to regress and to be looked after, although that may indicate an unresolved sense of being adult. I have found that in adolescents with cancer this struggle is particularly marked: their ways of complying, or not complying, with treatment depend on how securely established is their inner sense of being a young adult.

The following brief example (quoted from Judd, 1994) serves to illustrate a young adolescent's oscillating reaction, which, of course, we see in adults as well: knowing and not knowing, waves of awareness, for the stark reality can feel overwhelming.

Abigail, a thirteen-year-old with lymphoma and poor prognosis, soon after diagnosis, said "Some people, when they hear the word 'cancer', start digging your grave immediately". She was clearly trying to put her fears of death into others. I asked her what she thought "cancer" meant in terms of survival. She said categorically, "Most people have a ninety per cent chance of success". I said, "What about the ten per cent?" "That's the older ones", she replied.

She was able, however, to explore her own shock more readily in relation to the forthcoming chemotherapy and subsequent hair loss: "When I heard about that, people might have thought I fainted. I just lay there". She talked indignantly about those who regard her illness as frightening or contagious, and who should be "educated". It seemed adaptive at the early stage of her adjustment for much of the problem to be located elsewhere.

I will end with a series of six drawings by one girl, who I will call Ayesha: a slim sixteen- year-old from Egypt, who had come to London for an amputation of her leg and post-operative chemotherapy. The medical team knew she had extensive lung cancer secondaries, but I am not sure how much she understood that. Her father, with whom she did not appear to have a close relationship, accompanied her, whilst her mother had stayed back home to look after the other five children. Ayesha and her father spent hours reading the Koran, separately.

I first saw her five weeks after the amputation. As she could not speak English, and I could not speak Arabic, I used a dictionary occasionally, as well as mime.

Picture 1

She drew this picture in our first meeting. You can see how fragmented it is, and how immature for her age it looks. It conveys her regressed, impoverished state, with various symbols: an empty plate; a glass of drink, possibly water; a chair with only three legs; a very insubstantial person with one leg; and a sort of nipple/breast, which is the only thing that is coloured in—emphasised, as if it carries an emotional charge. All I said to her, with the help of the dictionary, and gesturing, was: "You miss your mother". Her face lit up in acknowledgement. I felt we were "in business".

Picture 2

In the next meeting, a few days later, she produced this drawing: a basket of five flowers, in a much more age-appropriate style, possibly because she began to feel contained by me. Ayesha wrote her five siblings' names down the side. I thought it was about her siblings back home being held in mother's "basket" without her.

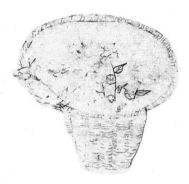

Picture 3

This sad drawing, made in the next meeting, begins to express her plight. She shows a helpless girl with arms behind her back, and inadequate feet with stylised high heels which look most difficult to walk on. The horizontal bands of the dress seem to cross out the site of the problem: the amputation. Perhaps she felt sufficiently understood (contained) to proceed immediately to the next drawing:

Picture 4

This clearly shows her longing for both the lost leg and for the prosthesis she so wanted, which was not forthcoming because of funding problems. She knew that there was a financial struggle to procure the leg, with which she longed to return home. Notice the two legs facing each other, as if keen to get together, and how the feet are more real, and the lost leg, or prosthesis, is solid and substantial and therefore desirable. The arms are more potent, possibly even angry.

Picture 5

She knew that she was probably not going to get the prosthesis, and that she would be returning to Egypt soon. Another girl from Egypt on the ward translated that this drawing was of the dolls of Paradise that they have at certain festivals. Notice, again, the horizontal bands on the dress, and the wings, and the blonde hair, when Ayesha herself had lost her dark hair from the treatment. It is certainly a beautiful girl or angel, and is quite idealised. It seems to be her way of coping with loss for the time being, perhaps by turning to Paradise. At this time she seemed to spend even more hours every day reading from the Koran.

Before the reader looks at the last picture that Ayesha drew before returning to Egypt the following day, I will comment on something I have often found in young people facing death: that is, a willingness to share, to leave some alive viable part of themselves with the recipient. It is as if this facilitates their facing death. We can understand this in many ways: in many cultures there is a wish to leave significant tokens or symbols with the person who had died, and to keep mementos of the one who has died. This is a concrete example of the more psychological process I am describing, which is a way of softening the extreme separation that death implies: if a healthy part of us lives on in others, in their memories of us, inevitably the finality of death is more bearable. Symbolically the therapist may carry this projection up to and beyond the patient's death, thus enabling him or her to relinquish this world. In an ideal, but excruciatingly painful, world, this function could be that of the parents. Through these pictures, and especially through the final one, and through shared understanding, Ayesha left me with her struggle to integrate the loss of her limb with a more whole, intact self, so that she could face going to her Maker. In Muslim culture it is extremely important to be buried with all one's body parts, and that partly explains Ayesha's desperation for at least a prosthesis, if not the actual limb. As that was not possible, she nevertheless found a psychological, symbolic, and, in a sense, more real intactness which I believe could only be arrived at *once she had acknowledged the reality of the loss and the lack of intactness.* This is a fundamental part of the mourning process.

Picture 6

This was the last picture she drew, before returning to Egypt the next day. The other Muslim girl on the ward translated the writing on the boat as "Ship of Allah" (although I later learned that in fact the words are usually translated as "Allah is the Greatest"). The girl in the drawing is certainly serene, and looks happy. The kite goes up towards Paradise, in a very striking yellow sky, which gives it a spiritual splendour. The boat is three-dimensional, with the girl securely within it. The sea, possibly representing the mother, from whom we all come, is very much a part of the picture.

It really does seem that this young woman was able to arrive at an impressive acceptance of her plight. Ayesha conveyed a capacity for an accelerated mourning which some people facing death are impressively capable of.

I learnt that she died a few weeks later, back home.

Postscript

I do not wish to idealise dying, for there is of course anguish and loss, and perhaps fear, but if it is not too sudden, and is not a death out of season, there can also be a heightened intensity, an awareness of the transience of life, and above all, the glory of living in the present.

I end with a quote from Dennis Potter, when he was interviewed by the broadcaster and author, Melvyn Bragg, in 1994. It may be what many people—whether dying or not—strive for:

> "That nowness becomes so vivid to me now, that in a perverse sort of way, I'm almost serene, I can celebrate life … the blossom is out in full … instead of saying, 'Oh that's nice blossom', looking at it through the window when I'm writing it is the whitest, frothiest, blossomiest blossom that there ever could be".

Acknowledgement

I am very grateful to Ricky Emanuel, who read a draft of this paper, for some extremely insightful comments, and alerted me to his paper (2001).

References

Bick, E. (1967). The experience of the skin in early object-relations. *International Journal of Psycho-Analysis, 49*: 484–486.

Bion, W. R. (1962). Learning from experience. In: *Seven Servants*. New York: Jason Aronson. (Reprinted London: Karnac, 1988.)

Bion, W. R. (1967). A Theory of Thinking. In: *Second Thoughts*. London: Heinemann. (Reprinted London: Karnac, 1993.)

Emanuel, R. (2001). A-Void—an exploration of defences against sensing nothingness, *International Journal of Psycho-Analysis, 82*(6): 1069–1084.

Fonagy P., Steele M., Steele H., Higgitt A., & Target M. (1994). The theory and practice of resilience. *Journal of Child Psychology and Psychiatry, 35*(2): 231.

Freud, S. (1916). On transience. *S. E., 14*: 305–307. London: Hogarth.

Freud, S. (1929). Letter to A. Einstein. In: Grubrich-Simitis, I. Letters between Freud and Einstein, *International Journal of Psycho-Analysis, 76*: 115–122 (1995).

Judd, D. (1994). Life threatening illness as psychic trauma: psychotherapy with adolescent patients. In: A. Erskine & D. Judd (Eds.), *The Imaginative Body: Psychodynamic Therapy in Health Care*. London: Whurr.

Judd, D. (1995). *Give Sorrow Words: Working with a Dying Child* (2nd edition). London: Whurr. (3rd edition: London: Karnac, 2014.)

Menzies Lyth, I. (1989). The aftermath of disaster. In: *The Dynamics of the Social*. London: Free Association Books.

Potter, D. (1994). *Without Walls: An Interview with Dennis Potter*. Channel 4 Television.

CHAPTER THREE

The emotional impact of cancer on children and their families*

Anthony Lee and Jane Elfer

The child and adolescent psychotherapy discipline at University College London Hospital (UCLH) is part of the Department of Child and Adolescent Psychological Medicine, which also comprises teams of clinical and systemic psychologists and child and adolescent psychiatrists. With two other child and adolescent psychotherapists and a child and adolescent psychotherapist in training, we provide a psychoanalytic psychotherapy service to children and their families and to young people referred from within the hospital. We dedicate a significant proportion of our time to work with the young people who are treated in the teenage and young adult service, as well to the many young children who are treated here for their cancer in the paediatric service. A high proportion of children with brain tumours come to UCLH for radiotherapy treatment.

In this chapter, we consider aspects of our experience of working closely with children with cancer. Through case material and with reference to the literature, we will attempt to construct a narrative around

---

*Throughout, unless referring to a specific case, we denote the masculine for the child, the feminine for the therapist, and use the term "parents" to refer to any adult or adults who may care for the child.

the emotional impact of cancer on children and their families. It is an account drawn from our close observations of the children and their families and from our countertransference responses from being in their company.

The emotional impact of cancer

A diagnosis of cancer immediately raises consummate anxieties both conscious and unconscious, around loss, dying, and death. This is in stark contrast to the more ordinary anxieties—and joys—around a child growing up that are associated with his emerging bids for independence. Children diagnosed with cancer may find themselves relying on their parents physically and emotionally in ways that may have been more typical of when they were younger. This may be the case for any child with a serious or disabling illness, but the anxieties surrounding thoughts of loss, death, and dying, bring a quality of omnipresent terror that can have profound effects on the child and his family. The diagnosis, the shock, the urgency of the treatment, the demolition of ordinary life is traumatising; the resultant uncertainty maintains the traumatic state and may leave the child and his family undefined, disorganised, and profoundly distraught.

For each family member, such trauma is met with the erection of powerful defensive structures, where the full impact of the shock is mitigated to prevent a collapse into despair and dread. Thus, for example, the child with cancer may appear oblivious to his illness and be thought of by others as "brave", "coping amazingly", "so grown up", but at other times seen as fretful, and clingy, frightened and terrified, and at other times unreasonably demanding furious and angry. The sibling may at times tenderly temper his needs in consideration of his brother's or sister's and parents' states; at other times be distant and withdrawn. The parents may find themselves in a surreal and exhausting "going through the motions" state, which serves to hold them together to do what needs to be done, but which from time to time is punctured by the horrifying reality of what is happening. Both children and parents will, in their own ways and with varying degrees of success, attempt to restrain themselves to protect the other—at other times not. Within the family, one person's shift in state of mind will affect all the others. The ongoing dynamic inevitably leaves everyone feeling at times wrong-footed, inept, and insensitive, guilty, and angry. It can lead the family members feeling at times dejectedly disconnected from one another. This complexity is in part explained by the fact that despite "cancer" being the common source of cataclysmic upheaval in the family, each family member will react uniquely to the trauma, both from moment to moment and in terms of their anticipation of what the future might bring.

Projective identification

Melanie Klein (Klein, 1974) showed how the infant, at a time in his development when he has limited capacity to integrate his experiences, instinctively deals with early anxieties and overpowering impulses by splitting off such experiences and projecting them into his parent. Betty Joseph (Joseph, 1993) writes that in its most primitive form "… projective identification is the attempt to get back into an object—to become, as it were, undifferentiated and mindless and thus avoid all pain" (p. 178). Projective identification continues to be used as a psychic defense, though to a lesser degree and for other purposes, as the child develops and grows. Wilfred Bion (Bion, 1959) felt that the process could also be understood as a means of communication, whereby the child casts the parts of his experience and inner world that are un-processed and un-digestible into the other—to have these parts received, processed, and returned in a form that makes the experience bearable and meaningful.

Irma Pick writes that the projective identifications have powerful effects on the recipient—the function of this process is to evoke a reaction: "… in so far as we take in the experience of the patient, we cannot do so without also having an experience. If there is a mouth that seeks a breast as an inborn potential, there is, I believe, a psychological equivalent, i.e. a state of mind which seeks another state of mind" (Pick, 1988, p. 35). As child psychotherapists, we must not only allow time to process these projections, but remain conscious of and process our own reactions to them. Given the inherent drive in all of us to move from discomfort, the child psychotherapist will come up against forces from within the child as well as herself, to enact—to avoid pain.

A child with cancer

Louis looks small and frail, but his rage was huge. He shouts at his mother and hits her with his small, balled fists. He did not want to go to radiotherapy. His mother patiently crouches down to speak to him. She gently encourages him to go down to the machine.

The machine is very large. It looks like the receiver of an old-fashioned telephone. It moves around the patient on the bed and pinpoints the beams to the diseased area. Radiographers help Louis to climb onto the bed and carefully adjust the height of the bed.

Louis has a brain tumour. He must lay very still, in exactly the same position each day, five days a week for six weeks. In order to do this he must have a head mask made—it is green with small air holes and a large hole at his mouth. The mask is screwed tight onto the bed to prevent any movement so the beams can be directed precisely at the tumour. Louis' mother helps and encourages him. The radiographers move around adjusting and correcting both the machine and the bed until all is set. They tell Louis and his mother that they are ready, and she says she will begin to count. Louis, now calm, puts his thumb in the air. He is six years old.

Everyone leaves the room. Louis, alone in the centre and fixed to the bed, stays in contact through the reassuring voices of his mother and the clinicians. The corridor from the room is long and winds round, back to the control room. This is because light travels in a straight line and the radiotherapy rays are of course dangerous. A warning sound begins. Once in the control room the mother and the clinicians can see Louis on the television screen and they speak to him through a microphone. "Okay Louis we're starting now!" The machine begins. Louis, like all the children before him, will feel and see nothing."Okay Louis, a little noise now! The machine is just moving round!" The thumb appears again, and Mother, who has been counting loudly for him, says "You're doing great Louis!" and resumes her counting. The machine moves across Louis. There is a flurry of movement as the clinicians run down to make small adjustments and then return to the control room and the radio-therapy continues. After a while: "All done Louis! We're coming down!" The treatment is finished for the day. Louis is freed from the confines of his mask and helped down from the bed. Mother congratulates him and tells him the number she had reached. It is about the same each day. "Well done!" she says and hugs him. He wriggles free and rushes to a sticker chart behind her. There are stickers ready for him and his drawing of a football pitch denotes how many "fractions" or treatments he has left.

This is a small part of Louis's treatment. He has had major surgery to remove the brain tumour—or as much as is safely accessible. Now six weeks of daily radiotherapy lie ahead of him to eradicate the remaining growth, to be followed by months of chemotherapy. This will make him sick, vulnerable to infections, and, for a time, hairless.

The journey is long and arduous for Louis and for all his family. The medical staff can also find it painful to subject children to such harsh treatments. (JE)

A diagnosis of cancer may follow on from a period of unexplained illness, where in the first instance aches and pains are treated with conventional, well-intended interventions to provide relief. Once a diagnosis of cancer has been confirmed, however, a specific treatment pathway is set out—depending on the nature of the cancer and its site. Children may often find themselves in a position of working to learn and understand about their illness during what is generally a massively disruptive period in their lives. In addition, they will be living in the company of parents who are themselves working to deal with the abject terror of such a diagnosis for their child. In essence, the child's world is turned upside down: what may once have been a life with a reasonable degree of certainty and order becomes one of huge uncertainty and disorder.

Amy, a bright and sensitive thirteen-year-old, had been experiencing increasingly severe headaches. It reached a point where she could no longer concentrate at school. The pain relief prescribed for migraine had little effect. Mother took Amy to the Accident and Emergency Department (A&E) at a weekend, where a scan showed the presence of a brain tumour. Amy's mother, a single parent of two children, was deeply distraught. Following immediate surgery, Amy underwent a lengthy period of daily radiotherapy.

Amy's consultant referred her to the service as he felt that Amy had become increasingly withdrawn. In the sessions that took place in the radiotherapy department, prior to her radiotherapy, Amy spoke of knowing the name of the cancer she had—a grade 4 glioblastoma—but not daring to look it up on the internet to find out what it meant. She lived in a pocket of frozen terror—not wanting to know, not wanting to ask questions, yet consumed by uncertainty.

Being in Amy's presence at this time, I found myself wanting to hold my breath—not daring to know. This primitive form of psychic protection adopted by Amy and projected out, served to evoke trepidation, anxiety for what being curious might reveal. The regularity of meetings helped to provide some certainty wherein I learned of Amy withdrawing from her friends so she did not have to face their questions, and withdrawing from her mother to protect her from even more distress.

After some four weeks, Amy reported in her session that she had searched on the internet to find out about her tumour. She had discovered hundreds of sites—some hopeful, others not. We sat in silence for a while. She eventually said that her cancer was a very aggressive type. She wiped the tears that streamed down both cheeks. After another period of silence, she asked me what she should do. I spoke about how she had felt she had to manage all by herself, but could now begin to think about turning to others. I said she was overwhelmed with what she had found out on the internet and that maybe it was to her consultant she should now turn. (AL)

The nature of trauma

We describe as "traumatic" any excitations from outside which are powerful enough to break through the protective shield. It seems to me that the concept of trauma necessarily implies a connection of this kind with a breach in an otherwise efficacious barrier against stimuli. (Freud, 1920)

Wilfred Bion described the role played by the parents in offering protection to the developing ego through their capacity to help the baby manage overwhelming emotional experiences through containment (Bion, 1967).

Melanie Klein has described an aspect of projective identification concerned with the modification of infantile fears; the infant projects a part of his psyche, namely his bad feelings, into a good breast. Thence, in due course they are removed and re-introjected. During their sojourn in the good breast they are felt to have been modified in such a way that the object that is re-introjected has become tolerable to the infant's psyche (Bion, 1962, p. 90).

Bion wrote, for example, of the terror that can engulf an infant if the mother is unable to contain her child: the experience of hunger can be felt by the infant as a terrifying pain that has no end. The mother who can help her baby to bear the wait for a feed can, over time, support the internalisation of a world that has order and is predictable and which supports the formation of a protective shield. In this way, the child is felt to be more able to deal with future adverse experiences.

When the ego's protective shield is broken through or shattered, the person is exposed not only to an external environment that feels unsafe, but an internal sense of disorder and chaos. The degree of devastation may be so complete that the traumatised person collapses completely. In most situations, however, the ego works to form a semblance of cohesion from the fragments. While cohesiveness is reinstated, the capacity to think is profoundly affected. The person traumatised may adopt a cognitive concreteness, that leads to the formation of a rigidly structured "traumatic organisation"—a "*second skin*" (Bick, 1968; Bick, 1986) that is defensively formed to encase the shattered ego. This organisation serves as the base for re-enactment of the trauma and thus impairs the ability to learn from experience (Bion, 1962).

Louis came into treatment with me for weekly psychotherapy after his period of radiotherapy. He attended regularly. Indeed, he missed only one session because he felt too ill to attend. Often he looked pale, and in the time after radiotherapy his radiated skin was burnt and sore. His scar from the surgery was prominent too. It induced in me a sense of pain and horror that such a small body should endure such hardship.

Initially, because Louis was exhausted by his treatment, he sat at the small table in the room and drew endless football pitches. He drew them carefully and when he made a mistake there would be sharp intake of breath and he would rub it out ferociously. I found myself at first commenting on the two sides battling it out—his team Liverpool and the opposing side, Newcastle, fighting for control of the ball. My mind whirled with the idea of a tumour and the fight to beat it. If I ventured a comment about this, he would just shake his head.

These drawings went on for some time. I found my mind going vacant at such times. I began to wonder about the safety of rules and regulations, of him needing to keep everything the same in

the face of such horrible things. Over time, I noticed that Louis'
drawings began to evolve—he began to depict places that required
colour and imagination. He drew a farm and a jungle, asking me
to help to colour in the sky or grass. I spoke about the life that he
had lived previously—full of colour and interest. He would not
respond to these thoughts—would not even look at me—but he
would continue to work industriously. (JE)

Being with Louis and seeing the impact the cancer and the treatment
was having on his small body evoked in the therapist a sense of injustice. Older children will often verbalise how unfair it feels—what did
they do that was any different to their friends? Louis' recurring drawings of a football pitch served to numb and deaden any thinking, with
his effort more directed at getting the perfect football pitch, though the
therapist finds a battle between life and death playing in her mind.
Over time, the rigidity of Louis' defences lessened and he was able to
bring variance into his drawings. Further, he turned to the therapist and
invited her to become involved, thereby enlivening the space between
them. In the therapist's experience, Louis was becoming more expressive, and she had a sense of a child re-emerging.

For parents dealing with their own horror, it is often hard to find the
right words to speak about what is happening to their child. How can
parents who themselves feel uncontained be expected to contain their
child? Ahmed was three years of age when he was referred to our
service—a small child with a brain tumour. His restless and aggressive
behaviour was making it almost impossible for staff to manage him and
to give him his medical treatment. Ahmed required daily radiotherapy
for six weeks, which meant for him a daily general anaesthetic.

I met Ahmed in the playroom. He was in his father's arms and
holding a large toy elephant. Without warning, he hit his father
hard in the face with the toy. His father looked shocked and pained,
but said nothing to Ahmed—not reacting or acknowledging the
attack. At that moment, one of the doctors arrived and asked to
speak to his parents. Ahmed was put down to play. He rushed
about the room, as if in a panic—pulling toys out, hardly looking
at them and casting them aside. He seemed not to have noticed
his parents having left the room. I sat on the floor and began to

take out some more of the toy hospital equipment—bandages, the stethoscope and syringes. I took some toy animals too—horses, giraffes, zebras, and lions and began to "play hospitals". After a few minutes, Ahmed joined me. He seemed interested in my play and listened to me as I spoke with sympathetic tones to the sick animals; watched me use the stethoscope to listen to their hearts and give them injections. Ahmed bandaged one of the animals and lay them all down as though they were in a big ward. He nodded as I stroked them and continued to speak softly about them. Ahmed's parents returned and he resumed his whirlwind, manic rush around the room.

I asked to speak with Ahmed's parents and discovered that they had not spoken with Ahmed about him being so unwell and the need for the treatment. They felt that he would not understand and would only be made afraid. They had tried to distract him with new toys, but his behaviour had changed completely from a sweet lively boy to an aggressive, angry child who lashed out at every opportunity. They were heartbroken, and believed that it was the brain tumour that had caused his change in character. They felt Ahmed would never be the same again. The consultant had confirmed that Ahmed's behaviour was unlikely to be caused by the tumour, given its location. I worked with the parents to think of a way of speaking about what was happening in a manner that Ahmed could engage with and understand. I spoke of how the current situation was much more frightening for Ahmed, as he had no idea why he was in hospital. He was being treated by strangers, who at times had to do painful things to him. He was also at times witness to his parents looking upset and afraid. I suggested that the wild behaviour exhibited by Ahmed might be linked to their feelings of fright and uncertainty. I helped them to acknowledge the importance of reinstating the more ordinary boundaries that could contain Ahmed's unmanageable feelings.

Over the next six weeks, Ahmed's parents worked with me, and Ahmed began to understand why he was in hospital. He settled down and managed his daily treatment without further difficulties. Ahmed's mother had found the support so helpful that I was able to refer her to a local team for continuing help. I recently learned that Ahmed had started nursery and that he had settled well. (JE)

Ahmed was only three and his parents feared that they would lose their only child, despite reassurances from their medical team that Ahmed's tumour was treatable and that he had a good prognosis. The parents felt that it would be best to hide the "truth" from Ahmed in the belief that he was too young to understand. However, they came to acknowledge that their sense of events was also coloured with their fantasies, and how their son, bathed in their anxiety, felt alone in his fear. With no one to contain his fear and anxiety, he resorted to a muscular defence, becoming overactive and aggressive as though trying to keep fear at bay and to crush any sense of feeling small and vulnerable. The psycho-therapeutic work provided them with a containing space to allow them, in turn, to contain their son.

Children below the age of ten may have only a limited understanding of their cancer diagnosis. Naturally, like Ahmed, they will look to their parents to make things right for them—to take their pain away. Children will naturally have a sense of things not being right and some may possibly know more than their parents can bear to acknowledge. The sense of the child protecting their parents was evident with Jake, who was five years old.

Jake had had many treatments. Lying in his hospital bed, he asked me to watch a DVD cartoon. He did not want me to watch it all, just a short sequence. It was an unsophisticated cartoon about some animals on a farm:

> One of the daddy animals had defended the farm from a ferocious pack of wolves and in doing so had been killed. The young son of the father was bereft and in his grief returned to a spot where days earlier he and his father had happily played together. He had recalled their closeness and their joy in each other's company and had smiled.
>
> At this point Jake turned to me to ask what I thought. I was full of sadness and a powerful sense of imminent loss. I said that Jake was letting me know how very sad it is when someone you love dies and how it was important to know that we always have those we love in our minds and in our hearts. He smiled at this in a way that conveyed a sense of relief. He turned off the television.
>
> Jake was to go home the next day and we said our goodbye. He left me a drawing saying "I love you". Some weeks later he died

and I felt that whilst we had not been able to speak directly about his knowledge that he would die, I had understood his hope that people who we love will remember us. (JE)

Working with trauma

For most children with cancer, and as was evident with Amy, there may be an unsettling state that exists in them of both wanting to know and not wanting to know. The general drive to avoid discomfort unconsciously elicits in the other an urge either to reassure or the opposite— to adopt a defensive stance whereby the depth of the terror is denied. In either case, the complex state being experienced by the child is not being acknowledged. Therapeutically, the ambivalence communicated calls for the presence of a mind that can remain aware of the dissonance created from the flow of disparate projections. Attuning to the child in this manner offers a deeper understanding of their internal struggle.

I felt that it was my commentary that Louis held on to, and so as well as speaking of what he was doing in a factual way, I weaved in the emotional charge stirred in me to bring into *what I said* something of what his play might mean. As Louis became stronger, he explored the room and began to play with the doll's house and the domestic and wild animals. In each session in this period, Louis carefully lined up the animals outside the doll's house—with all of them looking in. I was taken with a sense of being seized upon, invaded—an image of Louis having brain surgery—a forming sense of this most inner part of the self being looked into. I wondered about Louis feeling looked into, that he was letting me know that he felt he had no privacy. He started to place the baby animals on the backs of the adult animals. I had a sense of the smaller animals getting a better view, and I wondered if he felt able to see things more clearly with the help of Mrs. E.

Shortly after, the animals began to enter the house and jump on the dolls. I described the attack and how frightening it was. There seemed to be no escape. I linked this to times when he may have been frightened and felt there was no way out. Louis listened in his way, without looking at me or acknowledging what I had said. The animals stopped invading. A mother bear and father bear and their two cubs were picked out from the animals. The cubs magically flew around the room and had adventures climbing on the computer, landing on the door handles or light switches. As I commented, Louis maintained his silence, but seemed to attend closely to my words, in particular to the descriptions of the emotional states of the two cubs—fear if they fell, excitement when they could fly, anger when they fought, pleasure at returning to the mother and father bear. I spoke of the competition between the two cubs, especially when one fell and the other seemed triumphant. I wondered aloud about Louis' own feelings towards his sister.

Although Louis said very little, he was always keen to attend his sessions. His mother said that he looked forward to coming each week. As his treatment progressed, he became weaker and more tired—an inevitable consequence of the onslaught of the chemotherapy. Despite his physical state, in a session at this time Louis turned every piece of furniture in the doll's house upside down. He turned to his box and began to turn all the toys within this upside down. He turned the small table and chairs over. He looked at me and asked if he could turn the big chairs over too—and the doll's house. Over the course of the session, Louis had turned everything that he could upside down. I said that he was letting me know what his life was like, what had happened since he had been taken off in the ambulance.

His reaction on finishing this upside down world, was one of absolute delight. He asked if he could show his mother. At the end of the session he pulled her and his sister into the room. Mother was rather amazed. I said that Louis was perhaps showing us how upside down the world was for them all. Louis seemed proud and pleased and repeated this play during subsequent sessions. (JE)

Louis conveyed a sense of needing to be held by the concrete presence of the therapist—through her words that followed him. The therapist provided a curiosity and interest, which contained Louis and allowed him to explore the room and to use the toys to communicate to her. At each stage in his play, the understanding by the therapist seems to allow further elaboration, thereby gradually elevating the depth of the communication. The repetitive lining up of the animals, turning them all to look towards the house, seemed to show that Louis felt safe to bring the confusion he was experiencing, and evoked in the therapist a sense of intrusion, being looked into. The animals, domestic and wild, enter into the house and jump on the dolls within. The therapist felt the attack and reflected this back, making links to Louis' own angry feelings. Placing the baby animals on the backs of the adult animals seemed to convey Louis seeing what he could not see before—leading towards an understanding and clarity through the help of the therapist. Through this understanding, Louis seemed to link with something more connected to his external world, with the bear family representing his family and, through the play, his exploration of the close relationship he held with his sister.

The upside down world seemed to convey vividly the chaos Louis and his family were all experiencing at that time. His delight—and relief—on constructing this world was palpable. His need to share this vision with his mother and sister may have also been a means of letting them know that this was not unique to him, and that they too may be able to find some relief from seeing what he worked to show. Louis seemed to have genuinely taken in his experience of his therapist, of someone who worked to bring understanding.

In working with children with cancer and their families, we often bear witness to the shock and terror of the evolving trauma. We work to support the family by listening without reassuring; providing a presence for them to express, in whatever form, the myriad of different thoughts and feelings that may arise; to stay with the distressing, painful, and at times unbearable feelings that do not yet have words given to them. We particularly strive to understand the child's perspective and support them by amplifying their communications throughout their medical treatment. Sadly, we also confront the distressing fact that some of our child patients become terminally ill and will die.

> Lily is a bright fourteen-year-old. She has lymphoma, which presents as a mass in her lungs. I met her following a shockingly sudden relapse that occurred after a brief period of being in remission. The planned stem cell transplant was suspended. Instead, she had to prepare to undergo further cycles of chemotherapy with a different drug. She was angry with her consultant—who Lily felt had had no right to tell her that she was in remission. I was astounded as to how much Lily knew about the nature of her cancer, about the different drugs. She had a solid belief that she should remain fully aware of all aspects of her disease. She recounted how,

a couple of years back, she circumstantially missed a school trip with her classmates, among whom were a number of good friends. The coach the group travelled in had crashed and all but two of the children had survived. Lily understood that there must have been a reason why she was not on that coach—a purpose for her surviving this tragedy that she was yet to find. In her mind, it was not possible to succumb to the cancer. This belief gave her the strength to look the cancer in the eye, as it were.

I continued to meet with Lily weekly as an outpatient. Though unable to attend school, she maintained her desire to study, to go to college, to go to university. Lily was irritated that this illness was holding her back from her studies—from getting on with what was important. I felt somewhat intimidated by her knowledge and found myself needing to be precise in the words I used. I came to understand that the knowledge functioned as a "second skin" for Lily, for below the knowledge was a dread, as was occasionally evident when her attention was taken by the meaning of aches and pains.

Following the third cycle of the drug she had been on for the past twelve weeks, a scan revealed secondary tumours—the extent of the spread throughout her body was astounding. Lily was told a few hours before I arrived that she was terminal. She lay in her bed in a side room with the lights dimmed. Through occasional spasms of painful coughs and light gasps for air, she told me the sequence of events following her meeting with her consultant. Lily understood that she had a few weeks. She did not blame her consultant— she had done everything possible. There was a long period of no words—just intakes of breath. My throat restricted. I kept my eyes on her face. Lily stared at the ceiling. She turned and, looking directly at me, said that it was just shocking. As she articulated the unfairness, the waste of hope, I could also feel how angry she was. Suddenly, and with no warning, my mind was overwhelmed with a swell of anguish and utter despair. Lily held my eyes. A tear burst from the corner of her eye and fell on the pillow. (AL)

In working with children who are dying, the imperative is not so much to interpret, but to understand through the countertransference and bear the feelings evoked, so that the therapist can maintain her contact with the child and the family.

Conclusion

We have attempted to describe aspects of the emotional impact on children with cancer and their families through our work as child and adolescent psychotherapists. As part of the paediatric, adolescent and young adult cancer team, our discipline provides a component of the support that is offered to patients and their families. We work in a flexible manner that can range from single meetings following a child's consultation with their medical team, to more traditional regular contact through in-patient, in-clinic, or out-patient appointments.

At the heart of our thinking is how we work to retain a thoughtful presence in the face of the trauma we witness, in a way that best supports the child and his family through the diagnosis, their medical treatment, and often beyond. At times, we can help by separating out the different emotional experiences, with a view to keeping the family in touch with each other, by working with the whole family or sometimes the parents alone. At other times, it may help the child to feel attended to and to be with a person who is separate from their family, who they do not feel they have to "protect". At all times we endeavour to stay with the painful states if expressed and avoid the imperative to reassure. Our understanding of the emotional impact on the child and the family through these encounters is shared with the multi-disciplinary team to support a broader experience of containment for the family.

Acknowledgements

We would very much like to thank all the families mentioned here for their generosity in allowing us to use this material. We learn so much from our work about the extraordinary nature of the human spirit, of courage and endurance.

References

Bick, E. (1968). The experience of the skin in early object-relations. *International Journal of Psychoanalysis, 49*: 484–486.

Bick, E. (1986). Further considerations on the function of the skin in early object relations: Findings from infant observation integrated into child and adult analysis. *British Journal of Psychotherapy, 2(4)*: 292–299.

Bion, W. R. (1959). Attacks on linking. *International Journal of Psycho-Analysis, 40*: 308–315.

Bion, W. R. (1962). *Learning from Experience*. London: Heinemann (reprinted London: Karnac, 1991).

Bion, W. R. (1967). *Second Thoughts*. London: Heinemann (reprinted London: Karnac, 2004).

Freud, S. (1920). *Beyond the Pleasure Principle. S. E., 18*. London: Hogarth.

Joseph, B. (1993). Projective identification: Some clinical aspects. In: M. Feldman & E. Bott Spillius (Eds.), *Psychic Equilibrium and Psychic Change: Selected papers of Betty Joseph* (pp. 168–180). London: Routledge.

Klein, M. (1974). Notes on some schizoid mechanisms (1946). In: *The Writings of Melanie Klein (Vol. 3)*. London: Hogarth.

Pick, I. B. (1988). Working through in the counter-transference. In: E. B. Spillius (Ed.), *Melanie Klein Today: Developments in Theory and Practice, Vol. 2: Mainly Practice* (pp. 34–47). Florence, KY: Taylor & Francis/Routledge.

CHAPTER FOUR

What the illness may reveal

John Woods

Introduction

From his many years of therapeutic work with cancer patients, Lawrence Goldie likens the impact of a cancer diagnosis to that of a traumatic war experience, which may result in an overwhelming "fear of what is going to happen to me". Drawing on Bion's ideas he shows how a predicted future can become as fixed as if it were a past event. This psychological process, he maintains, has a tremendous influence on what happens to a person's capacity to deal with their illness. Psychoanalytic psychotherapy, he shows, can help the patient change in their experience from one of persecution and helplessness, to feeling "empowered to act in the present, out of concern for others" (Goldie, 2005, p. 25). The meaning of the illness may therefore be transformed from a death sentence to one of creative opportunity. But what happens if it is the therapist who has received the diagnosis? In this account I propose to show how a therapist's experience of cancer may have influenced the work with a particular patient.

My own cancer, which resided in the bone marrow and therefore affected the blood, is known as Waldenström's macroglobulinaemia. Currently I am glad to say it is in a state of "indolence", as it was when first it was discovered. However, five years ago it went on the march, causing anaemia, energy loss, and would, if not checked, have resulted in death. A five-month course of chemotherapy was prescribed. A good outcome was predicted, and so the news was not all bad. And I could be sure of the support and love from family and friends.

In preparation for the treatment, I considered whether I could continue to work as a psychotherapist. I was advised by doctors to avoid public places because of damage to my immune system, a side-effect of the chemotherapy, and that my energy levels would be much reduced. This meant that my NHS clinic job would have to be put on hold. However, to see one or two clients on a private basis should be perfectly feasible.

After four months it was clear that the illness had not been defeated, and that I needed a more powerful treatment. Managing this additional treatment, and its complicated side-effects, with repeated tests and appointments, became almost a full time job during that year. Often there was little time for reflection, but in retrospect I find myself strangely glad of the experience. I used to be surprised when I hear others say of some similar difficult experience, they "would not have been without it". (See also Goldie, 2005, Ch. 1). Maybe it is only possible to say this when and if there is a good outcome. It is also perhaps egocentric to say that an experience like this may be turned to a personal advantage. It ignores the worry and pain suffered by those nearest and dearest. But maybe others can benefit if the cancer patient allows some change, grows in emotional maturity, and becomes perhaps less prone to that besetting sin of the psychotherapist, overwork.

Ethical questions are raised by the therapist's continuing to work during his own illness. Each case is different and it is vital that any therapist makes decisions in consultation with a senior colleague. How much can the proper care of the patient survive the therapist's inevitable preoccupation with his own situation? Supposing the therapist begins to fail in his ability to work? If the therapist is perceived as a damaged or compromised container, the patient is in danger of having to look after the therapist. Indeed, another patient of mine, who had experienced family loss through cancer, opted to transfer to another therapist, to pre-empt such difficulties.

The opposite may also be the case. What I am suggesting here is that in certain circumstances it may be that the situation of the therapist's illness provides exactly what is needed. This can occur, I believe, when some important emotions, or recollections that have been inaccessible, may be reawoken as a result of the patient's perception of actual changes in the therapist. What is happening to the therapist may then be akin to what T. S. Eliot (1921) called an "objective correlative". This term was coined when Eliot was discussing the power of art to express emotion. The problem of Hamlet, Eliot thought, was one which Shakespeare could not "drag into the light, or contemplate, ... at least not in the same way that he can with Othello's jealousy, or Coriolanus' pride". He suggested that by finding an "objective correlative", a set of objects, a situation, or a chain of events, then shape could be given to a particular emotion. In a similar way there were elements of a particular patient's illness that were inaccessible until his treatment came into contact with my own. Bodily experiences resurfacing in the patient's mind may have been specific responses to physical changes in the therapist.

Mr. X

I had been seeing Mr. X for some three years already in three times per week psychoanalytic psychotherapy. He had begun treatment in his early fifties because of severe depression and suicidal feelings that he connected to his paedophilia. Some findings from the early years of his treatment I wrote up and published, with his permission (Woods, 2007). During that time we worked on both the management and the understanding of his sexual orientation to children. He was attracted to boys in the early stages of their puberty, and as a young adult had engaged in the seduction of many young boys. Working in education, there had been opportunities to indulge these desires, although at the time of coming into treatment he had not abused for more than twenty years. He had always been aware of the harm he was doing, as well as the illegality.

Although he had not committed a sexual offence for many years, nevertheless we made an agreement that he would report to me any signs of recurrence, and that he, or I if necessary, would take any action required to prevent the abuse of any child. I questioned whether he should return to the kind of work where he would be in contact with young boys and in due course he changed job. We did some work on the emotional factors that led him to his sexual behaviour, which in his twenties had seemed compulsive, and saw how his masochistic dependence on Mark had protected him. He had no recollection of being sexually abused himself but in his background there was abandonment and significant emotional neglect. At boarding school from around the age of eight (he was "not quite sure"), with a father whom he rarely saw, he also had a highly erratic mother who was at times over-close, but at others severely depressed. She committed suicide when Mr. X was eleven, and his feelings of guilt and anger about her were uncovered in treatment.

He was compliant throughout his therapy, though more open as time went on. He preserved me in the role of expert, and frequently acknowledged the support he derived from speaking of things he could not reveal anywhere else. We understood some of his fear of adult sexual relationships in which emotional intimacy would threaten to reactivate some traumatic feelings of loss.

I often noted a strange piece of behaviour as he lay on the couch; lifting his right hand (I was on his right side), he would appear to be fending off the possibility of physical blows coming to his head. Try as we might we could not understand this automatic reaction of his to being on the couch. He reported no associations to violence or the fear of violence. He could admit to a fear, not of my anger or violence but rather of rejection, which we readily linked to his chronic experiences of neglect by parents. I began to think of this habitual hand movement as one of concealment, since there were areas still to be explored. The deeper issue of his sexual perversion, and his sexual fascination with young boys, even if only in fantasy, remained unresolved at a point when the therapy was interrupted by my need to undergo chemotherapy. I discussed various options with a senior colleague. My patient was reporting much improvement in his emotional well-being, and less compulsion regarding sexual behaviour, but clearly there was more work that could be done. I felt it right to be open about my situation. I presented Mr. X with a choice; he could terminate his treatment at this point (the immediate answer was "No") or stop the therapy for the duration, returning when my medical treatment was completed; I offered also to refer him to another therapist. Or he could choose to continue his sessions with me for the months of my chemotherapy, because I had been advised I would be fit enough to undertake this.

In the event he chose the last of these, and continued throughout my treatment, which lasted longer than expected—eleven months—before I was finally in the clear. The effects of the chemotherapy did not interfere, ostensibly, with my ability to be there for sessions, pay attention, and continue to work with him, and, on some days, another such patient. Mr. X rarely commented upon the evident physical changes that he would have observed in me—papery skin and hair loss. He went from the consulting room door straight to the couch, giving me the most cursory glance. He said, yes, that he noticed these changes in my appearance but just assumed the chemo was going as expected. He had more pressing matters on his mind. Disturbing dreams were leading him to wonder if there was not something in his childhood we had missed ... and gradually it emerged that for a long period at boarding school he had been interfered with sexually on a nightly basis. The abuser, an older boy, interrupted the young Mr. X's sleep by demands to suck his penis and masturbate him. Eventually the older boy was reported by another child (a less compliant victim) and disappeared from the school. Mr. X never spoke out. The recollection of these experiences was extremely painful and disturbing to Mr. X, who relived the disgust, humiliation, and shame. And yet he could see it also made sense of his later sexual problems; we acknowledged the physical subjection, disgust at the older boy's body, the intrusion of unwanted sexual arousal, and subsequently, as a young adult, the need to master the traumatic fixation on the erect penis by taking on the role of initiator, and therefore, in effect, of abuser.

This work provided some relief and a sense of meaning to his life. He saw how he had always been terrified of adult sexual relations, and had felt more comfortable being around boys. Paradoxically he became less of a victim, as he was strengthened in his conviction of the wrongness of sexual abuse of the young. There were times when it still seemed that Mr. X was holding back, and I commented that he may well be anxious about my situation, but then he would plough on with his material. However, it felt to me that we were on some kind of parallel course, with me carrying my illness and him exploring the depths of his. I interpreted his reluctance to make demands of me because of the reality of the situation, just as he may have felt he could not make demands of vulnerable and unreliable parents. He could see that he was having to overcome a profound fear of rejection as he revealed more of himself.

As my hair and skin returned to normal Mr. X said that he had noticed these changes, and maybe I was a bit different in my energy level, he was not sure, but mainly he was concerned with getting his own "life back", as he put it. Indeed, he had found new work, which was much more appropriate for him, resumed contact with friends, and was clearly less depressed. He noticed that there was less sexual arousal at the sight or thought of young boys, and more of an interest in the positive aspects of friendship with both males and females. Nevertheless, he expressed a need for a further year of therapy following the end of my own treatment. Mr. X later acknowledged that he had needed to see me fully recovered before he could finish his psychotherapy. My comments that he needed to reassure himself that he had not been too much for me were met with wry amusement.

In a follow-up session one year after the end of his therapy, Mr. X informed me that he had accepted his fate, as he put it, of never being able to have a physically intimate relationship. He insisted there was no disappointment with the therapy or with me, because he always thought he was "essentially incurable". "But at least you have given me some kind of life," he said. He went on to reflect upon the process of his recovered memories. They were "strangely familiar", he said, even though he had always dismissed the idea that anything like that could have happened to him. "It was as if I had always known, but not seen it … But I couldn't ignore it any longer … It was now or never, especially since … ".

I ventured to complete his sentence " … you were going to lose your therapist, one way or the other?"

"No, no, I knew you would get better, but you did look like … I mean, you looked terrible".

I interposed, " … you were going to say, 'like death'?"
He went on to say, "Maybe all the bad stuff you heard from me had made you ill, … so I really wasn't sure. It was difficult … I mean, listening to all this poisonous stuff, it must get inside you, doesn't it? And so I felt I had to work harder and harder in the therapy, not waste time, keep on with all that stuff about boarding school. I wanted to say that it was *my* poison, the most shameful thing being how I learned to like it, and later wanted to do it again with other boys … I was having to fight something in myself. I mean, 'cancer', you could hardly say the word in those days. You couldn't talk about it, like 'paedophilia', I suppose, or 'suicide', all unspeakable. Put them all in a box, marked Death. For a long while I did not think about any of these and pretended things are not happening, but then I saw you losing your hair, and … I thought this could be it now and I think I realised now this is the last chance. I didn't decide it, it just happened at that time the

memories came back. I suppose it was different, I didn't push them away as I always have done. It was a horrible process, all that poison, but I suppose it had to come out. Now I am glad of it, but at the time! I don't know …".

Reflections

What is cancer? Known medically as a malignant neoplasm, the term refers to a broad group of various diseases, all involving unregulated cell growth, "an astonishing perversion of the normal cell" (Mukherjee, 2011, p. 38). In cancer, cells divide and grow uncontrollably, forming malignant tumors, and invade nearby parts of the body. As to its causation, some environments make destructive cellular mutations more likely to arise and propagate. Such environments can include the presence of disruptive substances called carcinogens, repeated physical injury, or genetic factors. A feature of this pathological proliferation of cells is a clonal quality; the reproduced cells are a clone of their predecessor, and so come to dominate other cellular tissue. The signals in normal cells that produce variation of functioning are obliterated by the unbridled growth of the cancer (Mukherjee, 2011, pp. 38–39).

What is paedophilia? A sexual orientation to children, this is a specific form of sexual deviation. It seems to arise from a pathological adaptation to various environmental factors such as neglect and abuse (Glasser, 1988). Certainly, such factors are always to be found in the personal history of the paedophile. It seems that the closeness and intimacy of an adult sexual relationship is fundamentally threatening. Instead, the unequal adult-child interaction offers an illusion of safety and control of the other. Sexual perversion acquires its virulent power because it originated as a form of protection against traumatic pain, and continues to function in that way, even though the original environmental stressor has long gone. The original pain of helplessness and victimisation is mutated into an illusion of satisfaction, perhaps by "identification with the aggressor" (Freud, A., 1936). Although repetition and compulsion abound in all sexual perversion, there is, in some views, a creative effort at overcoming trauma by creating a "neo-sexuality" (McDougall, 1995), though it is clearly malignant in many respects.

The enormous contrasts between my patient's psychological illness and my own physical one cannot, of course, be overlooked. And yet there may have been some connection during the course of this work we were engaged in together. His access to previously suppressed memories seems to be connected in some way to his changing perceptions of the therapist. Perhaps it is only in intensive analytic treatment that this could occur, because of the relative intimacy of the situation. Mr. X's treatment could have ended before that year, that is, after three years, or as soon as his behavioural improvements were noted. If they had been defined as treatment goals, the job could have been regarded as done. Some might regard it as entirely unnecessary to dig up past experiences of sexual abuse, unless we expect that the underlying causes of perhaps both the depression and the sexual perversion were, in different ways, rooted in his trauma of sexual abuse.

Perhaps I was something far removed from the benign father figure he would have wished for. Maybe these "recovered memories" were completely false? In the absence of any corroborating evidence it has to be asked whether these tales of abuse could have been manufactured by the patient not only to explain some of his personal difficulties, but in a more sinister way to express something abusive in the therapy he was receiving. Was the abuser in fact the therapist? Lulled into a sense of security over years of psychotherapy he had found supportive, the patient suddenly finds himself being exploited by a therapist who, for reasons of his own, imposes his "disgusting body" on the patient as he lies like a victim on the couch. In order to fend off this abuse by the therapist the patient concocts a fictional narrative of child abuse at boarding school in order to distance the abuse from the current reality, and appease the therapist's need for affirmation. For this to be true we would have to conclude the entire treatment became a hoax, which would very likely damage the patient. Fortunately there is little evidence for that, indeed the patient seems ultimately to have benefited. However, it may also be that the situation of that year was potentially abusive, although the degree of trauma, from whatever source, could be tolerated.

The box of "unspeakable things", though in some ways an ominous image, is at least a container of the otherwise unmanageable trauma of his abuse. In that undifferentiated realm his perception of my "unboundaried invader", as Parkinson (2003) dubbed cancer, merged with other split-off experiences. The recollected disgust at the older boy's body may have been explicitly evoked in a transference reaction to the physical changes in the therapist's body. Reaching into those childhood experiences, and the associated emotions, must be acknowledged as a dangerous business, particularly when he may have felt unsure of the robustness of the therapist. However, the urgency induced by the evident vulnerability of the therapist, and the threat of an enforced ending, seems to have combined into a drive to catch hold of elusive memories that were before easily denied. "No, but wait", he might have been saying. "You cannot leave me, I have this to deal with!" I remained, to an extent, the good father figure he so desired, but, with a tinge of bitterness, he could acknowledge that there was no cure for his predicament.

At the point of the follow-up session there seemed to be an equation, in Mr. X's mind at least, of the poison of sexual abuse and the poison of cancer, which has made me think of certain parallels in their insidious effects. Paradoxically, the chemotherapy employs a different type of poison which kills off healthy cells as well as diseased ones. Is this parallel to the way in which psychotherapy brings back the pain of recovered memories? Perhaps this paradox enabled Mr. X to bear the pain of the potentially harmful resurgence of the memories. In cases without therapy these memories may have to remain suppressed because they are capable of re-traumatising the sufferer. This kind of heavily controlled equilibrium may underlie much chronic depression, as the "real" illness remains hidden.

Working with sex offenders in general requires care in the countertransference, and I had, as in other cases, been able to put aside the revulsion I might feel against someone who had abused children, by allying my professional role with the side of him that was working to manage and control his sexual deviance. This is not a complete solution, because it splits off the sexual problem, and therefore the psychopathology, from the patient. It has to be admitted that sometimes this results in a certain emotional distance in the psychotherapy. However, in the year of my chemotherapy and his recovered memories, I began to see how the corruption of his mind had resulted from the abuse, how he had needed to adapt to an abusive and premature form of stimulation of his sexual desire, and I began to feel much more empathic concern for him. I already knew that his sexual orientation to children was most unwanted by him. He was no callous child abuser, but the persecuting guilt had persisted, and had its own destructive momentum. I began to feel a certain parallel here with my own process, dealing with my illness. Occasionally I could be subject to fears that the cancer may well be due to some psychological failing, that in developing this illness I was resorting to a somatic expression of something that should have been analysed, or at least expressed more appropriately in feelings. There is apparently little or no evidence that suggests a certain type of personality is more prone to cancer. However I felt that I was increasingly a fellow sufferer, not just from the objective problem, but from the emotional implications of our situations. Had we each in different ways brought our illness upon ourselves? And like Mr. X, eventually I came to see that self-blame was not a very health-giving position to take.

At that follow-up session I felt a certain kinship with Mr. X, that here we were, each having been helped a good deal, but not cured. The current "indolence" of my cancer is a constant reminder of mortality and the need to make the most of what time there is left. For Mr. X the acceptance of his paedophilia has meant a realisation that he will never have a sexual relationship as such, but he attains a better sense of value in himself and others. Any anger at the lack of a cure may have been dissipated in such therapeutic work, or perhaps it remains suppressed, along with the illness,—who knows?

In the absence of scientific certainty we may have to turn to the arts for illumination. As referred to earlier, T. S. Eliot (1921) described artistic endeavour as connecting emotion by finding an "objective correlative"; in other words, "a set of objects, a situation, a chain of events which shall be the formula of that particular emotion". Psychotherapy, as an activity perhaps closer to art than science, creates forms that reach emotional experience which previously has been unavailable, and the healing of trauma may result.

Neither his paedophilia nor my cancer has gone away. Each lurks in the wings awaiting its next opportunity to re-enter the stage. What has changed is the stance toward our respective illness, and the power of death it represents. Through being more known, accepted, and even familiar, each of our own particular nemeses becomes less frightening and less powerful over the rest of our lives.

Acknowledgement

The author acknowledges the support and guidance of Mr. Mannie Sher.

References

Eliot, T. S. (1921). Hamlet and his problems. In: *Selected Essays 1917–1932*. London: Faber & Faber.

Freud A. (1936). *The Ego and Mechanisms of Defence*. London: Hogarth. (Reprinted London: Karnac, 1992).

Glasser, M. (1988). Psychodynamic aspects of paedophilia. In: *Psychoanalytic Psychotherapy, 3*(2): 121–135.

Goldie, L. (2005). *Psychotherapy and the Treatment of Cancer Patients*. London: Routledge.

McDougall, J. (1995). *The Many Faces of Eros*. London: Free Association.

Mukherjee, S. (2011). *The Emperor of all Maladies: A biography of Cancer*. London: HarperCollins.

Parkinson, J. (2003). The intruder in the night: Cancer and the I within. *British Journal of Psychotherapy, 19*(4): 414–433.

Woods, J. (2007). Ethical problems in the treatment of paedophile patients. In: D. H. Morgan & S. Rusczynski (Eds.), *Lectures on Violence, Perversion and Delinquency: The Portman Papers* (pp. 203–219). London: Karnac.

CHAPTER FIVE

The ill psychotherapist: a wounded healer

Judy Parkinson

In this chapter I will consider the impact of cancer on the psychotherapist and his or her clinical practice, whether the psychotherapist is working alone or with colleagues in group, couple, or family therapy. I will draw upon my own experience and that of other psychotherapists who have written or spoken about how they were personally affected by a diagnosis of cancer. These include Helen Bender and John Woods, who related their own personal and professional dilemmas and challenges in a conversation before an audience at the London Centre for Psychotherapy (now part of a new organisation: the British Psychotherapy Foundation) in November 2011.

The experience of cancer

Cancer can leave us feeling that we have been invaded, our bodies taken over. Shock, fear, disbelief, and questions such as "Why me?" and "Why now?" are common in response to this unexpected intrusion into our lives. There may be a sense of dread about what the diagnosis means in the life of the individual and for the person's sense of "who I am", the "me" feeling vulnerable and exposed to the unknown (Parkinson, 2003). Some people with cancer will experience a sense of shame or guilt for something felt to be their fault (Burton & Watson, 1988; Parkinson, 2003).

A psychotherapist with many years of training and personal psychotherapy, and an understanding of how the body and mind work together, cannot, of course, be immune from the emotional impact of a cancer diagnosis. In my own case, I found a lump in my breast in December 2006 just as I was getting ready to go out to meet some close colleagues. I was able to tell two of my colleagues, and their concern and support helped me to absorb my initial shock. I was referred by my GP to a local hospital and after tests including a mammogram I saw a surgeon who confirmed the suspected diagnosis of breast cancer. In the New Year I was admitted to hospital for surgery. I stayed there for the inside of a week and returned to work after two more weeks to allow myself time to recover from the operation. I had four months of chemotherapy following the operation and three weeks of daily radiotherapy. I did not need to take much time away from my private work as I was able to fit most of the appointment times around my work schedule. I made a full recovery and I remain well.

These are the facts. I was aware that other people are more affected by the disease or by the treatment, or by both; and so I felt very fortunate to have had an uncomplicated recovery without ever having felt particularly unwell. As I went through my diaries and medical notes in preparation for writing this account, however, I realised I had forgotten how hugely anxious I had felt, even for a short time, about the systemic effects of the chemotherapy treatment on my heart, as I had had a minor stroke the previous year, a stroke that had occurred as a result of atrial fibrillation, secondary to my having a heart murmur. With my anxiety having focused on how the chemotherapy might affect my heart, any worry I had about being ill with cancer and losing my hair seemed to have been displaced. In retrospect, it seemed the "forgetting" was a forgetting aimed at minimising the emotional impact on me of the illness. It was a form of conscious denial similar to that commented upon by Arlow and Wong who, in separate papers, refer to the role of both conscious and unconscious denial manifesting as hypomanic mood swings or intellectualisation as well as denial, post-illness, of the effects on the therapist of having been seriously ill (Arlow, 1990; Wong, 1990).

When I became ill with cancer I was working as a part-time counsellor in a department of psychological medicine in a hospital specialising in the diagnosis and treatment of people with cancer. It was not until eighteen months after my treatment, however, that I realised that I could no longer help people who were struggling to cope with the emotional impact on them of the disease. I had become conscious of the fact that I was identifying too closely with my patients. Again, in retrospect, mine was a delayed emotional response to my illness and the seriousness of my condition.

In the course of working with people who are seriously physically ill I had come to appreciate how important it was to know about any experience of illness in childhood that the patient may have had, or fears concerning illness that might have an impact on how they would react to their current condition (Morrison, 1990). I looked for any conscious or unconscious indications of phantasy life (including dreams) that could affect their emotions and attitudes to treatment (Parkinson, 2003, 2006a). I found it was common for people to feel they had brought their illness upon themselves in some way.

Although I did not blame myself for my illness, I did feel that I had come "full circle", and could now know "from the inside" something of the reality of the experience of cancer, having previously written about how other people with cancer cope with the disease (2003, 2006a). Being diagnosed with cancer meant that I entered more fully into the experience of the patient and as a result I felt less concerned about being simply a witness to the situations of other people.

Self-disclosure

Following a diagnosis of cancer the practising psychotherapist has to decide who to tell, how to tell, and when to tell. Our training has taught us to be sparing about giving the patient information about ourselves so that the transference and countertransference dynamics might evolve with the minimum of interference from unnecessary external sources of information.

The classical position, arising out of the technique that Freud instituted, recommended the analyst remained "opaque" to his or her patients so that patients could project their conscious and unconscious desires, fears, or unfulfilled longings onto the analyst. Absence of self-disclosure was taken on as part of the emerging technique in psychoanalysis (Farber, 2006; Akhtar, 2011).

The emphasis on abstinence and the opaque "blank screen" therapist was, however, steadily challenged by a shift in thinking away from this ideal of analytic distance and the analyst as a removed observer of the process, and more towards a position whereby the analyst considers the part played by both parties in a joint examination of meaning and motives (Farber, 2006; Skolnikoff, 2011). Melanie Klein's theories of object relations placed the person and their relation to internal and external objects in the centre of the psychoanalytic treatment of the individual. The analyst was thought of as susceptible to the patient's unconscious communications and disowned feelings. Drawing the person of the analyst into the field of interaction between patient and analyst gave a foundation for perspectives on the influence of analyst and patient upon each other in an affective relationship. Paula Heimann traced the origin of this ideal of the "detached" analyst and in 1950 published her classic paper on countertransference in which she suggests that "this may possibly derive from a misreading of some of Freud's statements" (Heimann, 1950). In the same period C. G. Jung wrote that "it is futile for the doctor to shield himself from the influence of the patient and to surround himself with a smoke-screen of fatherly and professional authority" (Jung, 1958).

The contemporary relational and intersubjective schools of psychoanalysis and psychotherapy have been indirectly influenced by the object relations theorists and the work of Winnicott, Fairbairn, Harry Stack Sullivan, and others in which the importance of the relationship between patient and analyst takes precedence, while the works of John Bowlby and the modern attachment theorists underline the importance of our patterns and styles of relating.

Psychotherapists and their patients normally have a mutual agreement to co-operate with each other in the interests of the patient's well-being and mental health. The patient's side of the agreement is to talk to the therapist with as few self-critical restrictions as possible on what to say. The therapist will be making choices about what to say, if anything, and often about what not to say. Some self-disclosure is inevitable although what is generally not said usually includes revealing statements about oneself including details of children, political, or religious views. Though in part perhaps still an ideal, Rackman's suggested guidelines for the thoughtful use of self-disclosure in psychotherapy include: that the disclosure is given to aid the therapeutic process and not to meet the needs of the analyst; that it is guided by empathy and not acting out; that it should come from a conflict-free area of the analyst's personality;

and that its impact should be analysed with the patient (Rackman, 1998).

The ill psychotherapist

Related to the issue of self-disclosure is the finding that the subject of the ill psychotherapist is an under-discussed area of clinical practice and technique in Great Britain and the United States. Only a few writers have explored the subject (Skolnikoff, 2011), though a collection of papers by psychoanalysts practising in the USA offers first-hand accounts of the experience of illness in the psychoanalyst and its effects on both analyst and patient (Schwartz & Silver, 1990).

The personal and professional choice of the therapist not to make the facts of his or her illness known by others beyond immediate family or colleagues may, of course, account for the paucity of published accounts on the ill psychotherapist. The therapist may prefer not to dwell on the illness or its effects once recovery is established and a return to work is being considered. The therapist who supervises, runs workshops, or lectures may not necessarily want to be known for having had a serious life-threatening condition. It may also be that a stoical position with regard to illness in the analyst and disclosure to the patient might have been adopted by generations of psychoanalysts after Freud (Farber, 2006) whose experience of cancer is the subject of Chapter One. Naturally a practising psychotherapist who becomes ill with cancer might, like others with cancer, have concerns about his or her financial position and these will add to the emotional stress caused by the illness. A responsible ethical position on this question may be reached by talking with colleagues who have a good understanding of the kinds of emotional and financial pressures their colleague is under. In my own case I was not insured for illness and had to accept loss of earnings for a time. I was fortunate in having close friends and colleagues with whom I could talk about my concerns and who knew me well enough to know that I would want to return to work as soon as possible after my operation, motivated not by financial worries but by a desire to return to normal as quickly as possible. Discerning colleagues also knew that I was prone to minimise the seriousness of my condition, and inclined to throw myself into activity at the expense of enough recovery time. I knew myself that, having been ill with a stroke the previous year, I was reluctant to interrupt my professional contact with my patients again.

Whilst I was fortunate to have a range of support available to me, colleagues living in rural areas or in locations where there are few other psychotherapists available to consult face-to-face may need to rely on alternatives such as telephone and internet communication to maintain contact.

The wounded healer

The Greek myth of the wounded healer might be helpful to consider before reflecting on how psychotherapists and their patients may interact at conscious and unconscious levels when the "healer" therapist falls ill.

Martin Schmidt offers a contribution here by commenting on the archetypal "wounded healer" in Jungian thought being based on the myth of the centaur Chiron. He writes:

> In Greek mythology, Chiron, abandoned by his mother at birth (his first wound), was adopted by Apollo who taught him the healing arts. Having also been instructed by Diana, he became renowned for his skills in, amongst other things, medicine, and became a respected teacher and mentor to many, including Hercules and Asclepius (son of Apollo) to whom he taught medicine. As a result, some also see Asclepius as the archetypal wounded healer, but whether we talk of Chiron or his pupil Asclepius, the moral of the story is the same.
>
> During a wedding banquet, Chiron was accidentally shot by one of Hercules' poisoned arrows (his second wound) which inflicted an agonising and incurable injury. After his wounding, Chiron withdrew and became a recluse, desperately searching in vain for a cure for his ailment and, in the process, finding remedies for many others' illnesses. Those who visited him were not the rich and famous but the poor and sick who called him the "wounded healer". Here we see the resonance with psychotherapists who, as a result of their emotional wounding, dedicate their lives to helping others (and in so doing finding, hopefully, some healing for themselves). (Schmidt, 2012, p.c.)

Schmidt comments:

> The patient coming to see a therapist is likely to identify with being wounded—feeling more passive, dependent, weak, confused and

sick than the analyst … the therapist is more likely to identify with being a healer—feeling more active, independent, strong, knowledgeable and healthy than the patient in the area of wounding presented by the patient. This [last point] is important because we learn from our patients in relation to areas of life where we are more wounded than them.

The patient consciously identifies with being sick and his/her archetypal inner healer is projected onto the therapist, reinforcing the therapist as a healer figure. The therapist in turn, projects his/ her wounded part on to the patient and in so doing is able to be empathic, understanding and disposed to help. The work of the therapy is for both patient and therapist to enter into the crucible of this archetypal transference to explore the wounds of the patient, to detoxify toxic projections, or in Bion's terms, to transform beta elements into alpha function, so that the patient is able to no longer just identify with the wounded pole of the archetype but to reintroject the "healer" pole (i.e., be a healer to themselves again). This of course means that the therapist has to reintroject their "wounded" part and identify less with being a "healer" to the patient. The patient no longer needs us and is able to leave, while we are left, still wounded, waiting for the next patient!" (Schmidt, 2012, p.c.)

If we are to function well as psychotherapists, we need to be aware of ourselves as both healer and in the process of being healed. This requires an attitude of humility, along with a daily recognition of ourselves and our patients as having some qualitative aspects within us of both wounded and healer (Hauke, 2005). Our training analysis will have given us insights into how we relate to ourselves and others, an essential precondition for us to have experienced if we are to help our patients and survive the wounds which some patients will inflict upon us. By this I mean that a patient will unconsciously transfer his or her history of having been wounded, by an attitude of a parent for instance, onto us as the parent-in-the-present. We are then perceived as the original wounding parent. A patient who retaliates against a perceived slight causes us to feel emotionally wounded and it may be difficult for us to avoid the temptation of counter-retaliation, which would confirm to the patient the validity of his or her feelings in connection with the original wound. The cycle of being wounded on both sides continues, unless broken by the shared insights of patient and psychotherapist working together to understand and begin to heal the wounds.

The psychotherapist as wounded healer can help the patient with his or her wounds as long as there is a balanced attitude whereby the psychotherapist knows that he or she is both vulnerable and able to survive, as for a while the patient needs the therapist to be emotionally stronger. At the same time, the psychotherapist can help the patient to recognise the inner strength that brought him or her to seek help and to stay with the treatment. An imbalance on the part of the "healthy" psychotherapist in relation to the "sick" patient, whereby the patient is seen only as "needy", leaves the power or authority in the hands of the one who "knows" but who has projected his needy or sick self onto the patient. Conversely the patient might project all power and authority, all healing potential, onto the psychotherapist who is perceived as having all the qualities it will take for the patient to feel better (Groesbeck, 1975; Guggenbühl-Craig, 1971; Hauke, 2005; Samuels, Shorter, & Plaut, 1986).

The wounds we carry with us throughout our lives might arise in the body and these include memories of being unwell and the attitudes of those looking after us. They may be emotional in origin, our suffering being related to a poor self-image or a sense of fragility; or they may be existential, for example, the wounds of the person who loses his faith in God or in his life as having any meaning, significance, or sense of purpose (Clark, 2012).

The matrix

As psychoanalytic psychotherapists we are used to thinking about the unconscious mind, reflecting upon our own motives, thoughts, feelings, and phantasies, and those of our patients. It is a busy field of interaction, as there are internal psychic objects and projections carried by therapist and patient, all of which have unconsciously determined lives of their own. I have found it helpful to think of all these psychic relationships as similar to a matrix. A matrix, as defined by the Oxford English Dictionary, is the "mould in which [a] thing is cast or shaped; [a] place in which [a] thing is developed". I would like to suggest that just as the unconscious mind is apparently timeless, so is the matrix of illness not limited to the therapist who is actually ill, but extends in the work with the patient to embrace all the experience of "ill" that both therapist and patient carry with them unconsciously, undetermined by time boundaries.

The psychotherapist who has cancer is therefore carrying a heavy load: of actual illness and all this means for the therapist, and the meaning of unasked or unacknowledged questions (by patient or therapist) such as "Who is ill?", "Why are they ill?", "Who will look after me?". These questions become woven into the fabric of the dialogue between patient and therapist. If they can be consciously shared, then understanding and emotional relief can result and work with the patient deepen.

The psychotherapist might choose to consider the question concerning "who is ill" independently of the patient but the question remains the same. The one who is "ill", whether physically, emotionally, or both, can shift from the person of the therapist with cancer to include the possibility of other people in the life of therapist or patient in the past or present.

The ill therapist might be felt by the patient to be weak, lacking in mental strength, mentally preoccupied, unsafe and a threat to the patient's sense of equilibrium or to the stability of the work that patient and therapist have started. Alternatively, the patient may feel that the ill therapist became ill because of something the patient did, thought, or said. It can be important, and a relief for the patient, if the therapist can bear in mind all of these possibilities and be ready to explore what "ill" really means, in relation to the patient's life in the present and in the past.

Impact upon the patient and the clinical work

After a diagnosis of cancer has been given, the psychotherapist comes into his or her consulting room a changed person. There is an illness in the room that was not known about before, or at least not consciously known by either psychotherapist or patient, and which now contributes to what I have called the "matrix". The matrix is made up of a set of conscious and unconscious internal and external relationships that belong to, and within, patient and therapist and include the presence of the history of their current relationship. The illness, the cancer, becomes part of the matrix, ready to become conscious or, alternatively, to influence unconsciously the patient's or the psychotherapist's thoughts, phantasies, and their mutual dialogue.

Before I was diagnosed with breast cancer, my private patients and I had "lived" with a sudden illness, the stroke I had the previous year, which temporarily halted our work together. I had been away from work for ten weeks that year, having been taken to hospital as an emergency one early morning. My clinical trustee and another colleague informed my patients and between us we kept them informed of my progress and recovery until I was able to resume work. In my case, the initial disclosure to my patients was unavoidable and unplanned. I had to make quick decisions about how to inform my patients and what I wanted to be known about my illness. At the time I had a practice in which I had seen most people over a period of time from several months to a few years. They and I had settled into our work together so that my practice day by day was reasonably stable. With the support and agreement of my clinical trustee I decided to tell my patients in a letter jointly composed with my colleague that I had been taken ill with a stroke. Once I returned to work I talked with each patient about the effect on them of my sudden absence due to illness.

I learnt from this process that there had been no "best" way to break news of this nature although there may have been alternative ways. I learnt to be sensitive to the fact of my patients having lived their own lives whilst I was away. I became better able to detect the presence of those anxieties that related to my illness and to distinguish these from other anxieties that surfaced during the period I was away from work and that related to the patient's life outside the relationship with me. Both could be present together, or one more dominant in the patient's conscious or unconscious associations.

When I developed breast cancer I had time to think through how I would tell or not tell my patients that I was ill and needing treatment. The situation was different from a year previously but many of my patients were still with me in once or twice weekly psychotherapy. I decided that I would inform my patients that I would be away from work in February for some planned treatment and that I would be away for just under three weeks. I could have told my patients that I was having a break in February without mention of any reason, but I decided not to do this. I thought it was not true to my real situation and I did not want to pretend that I had been away on holiday when this was not the case. I decided not to tell my patients that I was ill with cancer and needing treatment however, because I did not want to cause alarm or burden those who had been affected by my illness the previous year with more worry about the state of my health. I was prepared to explore any concerns about my health should they be expressed and I decided to take up any anxieties expressed by individual patients as they arose.

There was in fact a short period of time during which I wore a head-scarf while waiting for my wig to arrive and when it did, my hair was different again. One or two patients commented on my new hairstyle but otherwise the reason for the change was not mentioned and I chose to wait for any references to illness to emerge naturally. I suspected that one or two of my patients may have sensed that all was not well with me but chose not to mention this, either because they felt it too threatening to contemplate or because they needed to focus on their own difficulties and not have to attend to my problems.

Mrs. A and Mrs. Z

My patients Mrs. A and Mrs. Z had mothers who were mentally unstable. My being physically ill became grafted onto each of their remembered histories concerning the mother who needed attention and looking after, whether in the form of vigilance in the instance of one mother who was prone to "mercurial" moods, or of the other mother who was eventually admitted to a psychiatric hospital.

I recognised a wish in me to be asked how I was feeling by Mrs. A and Mrs. Z, both of whom work in caring professions, but needed to bear in mind their histories of having mothers who needed their attention and to examine my motives when answering their questions about the state of my health.

Mrs. A asked whether my break for planned treatment had anything to do with my stroke. We had discussed many times how my being taken ill suddenly had affected her, relating this to her mother who had frequently "disappeared" upstairs to bed when Mrs. A was younger, leaving Mrs. A to look after herself. Mrs. A had developed a premature sense of responsibility and sensitivity to her mother's state of mind and preoccupation with her own need to be acknowledged and looked after. Over the years Mrs. A and I had developed a way of working with each other in which she and I were both aware of the transference relationship (and the different versions of this) whilst also acknowledging the existence of the "real" relationship between us, one in which she knew that I would not remain so "hidden" that in her mind I would be emotionally inaccessible like her mother. In the "arrangement" between us

I understood that she wanted to discover and make use of a different kind of relationship that was unlike her relationship to her mentally and physically unavailable mother.

When Mrs. A asked whether my going for planned treatment was related to my stroke I sensed the anxiety behind her question and in this instance I decided to tell her in a straightforward way that I had been diagnosed with breast cancer. I was conscious that I might be responding to her directly out of my own anxiety to make things clear for her and at the same time I knew her well enough to trust that we would be able to explore how she reacted to this news. I told her that I would be treated for my cancer in the first place by surgery. Mrs. A expressed her concern and her hope that treatment would be successful and she wished me well.

At the beginning of the second of her two sessions that week Mrs. A told me that she had been feeling "devastated" that I had cancer. She was glad I had told her about my illness as she would rather find out directly from me than have to guess or find out from another source. However, my news left her feeling that all her "inner resources" had disappeared (like her mother and like me when I was taken ill the previous year). In subsequent sessions she told me she felt vulnerable and less "safe" with me knowing that I was unwell again. She felt I had come back to work very soon after my stroke, identifying me as a hardworking person, like her father and also like herself. I took her feeling of "less safe" seriously and I wondered to myself whether it had been right to tell her about my diagnosis. I felt, on balance, that it was important to work with the history of the less safe feeling as having stemmed from the lack of emotional holding she had experienced in her relationship to a mother who could not look after herself or Mrs. A effectively. At the same time I acknowledged her very real concerns for me and for our continuing work together. The threat of devastation related to her fears of losing me and being left all alone again, perhaps at the mercy of devastating and devastated inner abandoning objects. The work with Mrs. A continued for some years after the event of my illness. Meanwhile, I kept in mind, and alive in our conversation, the effects upon her of my becoming ill where this seemed relevant, so we could carry on making links to her past and present circumstances and to her inner emotional life.

In Mrs. Z's case, she did not question me directly when I told her I would need to be away at the beginning of February 2007. She said that she did trust that I would be alright and she expressed her hope that I would be looked after whilst having my planned treatment. She wondered whether the treatment was related to my stroke, which had occurred several years into her beginning therapy with me, but she did not pursue her thoughts or ask any questions, and I decided to let her express any concerns about my health in her own time. It was important to Mrs. Z to know that I could look after myself independently, as she wanted to feel I could be emotionally and thoughtfully available to her when we resumed after the break this time, as at other times in the course of her therapy.

More of Mrs. Z's history is of note here: Mrs. Z had lost her sister in an accident when Mrs. Z was six years old. Her mother later had a serious mental breakdown and her parents divorced. Her father moved to another part of the country and her remaining sister moved eventually to another country far away. Mrs. Z had taken on a caring, responsible role in her family of origin and in subsequent relationships throughout her life. She appeared calm and thoughtful and she was seen as capable by those who knew her at work. I thought about her calm reaction to my planned break for treatment and I decided to watch for any signs that may indicate concerns about my health. She had developed a strong and stable attachment to me that helped to make her feel more secure, as she was discovering that she did not feel compelled to look after me. However, she sometimes commented that I looked tired and I thought she was concerned about whether I was well enough to be at work and able to look after both of us.

Following surgical treatment for cancer I was offered a course of chemotherapy which started in the spring. The treatment did not interfere with Mrs. Z's appointment times. I felt tired sometimes, and I began to lose my hair. As mentioned earlier, whilst I was waiting to be issued with a wig I chose to wear a headscarf for a short time. I was aware that this was a different form of dress for me although it was not necessarily out of place given that the weather was fine and the scarf was colourful and in keeping with my taste in clothes. I was not surprised however when Mrs. Z looked at me at the start of one session and said, "I think you may have cancer and you are having treatment. I will have to get used to the scarf". She then talked about being "surrounded by needy people" in her present life, including one person who was ill with cancer.

This conversation led to us to talking afresh about how responsible she felt for looking after other people. We discussed how important it would be for her if she could tell me about any anxieties she felt concerning my health as it became clear, in a stark example a few weeks later, that she felt very anxious indeed about whether I would survive the cancer. She had received a letter through the post with a stamp on it showing the name of the clinic where my practice is based and where I saw her for her sessions. It was the weekend. Her immediate reaction had been not to open the letter because she thought it was bad news. She thought someone might have written to her telling her that I had died. In reality, it was a letter from another kind of practitioner working in the clinic who practises a physical form of therapy (and who had originally referred Mrs. Z to me for psychotherapy).

One of the outcomes of the discussion after this event with Mrs. Z was that we were able to talk about her fears of expressing direct anger or aggression to me. She wanted to keep me "safe", out of concern for my well-being and so that I would be able to look after her properly, unlike her mother who had been so mentally unwell. Unconsciously she was afraid of the anger that had become hidden behind her apparently calm exterior. These fears were able to be explored as being related to unconscious feelings of irrational guilt for not preventing her sister's death and her mother from becoming ill.

I have chosen the above clinical material describing extracts from the work with Mrs. A and Mrs. Z so that the remainder of this section can be given over to identifying common themes that have emerged in my clinical work with these and other patients during and since I was ill with cancer, now six years ago.

Conclusions

There are, of course, a range of factors that will contribute to a psychotherapist who becomes unwell with cancer deciding whether to continue in her work with patients and, if so, for how long. These factors include how the therapist is affected by the illness, both physically and mentally, and whether the cancer is of a type that can be treated with the minimum of surgical or medical intervention or, alternatively, will require a long period of treatment.

In this chapter I have set out to explore some of the many thoughts, feelings, and experiences that a psychotherapist with cancer will undergo in the course of having cancer, a life-threatening condition which will also be life-changing in many ways.

The psychotherapist who is able to resume work with patients after having been treated for cancer may find that he or she is more sensitively attuned to experiences of illness, trauma, or loss in patients. Patients might also be changed by their having had to cope with their therapist being ill and perhaps discovering new aspects of themselves as a result.

Psychotherapists are used to coping with doubt, uncertainty, and not knowing. We can only hope to discover something new about ourselves and about our patients by listening to ourselves and our patients with open minds, hearts, and souls, with an attitude of humility (Hauke, 2005) and with the hope of being open to what we can learn about ourselves and our patients in a spirit of enquiry.

Acknowledgements

I would like to thank my patients Mrs. A and Mrs. Z for their permission to use examples from our work together; Martin Schmidt for his contribution to the section on the wounded healer; Margaret Clark and Christopher Hauke for their encouragement and support during the writing of this chapter. I am grateful also to Helen Bender and John Woods for generously sharing their experience of cancer with me and for their reflective insights, from which I have both learnt and been helped to think about the subject more deeply in the course of writing this chapter.

References

Akhtar, S. (Ed.) (2011). *Unusual Interventions*. London: Karnac.

Arlow, J. (1990). The analytic attitude in the aervice of denial. In: H. J. Schwartz & A. L. Silver (Eds.), *Illness in the Analyst* (p. 19). Madison, CT: International Universities Press.

Burton, M. & Watson, M. (1998). *Counselling People with Cancer*. London: John Wiley and Sons.

Clark, M. (2012). *Understanding Religion and Spirituality in Clinical Practice*. London: Karnac.

Farber, B. (2006). *Self-Disclosure in Psychotherapy*. New York: The Guilford Press.

Groesbeck, C. (1975). The Archetypal Image of the Wounded Healer. *Journal of Analytical Psychology, 20*(2): 128.

Guggenbühl-Craig, A. (1971). *Power in the Helping Professions*. New Orleans, LA: Spring Publications.

Hauke, C. (2005). *Human Being Human: Culture and the Soul*. London: Routledge.

Heimann, P. (1950). On countertransference. *International Journal of Psychoanalysis, 31*: 81–84.

Jung, C. G. (1958). *The Practice of Psychotherapy. Collected Works, Volume 16*. London: Routledge & Kegan Paul.

Morrison, A. (1990). Doing psychotherapy while living with a life-threatening illness. In: H. J. Schwartz & A. L. Silver (Eds.), *Illness in the Analyst* (p. 229). Madison, CT: International Universities Press.

Parkinson, J. (2003). Intruder in the night: Cancer and the 'I' within. *British Journal of Psychotherapy, 19*(4): 415–433.

Parkinson, J. (2006a). Experiences of selves in isolation: A psychodynamic approach to the care of patients being treated in a specialized hospital unit. *Psychodynamic Practice, 12*(2): 149–163.

Parkinson, J. (2006b). The search for meaning. In: R. Archer (Ed.), *Dual Realities: The Search for Meaning: Psychodynamic Therapy with Physically Ill People* (p. 123). London: Karnac.

Rackman, A. W. (1998). Judicious self-disclosure by the psychoanalyst. *International Forum of Psychoanalysis, 7*: 263–269. (In: A. Salman (Ed.), *Unusual Interventions*. London: Karnac.)

Samuels, A., Shorter, B., & Plaut, F. (1986). *A Critical Dictionary of Jungian Analysis*. Routledge & Kegan Paul.

Schmidt, M. (2012). *Personal communication*.

Schwartz, H. J. & Silver, A. L. (1990). *Illness in the Analyst*. Madison, CT: International Universities Press.

Skolnikoff, A. (2011). Talking about oneself. In: S. Aktar (Ed.), *Unusual Interventions* (p. 141). London: Karnac.

Wong, N. (1990). Acute illness in the analyst. In: H. J. Schwartz & A. L. Silver (Eds.), *Illness in the Analyst* (p. 39). Madison, CT: International Universities Press.

CHAPTER SIX

The cancer nurse specialists' caseload: "contending with the fretful elements"

Anne Lanceley

This chapter describes cancer nurses' experience of, to borrow from Shakespeare, "contending with the fretful elements" (*King Lear* III.i.4): the emotional storm of patients' feelings, as well as those evoked in nurses during care. The focus of the chapter originates from my experiences caring for people with cancer in hospital, experiences which confirmed to me that by listening and talking to patients, cancer nurses may help them express their feelings and achieve a more integrated understanding of their illness and its place in their lives. This form of communication can help patients cope and can lead to an improved sense of emotional well-being. Communication of this nature takes place within the overall context of nurses' work, including the accurate assessment of complex care needs, planning and provision of day-to-day physical care, and monitoring and evaluating patient outcomes. Though nurses may work in clinical areas that espouse a philosophy of patient-centeredness, and in teams which place a high value on supportive psychological care, nurses struggle to deal with the emotional problems of patients and relatives, people thrown off balance by demanding treatments and the trauma of cancer.

The chapter will explore the nature of nurses' communications with patients and expose the challenges that nurses face in their daily work.

93

It takes as its focus the caseload and "emotion work" of clinical nurse specialists (CNSs), a group that has not previously received attention in the cancer literature. The chapter is illustrated with material from my clinical work with women with gynaecological cancers to reveal something of the felt nature of a CNS's caseload. The chapter explores the influence nurses' emotional experience has on the way they care for patients, and the impact the work has on nurses' psychological health.

Clinical nurse specialists

The CNS is considered to be a cornerstone of good cancer care in the UK (National Cancer Action Team, 2010a). The role was developed in the 1970s to help meet the needs of cancer patients. Often referred to as "Macmillan Nurses", because the CNS was employed with initial financial support from the UK charity Macmillan Cancer Relief, CNS posts in palliative care were among the first to take root in both hospital and community settings. Since then there has been increased recognition that failure to address patients' complex needs at an early stage can affect how the person copes with their cancer treatment and how they make the transition from cancer patient to cancer survivor (National Institute for Clinical Excellence, 2004; Department of Health, 2007). CNS posts were set up to meet these needs, and there are now approximately seventeen cancer site-specific CNS roles across the UK, for example in breast, colorectal, gynaecological, and lung cancer, as well as CNS posts in palliative care. A recent census found there to be about 2,800 clinical nurse specialists in post today (National Cancer Action Team, 2012).

Role

Patients with cancer face not only the dramatic impact of their cancer diagnosis but also prolonged multiple modalities of treatment: surgery, chemotherapy, and radiotherapy. These can have a profound impact on the person—physically, psychologically, sexually, spiritually, and financially. CNSs work in acute hospitals, community settings, and in hospices to ensure patients have expert information, knowledge, and emotional support to deal with difficulties at each stage in their cancer pathway (National Cancer Action Team, 2010a). It is a National

Health Service (NHS) requirement that every person diagnosed with cancer has a "key worker" from the health care professional team to co-ordinate care, ensure patient preferences for treatment and care are prioritised, and to provide continuity throughout the illness, including the dying process. More often than not a CNS fulfils the "key worker" role over an extended period of time, a role which includes providing expert advice to colleagues.

The CNS is usually the patient's first point of contact for any cancer-related worries or concerns (National Cancer Action Team, 2010b). They meet the patient at the point of diagnosis when the person may feel especially vulnerable and subject to strong emotions. Often this meeting is the beginning of a therapeutic relationship which extends over many years, during which the patient may become unwell or suffer a relapse.

The therapeutic relationship

The sheer sensual bodiliness in the intimate nursing care of patients is not generally acknowledged by nurses, yet it is crucial to an understanding of the grounds and expectations of the relationship between nurse and patient. The nature of the body fluids encountered during care—blood, sweat, saliva, tears, urine, and faeces—recalls the primitive mother-child relationship. For the nurse, the emotional and sensual experience of giving patient care evokes the nurse's own infantile experiences, and these may provide a basis for empathic understanding and sensitivity to patients. Indeed, powerful unconscious knowing lies at the very heart of nursing and partly accounts for what nurses often represent to patients, namely, the "all giving, caring maternal figure" who will protect and buffer them from stresses throughout the cancer journey.

In some cases, however, in caring for a person damaged by cancer, the nurse may be overwhelmed by these identifications (Wiltshire & Parker, 1996). It may in fact be very difficult for the nurse to give the care, especially if there is no one available to support the nurse.

Although a focus of the CNS's work is on the external physical dimensions of the illness, the nurse will also be exposed to problems in the patient's internal, psychic world and will need to acknowledge and address the person's ability to manage the feelings that the illness evokes (Rodin, Mikulincer, Donner, Gagliese, & Zimmermann, 2009). A constant interplay of internal and external realities characterises the nurse's work, and this can be profoundly challenging given the depth and intensity of the psychological disturbance which may accompany cancer. In this regard Erskine and Judd (1994) have underlined how the diagnosis and treatment of life-threatening illness "constitutes a psychic trauma" (p. 87).

The therapeutic relationship between patient and nurse is one in which the nurse needs to remain sensitive to the specific support needs of the individual patient and to engage as an active participant in the patient's cancer journey. It is this approach that is considered most likely to sustain hope, and counteract problems of demoralisation and depression (Rodin, et al., 2007). Remaining actively engaged with the patient is especially challenging in advanced cancer when there is increased frailty and dependence. Yet if CNSs strive to communicate during this phase, so that patients feel understood and supported, even when time is brief, patients may be more confident that hope, dignity, and a sense of personal meaning can be sustained to the last (Goldie, 2005).

Thus the role of the CNS involves forming a stable and continuing relationship with the patient (Savage, 1995). The relationship may provide emotional containment particularly if a secure attachment is made with the nurse. In researching patients' relationships with health care professionals, Kahn, et al. (2010) found that a patient's early life experiences of caring, supportive relationships lead to an internalised belief that one is competent and deserving of support, and that such support will be available when needed. In serious illness this system of attachment comes naturally to the fore, with most patients then able to seek and gain support. For those who may not have experienced secure attachments, increased dependency may be intolerable. Such patients may fear rejection, abandonment, or loss of dignity because of what they experience as their inescapable need of others' help (Parkes, Stevenson-Hinde, & Marris, 1991). These notions may be foremost in the minds of patients anxious about separation and contact with the nurse (Bowlby, 1997).

As Main considered in "The ailment" (1957), there are deep personal reasons nurses choose to work with cancer, including abiding unconscious determinants such as the need to heal sick parts of the self. In relating to patients, nurses naturally respond with emotions expressive of their own psychic inner worlds (Jones, 1999, 2003, 2005). Of course a range of feelings can invade their work, including anxiety, guilt, depression, and compulsive reparative wishes. As Menzies Lyth (1988) and Fabricius (1991) have suggested, there will be times when nurses feel deeply defended against the stresses and anxieties of caring for people with cancer.

Caseload

CNSs are generally either hospital or community-based. They will see patients in a variety of settings: medical clinics, nurse-led clinics, wards, and patients' homes. Their caseloads will contain a mixture of newly diagnosed patients, those needing support through treatment, and others with whom they maintain contact for extended periods after treatment has finished. Consequently the CNS may need to hold many patients in mind at any one time. Indeed, of late there has been concern about the number of referrals to CNSs, the size of their individual caseloads, and the impossibility of managing a very large caseload (Whittome, Richardson, & Trevatt, 2009). Community palliative care nurses, for example, are often overburdened with caseloads of between twenty-five and thirty patients of whom ten are, at any one time, likely to need regular visits for complex symptom management. An added complexity for these nurses is that they are not only involved with cancer patients but with patients who have other life-limiting conditions such as cardiac, neurological, and respiratory diseases.

It is important to recognise that the caseload experience of community-based CNSs is not framed by the containing, almost shielding environment of a hospital or hospice with its wards and departments. Rather the experience is in the home where the usually lone nurse encounters the patient surrounded by the trappings of his or her everyday life, and where the recognition of loss is often magnified. The nurse enters the territory of the patient and cannot fail to be aware of the changed, ill person as someone different from his or her former self.

This is, of course, a general feature of a CNS's role. The CNS gets to know patients over an extended period and bears witness at times when the patient flourishes and is physically well and at other times when the disease is active and causing considerable bodily change and physical problems. Simply taking a patient's hand can be poignant and meaningful for both nurse and patient if there has been wasting and the hand taken is skeletal and frail when once it was strong and healthy.

A CNS's caseload also exposes him or her to powerful transference feelings and projections from patients and their families, feelings which may be felt very personally (O'Kelly, 1998). The nurse is made to be a "good" or "bad" figure for the patient and family, or made to feel different roles at different times. Often the mix of individual cases can help the nurse with patients who project painful feelings, or feelings of despair or anger for the nurse to carry. These are balanced by others who have a more integrated sense of themselves and the part they play in their care.

Another aspect of the CNS's caseload, particularly in hospital settings, relates to the patient's reactions to the CNS's other patients. Whilst these reactions can provide the nurse with important clues for the patient's care, they can also possess multiple layers of meaning that may, in some instances, point to the patient's displacement of his or her transference feelings onto other patients. Such feelings can sometimes be very difficult to grasp and nurses are not generally trained to work with them. Patients' watchfulness of other patients is nevertheless *felt* by the nurse who may need to carry, for example, jealous or spiteful feelings, or feelings of unworthiness.

I have selected three case-vignettes and with these aim to show something of the dynamic of the CNS's work of listening and talking to people with cancer, and how it feels to carry such a patient caseload. The cases illustrate some of the challenges described above. The work was done in a London gynaecological cancer centre. Goldie provides a useful introduction to the potentially devastating effects that a gynaecological cancer can have on different parts of the body and the woman's conception of her body (2005, p. 78). Overall, my work was to assist the women to adjust to their cancer illness and help identify care strategies to support and enable them to improve their health outcomes, well-being, and quality of life. During my encounters with the women I encouraged them to think about themselves and was always interested and listened carefully to what they thought and felt. I believe psychoanalytic principles help in understanding patients and their reactions and interactions, and I also believe that their application in communication has therapeutic benefits. I am, however, not trained in these techniques and I acknowledge that my understanding and insights in the following vignettes are limited. Names have been changed and every effort taken to maintain the confidentiality of the patients.

Maintaining control

Enid was a seventy-year-old woman with womb cancer and when I first met her she was midway through her chemo-radiation treatment following surgery. She was tall, stylishly dressed, and her face carefully made up. She told me she had retired ten years previously from her job with the Citizens Advice Bureau and that she had been a very active union member. Her husband had left her some years before that and her two sons, aged twenty-six and thirty-five, lived abroad. Enid admitted feeling rather alone though she had a number of close friends living nearby. Her brother, aged eighty, had died the year before with cancer. Enid completed her initial treatment successfully but the cancer became active again a year or so later and further treatment was needed.

Over a period of two years I spoke with Enid regularly when she telephoned, and I saw her when she came for follow-up appointments. Enid invariably explored her feelings about being ill during our telephone conversations: how restrictive it was and how vulnerable and miserable she felt because of her "hopeless physical state". She "wanted and needed to feed her spirit" and had so little energy to do this. On several occasions we talked through plans for short "spirit trips": a lunchtime concert "to hear the human voice", a public garden visit to see a favourite plant in flower.

Enid remarked once in relation to her need for cancer treatment that it "would be nice to have something which was done and all done". She reminded me that she was realistic about the disease coming back though she did not want to talk about that generally, "only with me". Enid was tearful in the clinic when the doctor gave her the news that the cancer was active again. When he suggested "talking to Anne about it" she exclaimed that she "should not have to be nursed by Anne!" Enid had always been sensitive to any intimation of sympathy on my part and had said on occasions "Don't give me sympathy—that will make me cry". When Enid was admitted to the ward for what proved to be the terminal stage of her illness she asked to wait until she looked and felt more like herself before seeing me. Enid knew through the messages I relayed via the ward nurses that I was thinking about her, but there was no leave-taking between us.

Enid was a strong person and the helplessness and lack of control brought about by the cancer came through powerfully in our talks. I recognised that she could not bear losing control and this was a source of distress. Her resistance to expressions of sympathy and to being nursed was part of her need to remain in control. It was, it seemed, the very thought of not having to be nursed that would set her apart from "patients", with whom she refused to be included. Enid seemed to use me over the years to maintain hope and help muster her strength of spirit and psychological resources in an effort to retain control and not to let the illness get the better of her. In the final stages of her illness and with the inevitable regression that illness causes, Enid found comfort and safety in the care delivered by compassionate and experienced ward nurses.

Over time, arrangements were made for Enid to go to a hospice. She had always expressed ambivalent feelings about "hospice" and I was therefore not surprised to hear that Enid died the day before her transfer. This case highlights another difficult feature of CNS work, namely that the opportunity to say goodbye or make an ending may be missed for practical as well as psychological reasons. I was saddened by Enid's death and felt her withdrawal very personally.

Bearing rage

The next case also concerns a woman's fear and anxiety of losing control and was a reminder to me that I cannot hope to have good feelings from patients all the time; I will also have to manage the bad feelings.

Thirty-six-year-old Joan had advanced cervix cancer and when I first met her was responding very poorly to chemotherapy treatment and its side-effects. Symptom relief for her disease-related problems, including pain, was also a problem. I worked closely with the palliative care CNS and ward nurses to relieve Joan's symptoms and provide support to her family. Joan needed nurses to help her wash, go to the toilet, and sit up in bed.

Divorced from her husband, Joan was visited in hospital at weekends by her sister who would bring Joan's children, John aged five and Lucy aged seven, to see her. I watched helplessly with ward nurse colleagues as Joan would shout at her children to "stay there" at the foot of the bed, out of arm's reach. Joan would lift her hand as if to strike them if they crept closer.

The children hung off the bed-end, messing around, scuffing their feet and taking anxious glances at their mother who looked paler and sicklier each time they visited. Joan did not respond to her children or engage them, though she gave them a quick kiss as they left.

Members of the multi-disciplinary care team who witnessed the children's plight were distressed but Joan insisted to the social worker and her consultant that she did not want any "interference in bringing up *her* children". At the same time she would not allow any acknowledgement of how close she was to death. Pressure to do something surfaced in the multi-disciplinary team meeting and it was agreed that I should attempt to speak with Joan about her feelings and thoughts and her wishes for the care of her children. The team was concerned that I speak to Joan soon because it was thought her death was not far off.

When I approached Joan, she reacted with fury at what she termed my "interference". She was angrily abusive in her condemnation of me and, until she became too weak and ill to do so, continued to denigrate me to the nursing team weeks after our conversation. She refused to allow me near her and, if I was passing her bed, would never fail to turn her head quickly on the pillow to avoid meeting my eye.

Joan did talk with other nurses and confided in them. Meanwhile I felt desperate, upset and angry that my good intentions on behalf of the team had not brought about the outcome the team had hoped for. The wish for wholeness and a desire for repair and to make good the ill person is recognised as a primary motivation for nurses entering the profession and the idea that nurses may wish to heal sick parts of themselves in others was referred to earlier. That repair is sometimes the outcome of care is one of the sources of immense satisfaction in the job. It can, however, prove persecutory to the nurse and this, I think, was how I was experiencing my encounter with Joan.

I felt utterly powerless in my role as the bearer of her rage. The transference was unwelcome and really "got to me". In the situation, I had been asked to carry hatred, terror, anger, and impotence, and I was slow to realise that this was in fact the very work that was needed, the work that I actually did for Joan. It was only much later, when I understood that the split of "bad nurse/angel of death" and "good kind nurse" served a vital function for Joan, that I came to appreciate more fully the nature of my task. It was her way of dealing with the intolerable anxiety of her situation and of expressing sadness and guilt as a mother who would soon abandon her children. Given the splitting of Joan's difficult feelings, it was vital to her care, my functioning and our team work, that we could think together about her very powerful projections.

As noted earlier, the patient–CNS therapeutic relationship can extend over the course of several years. During this time it may develop in depth and intensity depending on the patient's situation, his or her needs, the nurse's skill and preparedness to enter into the relationship and, generally, the quality of the attachment. The relationship not only involves the nurse in powerful projections but in the physical ups and downs of the cancer illness. In the next vignette I summarise a patient's difficulty in holding onto hope as treatment repeatedly failed. The account also highlights my dilemma in trying to remain close enough to the patient's experience to feel the impact of it, whilst preserving some distance so that I could contain her feelings, including her anxieties.

Holding onto hope

Dawn was a fifty-year-old single woman with ovarian cancer. Her mother had died of this cancer two years before and Dawn vividly recalled her mother's painful death and spoke to me early on of her "terror of going the same way". Dawn had a large family with many siblings. She was particularly close to the women in her family.

When I met Dawn she was raw-boned and strained. Her bald head was concealed under a scarf. At the end of Dawn's initial surgery and chemotherapy treatment there was still cancer visible on her scan. Indications for giving optimally timed further treatment not only depended on Dawn's scan result but, amongst other things, on whether she was experiencing any symptoms. The agreed plan was to monitor Dawn's condition carefully and if she became symptomatic or had raised tumour markers, to re-scan. Dawn was perturbed by this "watch and wait" approach, saying it was "bizarre to be told you still have cancer, but to go away". She told me she was very frightened and worried by the uncertainty of the year ahead and how she would manage at home especially during the night when she felt "most depressed and terrified". She also said she was not helped by "seeing her future" in very ill women when she attended clinic. We agreed that I would telephone her at prearranged monthly intervals between her clinic appointments to assess her symptoms, discuss how she was feeling, and address any concerns she might have. Occasionally I would ring Dawn in between our prearranged telephone appointments to see how she was. Once or twice I happened to telephone when my attention was most needed. Dawn thought of these occasions as nothing short of miraculous, saying to the doctors, "How did she know I needed her to phone me?!" I felt that this was Dawn's way of letting me know her desperate wish that she needed me to be really *in touch* with what she was going through.

One thing that Dawn repeatedly went through was fluid collecting in her abdomen (ascites). This can be a very troublesome symptom of ovarian cancer and several litres of fluid can accumulate. Dawn became very bloated when this happened, had problems getting around, and "felt very awful and sick". Dawn recognised the cruel irony of her state when she said, "with the fluid on board I look pregnant". She also likened the ascites to the cancer itself, describing it as "something within that you can't control". Dawn became very anxious each time the fluid gradually re-accumulated, and every morning she looked at herself in the mirror and measured her girth with a tape measure to assess how much fluid was in her abdomen. When she considered herself "ready" she would call me to make arrangements for the fluid to be drained off. This plan worked well and Dawn retained control of her care as long as I was successful in organising the drainage.

The time came when Dawn could not bear to look at herself in the mirror. She tried to walk to the corner of her street and felt dizzy and sick and had to return home. Feeling so weak and tired was depressing her yet she resisted anti-depressants and did not wish to see a psychologist. She hoped that the next treatment would work because she was "not ready to lie down and die". Her terror was that she would not be offered any more treatment, and she repeatedly asked anxious questions about this and what would happen if she was not treated, saying "Well you can't just leave me like this, can you?" Dawn's questions made me feel inadequate, at a loss to know what to answer. I felt discomforted also by the emotions that I sensed were being projected, the feeling that I was to be the one to leave.

The consultant wanted to discuss treatment options to relieve some of Dawn's symptoms. Dawn's family had read about a new drug available only in Germany and had brought the information to the consultation. They urged Dawn to go to Germany for this treatment. Though the new treatment was not endorsed by Dawn's consultant, the idea of travelling to Germany took on a life of its own, with plans for the trip soon dominating conversations with Dawn and her family. I wondered if this might be a way of shutting off what Dawn was experiencing; or if perhaps Dawn's family were "sending her away" because they were unable to cope with how her distress made them feel. Maybe Dawn, in her very changed state of illness, also wondered if I too wanted her anymore since I had suggested she *go away* to a psychologist.

I spoke with Dawn's consultant and arranged for him to see Dawn and her family. In the consultation Dawn sat wide-eyed with anxiety, her family flanking her, with the new treatment information on their laps. The doctor said that we wished to continue to treat her and that he believed there were several treatments that would ease her symptoms. Eventually the consultant said, "I don't want you to go to Germany". Dawn cried then and was able to tell him how frightened she was. Her family visibly relaxed and, in a strong voice, Dawn said, "I want to stay here and be treated by people who know me".

This consultation was in some ways pivotal in Dawn's care. It showed her that her anxieties and fears could be held by another person and found to be manageable. Afterwards her fear of death was tolerable most of the time, and she hoped for more days with friends, more trips to her favourite cafés, days to bake just one more cake and, above all, to be pain free to enjoy time with younger family members. I only wish I had been able to understand Dawn's projections better and been better trained and supported at the time to use these communications in my responses to her.

Future directions

In this chapter I have tried to show the emotions aroused between nurses and patients and the particular ways patients may use a CNS psychologically, for example, to contain anxiety, relieve anger, and maintain hope. Though the CNS-patient relationship is often some-thing far more intimate and richer than I have managed to capture here, the vignettes give a sense of the difficulties that nurses face when working in death-haunted situations, situations where it is important to keep death in mind yet remain on the side of life. As Menzies Lyth identified fifty years ago, "by the very nature of her profession the nurse is at considerable risk of being flooded by intense and unmanageable anxiety" (1988, p. 50). Whilst the nurse may try to defend against this anxiety (Brown & Pedder, 1991) the milieu and thrust of twenty-first century cancer care increasingly presents challenges to these defences. More and more patients today are being offered complex combinations of treatments (including maintenance treatments aimed at keeping the cancer in remission for as long as possible), new technologies are being introduced, consumer expectations and competition for patient contracts and research funds are growing, and illness trajectories are lengthening. As the challenges grow, nurses' anxiety is likely to increase and with it the risk that rather than being aware of their defences as a normal protection from excessive anxiety these become barriers to thoughtful and responsive nursing practice.

I have shown how invaded I was by Dawn's emotions and fear of dying, and highlighted my attempts to use these feelings in my response to Dawn's distress. Yet CNSs, and nurses generally, exemplify a relative mistrust of their own personal feelings in understanding and reflecting on the emotional distress of cancer patients, and as a basis for responding to patients' emotions. It is important for CNSs to examine their feelings and learn how to identify and assess them consciously. They need support and training to do this. Recognising and symbolising feelings in words will help them accept and use their feelings meaningfully in their work. It will also help avoid the inadvertent harm to patients in care that can follow from feelings remaining unexamined.

In the UK levels of therapeutic intervention for specialist cancer nurses have recently been articulated. Specialist nurses work at level two of a four-level psychological intervention model, "using empathy, knowledge and experience to assess and alleviate the psychosocial suffering of cancer including referring to other agencies or disciplines as appropriate" (National Cancer Action Team, 2010a, p. 4). This clinical guidance has resulted in increased recognition of the need for supervision for nurses, and in the United Kingdom supervision is mandatory for CNS roles. These changes bring promise for future nurse training in conscious and unconscious communications and for supervision provided by experienced psychoanalytically orientated individuals who are skilled at examining the more profound emotional aspects of cancer care.

Acknowledgements

This work was done at the Department of Women's Cancer, UCL Institute for Women's Health and NIHR University College London Hospitals Biomedical Research Centre, London.

My thanks to Maggie Cohen for her invaluable supervision.

References

Bowlby, J. (1977). The making and breaking of affectional bonds. *British Journal of Psychiatry, 130*: 201–210.

Brown, D. & Pedder, J. (1991). *Introduction to Psychotherapy: An Outline of Psychodynamic Principles and Practice*. London: Routledge.

Department of Health. (2007). *The Cancer Reform Strategy*. London: HMSO.

Erskine, A. & Judd, D. (Eds.) (1994). *The Imaginative Body*. London: Whurr.

Fabricius, J. (1991). Running on the spot or can nursing really change. *Psychoanalytic Psychotherapy, 5*(2): 97–108.

Goldie, L. E. (2005). *Psychotherapy and the Treatment of Cancer Patients: Bearing Cancer in Mind*. London: Routledge.

Jones, A. (1999). Listen, listen, trust your own strange voice: psychoanalytically informed conversations with women suffering serious illness. *Journal of Advanced Nursing, 29*(4): 826–31.

Jones, A. (2003). On projective identification, containment, and feeling special: some thoughts about hospice nurses' experiences. *American Journal of Hospice and Palliative Care, 20*(6): 441–446.

Jones, A. (2005). Transference, counter-transference and repetition: some implications for nursing practice. *Journal of Advanced Nursing, 14*: 1177–1184.

Khan, L., Wong, R., Li, M., Zimmermann, C., Lo, C., Gagliese, L., & Rodin, G. (2010). Maintaining the will to live of patients with advanced cancer. *Cancer Journal, 16*(5): 524–31.

Main, T. F. (1957). The ailment. *British Journal of Medical Psychology, 30*: 129–145.

Menzies Lyth, I. (1988). The functioning of social systems as a defence against anxiety. In: I. Menzies Lyth, *Containing Anxiety in Institutions: Selected Essays* (pp. 43–94). London: Free Association Books (1959, 1961, 1961b, 1970).

National Institute for Clinical Excellence. (2004). *Improving Supportive and Palliative Care for Adults with Cancer*. London: National Institute for Clinical Excellence.

National Cancer Action Team. (2010a). *Excellence in Cancer Care: The Contribution of the Clinical Nurse Specialist*. London: Department of Health.

National Cancer Action Team. (2010b). *Manual for Cancer Services 2008: Psychological Support Measures*. London: Department of Health.

National Cancer Action Team. (2012). *Quality in Nursing. Clinical Nurse Specialists in Cancer Care; Provision, Proportion and Performance. A census of the cancer specialist nurse workforce in England 2011*. London: Department of Health.

O'Kelly, G. (1998). Countertransference in the nurse-patient relationship: a review of the literature. *Journal of Advanced Nursing, 28*(2): 391–397.

Parkes, C. M., Stevenson-Hinde, J., & Marris, P. (1991). *Attachment Across the Life Cycle*. London: Routledge.

Rodin, G., Lo, C., Mikulincer, M., Donner, A., Gagliese, L., & Zimmermann, C. (2009). Pathways to distress: the multiple determinants of depression, hopelessness, and the desire for hastened death in metastatic cancer patients. *Social Science & Medicine, 68*(3): 562–569.

Rodin, G., Walsh, A., Zimmermann, C., Gagliese, L., Jones, J., Shepherd, F. A., Moore, M., Braun, M., Donner, A., & Mikulincer, M. (2007). The contribution of attachment security and social support to depressive symptoms in patients with metastatic cancer. *Psycho-oncology, 16*(12): 1080–91.

Savage, J. (1995). *Nursing Intimacy: An Ethnographic Approach to Nurse-patient Interaction*. London: Scutari Press.

Whittome, J., Richardson, A., & Trevatt, P. (2009). *Prime Minister's Commission on the Future of Nursing & Midwifery in England: Summary of Responses from the Cancer Nursing Community*. London: National Cancer Action Team, Department of Health.

Wiltshire, J. & Parker, J. (1996). Containing abjection in nursing: the end of shift handover as a site of containment. *Nursing Inquiry, 3*: 23–29.

CHAPTER SEVEN

On survivorship

Adrian Tookman, Faye Gishen, and Jane Eades

Introduction: the changing nature of cancer care

Over the past twenty-five years there have been significant changes in cancer treatment and outcomes (Cancer Research UK, 2012a, 2012b; Office of National Statistics, 2003). Prolonged, more effective multimodality treatments for cancer are now commonplace, resulting in increasing numbers of "cancer survivors": people "living with or beyond" their disease (Cancer Research UK, 2012a, 2012b; Health Statistics Quarterly, 2004; Office of National Statistics, 2003). Treatments are often arduous, and in many instances "survivors" have disabilities as a legacy of surgery, chemotherapy, radiotherapy, and the disease itself. Many are in need of physical and emotional support (Macmillan Cancer Support, 2008).

There has indeed been an increase in cancer survival figures, with more patients ultimately being cured. However there are approximately 1.6 million people in England today who are living with cancer, and this figure is estimated to rise to almost 4 million by 2030 (Macmillan Cancer Support, 2008). This number includes those who have completed their treatment as well as those having ongoing treatment for cancer. This change in the patient demographics, although acknowledged in UK national publications, has traditionally not received adequate attention, leading to poorly developed services to support the cancer survivorship population (Armes, et al., 2009; Calman & Hine, 1995; National Council for Hospice and Specialist Palliative Care (NCHSPC), 2000; Nocon & Baldwin, 1998).

Current UK data (nationally collected) reflects these changes, but also demonstrates the growing burden of disability. Life expectancy for males is currently seventy-six years old, of which fourteen years on average will be spent with significant disability. The corresponding figure for females is eighty-one, with seventeen years spent with disability (Cancer Research UK, 2012a and 2012b; Office of National Statistics, 2003). These figures demonstrate increasing life expectancy of which a significant proportion will be spent living with disability. There is also clear evidence of increased ten-year survival data for many cancers, with nearly fifty per cent of cancer patients surviving more than ten years from their initial diagnosis (compared with the 1970s data where only twenty-two per cent of patients survived this long). Of particular interest, cancer survival now matches the survival outcomes for patients with many of the common long-term non-malignant illnesses (Solano, Gomes, & Higginson, 2006; Vestbo, Prescott, Lange, Schnohr, & Jensen, 1998). The consequence of these demographics is a growing cohort of cancer survivors who have a significant burden of symptoms and disability related to their disease, medical interventions (iatrogenic) and co-morbidities.

The consequences of improved survival

People who have finished cancer treatment report many difficulties (Macmillan Cancer Support, 2008; Stewart, MacIntyre, Hole, Capewell, & McMurray, 2001). They may struggle both physically and emotionally to adjust to changes that treatment has produced to their bodies. Short- and long-term side-effects of cancer and/or its treatment may be difficult for the individual to adapt to. In some instances it may be challenging for a person to live with the knowledge that their cancer cannot be cured even though they may feel healthy; these feelings of uncertainty can be extremely difficult to manage.

In addition to the physical and emotional consequences of cancer and its treatment, individuals and their families can struggle financially as household income decreases as a consequence of lost earnings. Returning to work can be challenging because of loss of confidence. In addition, employers can have prejudices about employees who have had time off for ill health. Employers tend to have little understanding of the length of time that rehabilitation can take after treatment.

Management of those living with and beyond cancer needs rethinking

Traditionally, the focus of cancer services has been on cancer as an acute illness with an emphasis on the acute treatment phase. Follow-up care has tended to focus on monitoring individuals in an outpatient setting, looking for signs of further disease (recurrence). These "follow-up" services are invariably health-professional led, and usually involve periodic hospital-based appointments.

A body of evidence now exists which suggests that current follow-up arrangements for those living with and beyond cancer does not fully address a wide range of physical, psychological, social, spiritual, and financial issues. Information needs have also been neglected. A study by Armes, et al. (2009) of 1,152 people with breast, colorectal, haemato-logical, and gynaecological cancers treated at sixty-six UK cancer centres suggested that thirty per cent reported more than five moderate or severe "unmet needs" at the end of treatment. Most commonly these were psychological needs and fear of recurrence.

One of the main reasons that clinicians follow up patients routinely is to detect disease recurrence. This has recently been challenged since routine surveillance appears to have little bearing on early detection of recurrence; for example less than one per cent of breast cancer recurrences are detected by this approach. In addition, a medically orientated follow-up service is costly for patients and their carers in terms of time, and can induce a significant financial, social, and psychological burden.

Clearly the impact of cancer does not end after treatment has been completed. The "Health and Well-Being Survey" by Macmillan Cancer Support in 2008 found that cancer survivors reported poorer health and well-being than the general population. The health and well-being profile of the cancer survivor population (without active cancer) is comparable to the population of people with a chronic condition such as diabetes or arthritis. The Macmillan survey showed ninety per cent of cancer survivors had visited their primary care physicians in the last twelve months, compared to sixty-eight per cent of the wider population.

We can therefore conclude that patients who are living "with" or "beyond their cancer" can have a complex burden of symptoms including the late effects of disease and treatment. This is often not well managed by a health care system that is understandably focused on managing the treatment phase of cancer and the early detection of recurrence. In addition, this population is ageing and cancer is more common in the elderly. Consequently, it is not unusual that a cancer patient suffers co-existent illnesses (co-morbidities/multi-morbidities). This increases the complexity of need and the breadth of symptoms that have to be addressed. There is therefore a need to rethink ways in which patients can access appropriate support throughout their cancer journey.

Survivorship and rehabilitation: the new agenda?

Survivorship is a confusing term that can be interpreted differently by different people. It is a term that is meaningful to some but considered unhelpful and negative, even pejorative, by others. In general, patients do not like the term since they feel it infers that they are labelled a "survivor" rather than someone who is aiming to return to normality. Returning to normality is a laudable aim; however, the reality is that many people have to, and need to, adjust to significant disability. These disabilities can be wide-ranging: physical, emotional, psychological, sexual, and spiritual. To assess need adequately and to develop an appropriate management plan requires awareness of the full spectrum of symptoms and an ability to triage patients to the optimal interventions. Accordingly, an appreciation of a multi-professional team approach is vital to manage the resultant complex problems.

An approach to survivorship that is focused on rehabilitation may be a more effective way of understanding and managing this cohort of patients. Whilst the need for support and rehabilitation during and after treatment is well recognised, the resources available to address this are, at best, limited. The following overlapping categorisations can be helpful to understand the wide range of patients that could benefit from a rehabilitative approach (Koocher & O'Malley, 1981):

Patients who have undergone treatment and may be cured: These patients need a range of psychological and physical therapies to enable them to recover, re-socialise, and adapt to any disability that may be present.

The object is to enable patients to live as normal a life as possible. Setting time frames for recovery is important here, and the aim is usually a relatively limited intervention.

Patients who have had treatment, are in remission, and are not cured: These patients may have disability. They are living with great uncertainty and need support to manage this. They have often had arduous treatments and when their disease recurs can feel disappointed, angry, cheated, and resentful that the treatment hasn't worked. They need the full range of rehabilitative resources to reframe their lives and maximise their potential.

Patients with progressive disease: Often these patients have had multiple courses of treatment and feel defeated by their cancer. They have complex physical and emotional problems and can feel cheated of a healthy future and resentful that things did not progress as anticipated. These patients often have a disease trajectory that is of gradual decline and progressive frailty. As care transfers into a palliative setting these patients can feel abandoned by their oncology teams. Frail patients often "fail to thrive" and need support from a full range of rehabilitative therapies. Despite frailty much can be done to maximise potential, optimise symptom control, and reassure patients that they can have control of their future and will be supported.

Patients who are close to death: Goals of treatment here relate to ease and solace in which giving patients a sense of control and negotiating care is important. These goals can be achieved by a rehabilitative approach to care, even at this stage of the illness.

The patient: assessing patients and managing challenging symptoms

With a new chronic illness emerging in patients living with cancer there is a growing healthcare issue. These patients have increased survival, and a significant proportion have disability and a need for support and rehabilitation. They may have symptoms related to their initial diagnosis and their treatment. They either have, or are likely to develop during their cancer journey, co-morbidities that further add to the burden of symptoms.

New paradigms of assessment and care must be considered to manage optimally this population. No longer can we focus on the cancer alone but there is a need to assess people holistically and develop strategies that address the complexity of their needs. Doing this demands a growing understanding of the importance of areas that were previously considered "taboo" or "too trivial" in the context of a person seriously ill with cancer.

There are "new" constellations of symptoms that are becoming recognised as issues that significantly affect an individual's quality of life. These include suffering, frailty, and complex chronic and severe pain. We must learn to look at "symptom clusters" rather than the effect of specific cancers on specific body parts. In assessing people with cancer we must also explore the values patients have, help manage expectations, set realistic goals, and discuss likely time frames for recovery. At all times we must be mindful that some individuals need to look into the future and discuss what control they may have in determining how their healthcare is managed (Advance Care Planning).

Many paradigms exist to assess patients holistically, and a framework for assessment of need is helpful. Below is an adaptation of the classification of symptoms originally defined by Dame Cicely Saunders (founder of the modern hospice movement), which remains relevant today (Tookman, et al., 2004). When assessing patients who have symptoms, the following domains must be considered:

Physical domains: Physical symptoms related to the disease, its treatment and co-morbidities.

Emotional domains: Psychological and emotional symptoms can include depression, fear, panic, despair and anger. Fear of uncertainty can fuel these symptoms. There is recognition that these are equal in importance to physical symptoms.

Social domains: The impact of housing, unemployment, and finances on health and well-being can be underestimated, and needs to be explored.

Spiritual domains: Whilst religious considerations and adherences can be important for many, spiritual unrest/distress can be expressed by anyone exploring their existential world, and looking for meaning in a *new* world, that is to say, one in which dealing with uncertainty has adopted a new level of priority. Here the concept of suffering needs understanding. Suffering may encompass unanswered questions, fears for the future, uncontrolled symptoms (physical or emotional), and the inability to manage distress. Addressing suffering is challenging; however, acknowledgement may, in the first instance, be key.

Sexual domains: Symptoms related to physical relationships are often ignored. This is an important area as it may well be a source of anxiety.

Tackling taboo topics

This chapter does not aim to be a comprehensive guide to symptom management; however there are a few areas that are important to address in more depth. The following are common issues seen in this cohort of patients; and they are focused on since they can be ignored by health care professionals because they sit in the "too difficult to tackle" box. This section will discuss managing uncertainty, long-term effects of strong painkillers (opioids), and sexual function.

Despite the fact that cancer is, for many, a long-term illness with a reasonable outcome, it remains a very frightening diagnosis to patients and their families. A diagnosis of cancer usually disrupts one's view of the future and challenges one's approach to mortality. This can have huge emotional implications. Dealing with uncertainty is difficult enough but when one considers the additional physical assault that comes with complicated and often demanding cancer treatments, it is not surprising that patients feel traumatised by their cancer and its management.

There are many uncertainties that are expressed by patients and their families: How complete will recovery be? How much energy might I have? Will I be able to get back to a normal life, and if so, when? For many people faced with a potentially life-threatening illness, the feeling of control is lost and a sense of control is sought. This can be facilitated in many ways: through factual information, knowledge, and submission/acceptance.

The impact on people who live with significant feelings of uncertainty is to experience anxiety, stress, and difficulty planning for the future. In addition, the patient's partner, children, other family members, friends, and employer may all share in the burden and may react in different ways. The emotional impact can be wide-ranging, with some people exhibiting the classic features of post-traumatic stress.

For many the "Damocles Effect" is real. This was described by Koocher and O'Malley (1981) in a study involving 117 young adults treated for cancer. They described the young adults as having a dread of disease returning and difficulty thinking positively about the future. These negative thoughts considerably disrupted their normal lives. This phenomenon is seen in many patients post-cancer treatment, where the inability to give absolute guarantees can hinder people in progressing with their lives.

The management of uncertainty is challenging. People deal with uncertainty in different ways, often based on their previous experiences. For example, some manage uncertainty by seeking information, whilst others avoid information. The skilled practitioner works with the patient, allowing difficult feelings to be shared, respected, and given weight. Indeed it is only by talking about the inability to plan and the tension that uncertainty creates, both in one's external world and in one's internal life, that patients can be encouraged to move forward in their lives. Psychological/psychotherapeutic intervention can assist in this process.

As with any long-term condition, pain and other associated symptoms are frequent and these require a range of interventions to optimise patients' management (Jones, et al., 2012). Drug interventions are commonplace, and in many cases patients can be on high doses of drugs for long periods of time. One area that needs further discussion is the consequence of using strong analgesics long term.

Pain is widely prevalent and generally poorly managed. Strong painkillers (often termed "step 3 opioids") are used frequently; this is good practice. If pain is poorly managed, the consequences can be devastating. However, we must appraise long-term opioid use, since in patients living with and beyond cancer they may be on such medications for prolonged periods of time. "Step 3 opioids" have an important role in improving quality of life; however there are some side-effects that are poorly recognised, such as the impact on cognitive and sexual function.

Many patients on strong painkillers have problems with concentration and memory, especially working memory. This type of memory is used for ordinary, everyday concentration and is the component of memory that is also most likely to be affected when patients have chemotherapy. The impact of drugs on cognition is usually transient but it is important to recognise since patients with poor cognitive function may be anxious about this. Reassurance can be offered that drug-related memory loss is common and invariably transient if the drug can be stopped.

Opioids also affect sexual function. In some patients, long-term opioids can cause a reduction in testosterone (Rajagopal, Vassiliopoulou-Sellin, Palmer, Kaur, & Bruera, 2004). This hormone has an impact on libido in both men and women; if low, fatigue and loss of muscle bulk can result. It is easily replaced and this should be considered in patients with non-hormone dependent cancers.

Sexual function is one area of the narrative that is often avoided (Ananth, Jones, King, & Tookman, 2003). Research confirms, however, that patients living with and beyond cancer consider that this is an important area of their lives. Yet there is a reluctance to discuss this with their clinical team, who in turn invariably do not broach the subject with their patients. Advice would be that it is important to be proactive when discussing sexual function since there are simple interventions that can be highly effective and positively impact on patients' quality of life.

The patient: changing perceptions and behaviours

Patients who have cancer treatment have very active management in an acute medical setting. Expectations at the beginning of the "cancer journey" are often that there will be a return to normality; however the reality may be quite different. Accepting this reality and focusing on areas of a person's life where changes can be made are the foundations of effective rehabilitation. These frameworks are useful in managing complex symptom control issues in cancer survivors where acceptance of disability and living with uncertainty can be difficult. Different approaches to this can be adopted, from simple interventions in community/primary care to very focused interventions in managing long-term effects of cancer.

Patients, following cancer treatment, can feel cheated of a healthy life, defeated by the burden of treatment, and uncertain of their future. Their sense of "personhood" may be disrupted, which can be distressing as they wrestle with retaining control in an altered physical and emotional persona. A feeling of abandonment by clinical teams can be perceived when the acute phase of treatment has been completed since the previous frequent hospital visits may cease, leaving a perceived "void". This can be particularly marked at the end of a clinical trial, during which time patients tend to be even more closely monitored.

In rehabilitation the situation can be further complicated: patients may not wish to change behaviour even if there is a clearly observed need. Healthcare workers may not facilitate a rehabilitative approach. They are often accused of using didactic, inflexible models of care, persuading patients to adopt a defined and pre-determined plan. It is here that clinicians clearly need to work closely with patients to assess the perception and feelings that the patient may have about whether or not to become engaged in a programme of care.

Understanding "change behaviour" can influence patient management. This is the theory behind motivational interviewing techniques (Rubak, Sandbaek, Lauritzen, & Christensen, 2005) whereby a patient's engagement in a rehabilitation programme, or the formulation of an advance care plan, is predicated on their acceptance that they have become disabled and are in a position to contemplate an active change in their behaviour to manage this. The transtheoretical model of change proposed by Prochaska and Velicer can be useful in this regard (Prochaska & Velicer, 1997). A modified form of this model is summarised below:

The patient who expresses "pre-contemplative" behaviours: The patient has no intention to change. They may not wish to have any involvement with a rehabilitation programme. Options are limited to interventions that are perceived by the patient to be relevant and useful.

The objective is to reassure the patient that they will not be burdened or forced into treatments. The aim is to gain patient's confidence. Intervention may be limited to outpatient follow-up, or the suggestion that re-referral at a future date may be appropriate.

The patient who expresses contemplative behaviour: There is an intention to change. Concepts of new therapies/goals can now be discussed. The patient is introduced to the programme. The objective is to inform the patient about the services available and guide them accordingly.

The stage of preparation: At this stage a care package is discussed with the patient and the team. The team may have useful input at this stage where treatment is often confined to limited interventions.

The stage of action: Rehabilitation therapies appropriate to the patient's need are organised and goals set.

The stage of maintenance: Strategies are employed to sustain change. The rehabilitation programme is underpinned by regular monitoring and assessment to ensure that therapies are appropriate to changing needs.

Relapse: Changing physical or emotional needs may make a patient disillusioned and reluctant to continue the rehabilitation programme. The consequence can be a return to contemplation or pre-contemplation. Flexibility in programme is fundamental to manage relapse.

The healthcare system: delivering the survivorship and rehabilitation agenda

When planning interventions for people surviving with and beyond cancer the needs of the wider healthcare economy must be considered. Knowledge of the national, system-wide agenda leads to a more complete understanding of what is necessary in order to deliver a service for cancer survivors that is fit for purpose and meets national standards.

There is a UK national framework for changes in cancer care that is outlined in a document entitled "The Model of Care" (NHS, 2010). This is the blueprint for reconfiguring cancer services and is underpinned by ten guiding principles:

1. Services should provide informed choice, quality outcomes, and a high-quality experience for cancer patients.
2. Patients should be at the centre of services, which will be based on patient pathways and will be commissioned to meet their needs.
3. Services should aim to exceed national, regional, and local care and quality standards, such as the National Institute for Clinical Excellence (NICE) improving outcomes guidance, and national policies including the Cancer Reform Strategy.

4. Health services should be delivered locally where this is clinically appropriate and delivers value for money.
5. Healthcare should be delivered close to home and in ambulatory care settings where possible, avoiding or reducing the need for patients to attend or be admitted to hospital.
6. Services should be centralised where clinically appropriate.
7. Tertiary, secondary, and primary care services should work closely together, with partners such as local authorities, to provide more cohesive and better care for cancer patients.
8. Services should deliver improved outcomes for cancer patients while being productive and providing value for money for taxpayers.
9. Services should meet the needs of the populations they serve and be innovative and continually evolving.
10. Cancer research, both basic and clinical, should be strongly supported and fostered.

For common cancers the evidence suggests that elements of cancer care, such as chemotherapy and patient follow-up, should be provided outside of hospital settings wherever possible. The evidence also makes the case for improving outcomes by centralising complex investigations and treatments in only a few specialist centres. All non-hospital based services should be integrated with other services in the network of cancer providers in a co-ordinated and regulated fashion. This ensures that services are high-quality and as safe as possible. The reality is that there are increasing numbers of people surviving with cancer and the current model of long-term hospital-based follow-up is not sustainable or financially viable. The aim is to move from the current clinician-led and largely hospital-based model of care for those living with and beyond cancer, to a more collaborative model which recognises people as experts in their condition and, as such, "partners" in the development and implementation of plans for their future care.

There have been national initiatives to facilitate a rehabilitative approach. These include the National Cancer Reform Strategy that incorporated rehabilitation within its wide-ranging, aspirational framework (Department of Health, 2007). This element of the Cancer Reform Strategy led to the development of The National Cancer Survivorship Initiative (NCSI). This identified the need to shift a greater focus of care and support onto recovery, rehabilitation, and health and well-being after cancer treatment. The proposal was to move away from a clinically led approach and follow-up care, to supported self-management, based on individual needs and preferences. For example, it has been estimated that seventy per cent of patients with breast cancer do not need hospital follow-up. Such patients have been deemed able to monitor their condition themselves. It is estimated that sixty per cent of people with lung cancer can have their condition monitored with shared care protocols, and that similarly sixty-five per cent of men with prostate cancer can be seen in the community for blood tests that are regularly fed back to the treatment (hospital) team. Naturally, patients with more complex needs will still be seen in hospital outpatient departments (NHS Improvement, 2009).

A future development will be "risk stratified follow-up". At its simplest, this is a new way of triaging and following up patients' postcancer treatment that is not dependent on hospital outpatient services. The model involves assessing and directing patients into different pathways: self-management, shared care, or complex care (NHS Improvement, 2011). Patients will need to have a clearly defined, rapid way of accessing hospital care if their condition changes. All patients will be given a care plan that requires regular updating and will include an assessment of need that is not only focused on physical problems. It will stipulate who will be following up the patient, and how and when this will occur, with the plan disseminated to key health care professionals.

Self-management is encouraged and facilitated by: health and well-being clinics, supported self-management, physical activity programmes, and vocational rehabilitation.

Conclusion

Surviving cancer is becoming commonplace, with patients living with and beyond cancer facing complex problems. Many individuals are left with a long-term condition and significant symptom burden. New conditions are emerging, such as "frailty", that reflect an illness trajectory where patients decline slowly, fail to thrive, and develop cascading health care problems. Cancer survivors often have multiple co-morbidities, chronic pain, fatigue, and suffering which need a new approach to management since people who survive cancer will live for many years. Managing the psychosocial elements poses new challenges as patients and their families have to live with uncertainty. The resources to manage these patients are limited at present; however, there is a growing awareness that a co-ordinated approach is needed to bring about changes in health care to accommodate these problems.

Cancer clinicians and healthcare systems are becoming aware that planning effective future care that is centred on the needs of patients must take account of the large numbers of patients who are living with and beyond their cancers. There is recognition of a need to develop new ways of managing patients and advance a flexible health care system that will allow patients to achieve their maximum potential.

References

Ananth, A., Jones, L., King, M., & Tookman, A. (2003). The impact of cancer on sexual function. *Palliative Medicine, 17*: 202–205.

Armes, J., Crowe, M., Colborne, L., Morgan, H., Murrells, T., Oakley, C., Palmer, N., Ream, E., Young, A., & Richardson, A. (2009). Patients' supportive care needs beyond the end of treatment: a prospective and longitudinal survey. *Journal of Clinical Oncology, 27*: 6172–6179.

Calman, K. & Hine, D. (1995). *Policy framework for commissioning cancer services: a report by the expert advisory group on cancer to the chief medical officers of England and Wales.* London: Department of Health.

Cancer Research UK. (2012a). Ten year relative survival (%), adults (15–99 years), selected cancers, England and Wales: survival trends for selected cancers 1971–2007. Available from: http://info.cancerresearchuk.org/cancerstats/survival/latestrates/.

Cancer Research UK. (2012b). Relative five-year survival estimates based on survival probabilities observed during 2000–2001, by sex and site, England and Wales. Available from: http://info.cancerresearchuk.org/cancerstats/survival/latestrates/.

Department of Health. (2007). *The Cancer Reform Strategy.* Department of Health.

Health Statistics Quarterly. (2004). Report: Healthy life expectancy in Great Britain: 2001. *Health Statistics Quarterly, 23*: Autumn 2004.

Jones, L., Fitzgerald, G., Leurent, B., Round, J., Eades, J., Davis, S., Gishen, F., Holman, A., Hopkins, K., & Tookman, A. *Rehabilitation in Advanced, Progressive, Recurrent Cancer: A Randomized Controlled Trial. Journal of Pain and Symptom Management. November 2012. [Epub ahead of print].*

Koocher, G. P. & O'Malley, J. J. (1981). *Damocles Syndrome: Psychosocial Consequences of Surviving Childhood Cancer.* New York: McGraw-Hill.

Macmillan Cancer Support. (2008). *Macmillan Study of the Health and Wellbeing of Cancer Survivors.* Macmillan Cancer Support.

National Council for Hospice and Specialist Palliative Care. (2000). *Fulfilling Lives: Rehabilitation in Palliative Care*. London: National Council for Hospice and Specialist Palliative Care.

National Health Service. (2010). *A Model of Care for Cancer Services Clinical Paper*. National Health Service.

NHS Improvement. (2009). *Rapid review of current service provision following cancer treatment*, NHS Improvement, Leicester.

NHS Improvement-Cancer. (2011). *Effective Follow Up: Testing Risk Stratified Pathways*. NHS Improvement, Leicester.

Nocon, A. & Baldwin, S. (1998). *Trends in rehabilitation policy: a review of the literature*. Audit Commission and Kings Fund.

Office of National Statistics. (2003). *Cancer Survival, England and Wales 1991–2001*. Office of National Statistics.

Prochaska, J. O. & Velicer, W. F. (1997). Behaviour Change: the Transtheoretical Model of Health Behaviour Change. *American Journal of Health promotion. September–October 2012(1)*: 38–48.

Rajagopal, A., Vassiliopoulou-Sellin, R., Palmer, J. L., Kaur, G., & Bruera, E. (2004). Symptomatic hypogonadism in male survivors of cancer with chronic exposure to opioids. *Cancer 100(4)*: 851–858.

Rubak, S., Sandbaek, A., Lauritzen, T., & Christensen, B. (2005). Motivational interviewing: a systematic review and meta-analysis. *British Journal of General Practice, 55(513)*: 305–312.

Solano, J. P., Gomes, B., & Higginson, I. (2006). A comparison of symptom prevalence in far advanced Cancer, AIDS, heart disease, chronic obstructive pulmonary disease (COPD), and renal disease. *Journal of Pain and Symptom Management, 31*: 58–69.

Stewart, S., MacIntyre, K., Hole, D. J., Capewell, S., & McMurray, J. J. (2001). More "malignant" than cancer? 5 year survival following a first admission for heart failure. *Euopean Journal of Heart Failure, 3*: 315–322.

Tookman, A. Hopkins, K. Scharpen Von Heussen, K. (2004). Rehabilitation in Palliative Medicine. In: D. Doyle, G. Hanks, N. Cherny, K. Calman (Eds.) *Oxford Textbook of Palliative Medicine, 3rd Edition*, Oxford: Oxford University Press.

Vestbo, J., Prescott, E., Lange, P., Schnohr, P., & Jensen, G. (1998). Vital prognosis after hospitalization for COPD: a study of a random population sample. *Respiratory Medicine, 92(5)*: 772–776.

CHAPTER EIGHT

Palliative care: what, when, and how?*

Robert Twycross

What and when?

The World Health Organization (WHO) defines palliative care as:

> An approach that improves the quality of life of patients and their families facing the problems associated with life-threatening illness, through the prevention and relief of suffering by means of early identification and impeccable assessment and treatment of pain and other problems, physical, psychosocial and spiritual. (World Health Organization, 2002)

However, for most purposes a shorter definition is adequate, such as "end-of-life care" or "comfort care at the end of life".

Initially palliative care evolved mainly in relation to incurable cancer. Indeed it can be viewed as a protest movement against the attitude that "There's nothing more we can do for you", either stated or implied by the oncologist. Inevitably patients felt abandoned, and all too often suffered

*An expanded version of this paper was first presented at the London Centre for Psychotherapy (now part of a new organisation: the British Psychotherapy Foundation) on 29 October 2011.

agonising pain and other distressing symptoms for many weeks, even months, before their death. Then, in 1967, St Christopher's Hospice opened in London, an event often used to date the inauguration of specialist palliative care. Its founder, Dr. (later Dame) Cicely Saunders, was a unique catalyst in the evolution of compassionate, scientific end-of-life care in the UK and many other countries. Her dynamism and commitment inspired thousands of health professionals and members of the general public, and set in motion a global movement for improvement in the care of people with progressive end-stage diseases.

The message that you do *not* have to die in agony was central to Saunders' teaching, and is what most people associate with her. She was the pre-eminent proponent of "efficient loving care" characterised by attention to detail, the regular prophylactic use of analgesics and other symptom relief drugs (Twycross, et al., 2009; Twycross & Wilcock, 2011), close monitoring of the impact of the prescribed treatment, and the exploration of the patient's fears and anxieties, and those of the family.

Credit for the development of the field is also due to an increasing body of enthusiasts in an increasing number of countries. In the UK a second major catalyst was the National Society for Cancer Relief (now Macmillan Cancer Support) with the advent of Macmillan inpatient units, specialist community Macmillan nurses, Macmillan palliative care support teams in district general hospitals, and Macmillan sponsored university posts. Worldwide, the second major catalyst was the Comprehensive Cancer Control Programme initiated by the World Health Organization in 1980 (World Health Organization, 2002). This three-pronged programme comprises:

- prevention
- early detection and curative treatment
- pain relief and palliative care.

The incorporation of the third component led directly or indirectly to the founding of an increasing number of national and international professional organisations including: the European Association for Palliative Care in 1988, the State Cancer Pain Initiatives in the USA in the 1990s, the Indian Association for Palliative Care in 1994, the International Association for Hospice and Palliative Care in 1997, and the Asia Pacific Hospice Palliative Care Network in 2001. Academic departments have been established in several countries, notably the UK and

Germany. Journals and academic courses (diploma and Master degree programmes) abound.

For many doctors, the entry point into palliative care was through the WHO *Method for the Relief of Cancer Pain* which can be summarised as:

- the right drugs (evidence-based choice)
- the right route (preferably by mouth)
- the right dose (individual dose titration)
- the right time (prophylactically "by the clock" *and* "as needed") (World Health Organization, 1986).

The *3-Step Analgesic Ladder* was a crucial component of the WHO Method; the third step comprising morphine (or a comparable alternative). Sadly, even now, thirty years later, globally it is still impossible for most of those who need morphine to access it. Fortunately, in the UK, medicinal morphine is readily available and freely used when medically necessary.

Palliative care has changed considerably over the last forty years. Originally, almost all patients had cancer, and admission to a hospice, with few exceptions, was a one-way ticket. Today palliative care is more generic, and is considered a concept of care applicable to all types of end-stage disease. In the UK there are more than 200 adult inpatient units with a total of over 3000 palliative care beds, with cancer patients still in the majority. There are also about forty children's hospices with a total of about 300 beds. (At these, the norm is for repeated "respite" admissions over five to ten years for children with a range of neurodegenerative disorders, who often live into their teens, and sometimes beyond.).

In the early years, few patients went home. For my own part, following my five-year research fellowship in therapeutics at St Christopher's Hospice, I worked, from 1976 to 2001, at Sir Michael Sobell House at the Churchill Hospital in Oxford. Although initially just an inpatient facility, the emphasis at Sobell House increasingly shifted to care in the community: with twenty inpatient beds but, at any one time, some 500 people on the register of those in contact with some aspect of the service. Indeed twenty-first century palliative care today is mainly in the community with back-up inpatient beds to provide respite admissions (primarily to allow the family to "recharge their batteries"), for symptom management, and for those who, for various reasons, cannot continue to be cared for at home.

Looking back over forty to fifty years, the progress has been truly remarkable. Yet in many other ways we are only just beginning:

- Globally, the provision of palliative care is still patchy.
- It is not an essential component of most national health services.
- In most countries palliative care is not fully accepted by the medical profession generally.
- It is not available for most of those who need it.

How?

Broadly speaking, the essential task underlying palliative care can be described as helping people with progressive end-stage disease, at the appropriate time, to make the difficult transition from being *seriously ill and fighting death* to being *terminally ill and seeking peace*. How this is done varies from country to country because the "how" depends on human and financial resources. This point is well made by the WHO in its series *Cancer Control: Knowledge into Action. WHO Guide for Effective Programmes* (World Health Organization, 2007). Despite the inevitable variation in its delivery, it is possible to build up a "pen portrait" of palliative care having the following features:

- Active total (whole-person, holistic) care: physical, psychological, social, and spiritual.
- Patient-centred, not disease-focused.
- Partnership with and empowerment of the patient and family.
- Openness and honesty in communication.
- Death-accepting, but also life-enhancing: improving quality of life, not quantity.
- Concerned with healing, not curing.
- Goal-setting and hope restoring.
- Multi-professional teamwork and community (volunteer) involvement.

Each of these features is discussed below.

Active total care

Saunders' now classic four-compartment model of "total pain" (a synonym for suffering) enabled health professionals, almost without realising it, to move from a narrow physical outlook to a whole-person (holistic) approach which takes into account a range of factors, as illustrated in Figure 1 below.

It is important to remember that suffering, defined as a state of severe distress caused by events which threaten the integrity (intactness) of a person (Cassell, 1983, 2003), and physical pain are *not* synonymous. On the other hand, it is essential to appreciate that pain is "somato-psychic": it originates in the perception of a physical discomfort but is *always* modified by a person's cognitive and emotional reaction to the discomfort.

The difference between pain and suffering (and between the observer's and the subject's perception of things) is well illustrated by the following account:

A sculptor in her mid-thirties developed breast cancer. Treatment with radiotherapy resulted in disfigurement; this caused her suffering. Later, after her ovaries were removed, she became hirsute, obese, and lost her sexual libido; this caused her suffering. Progression of her disease subsequently resulted in weakness in her

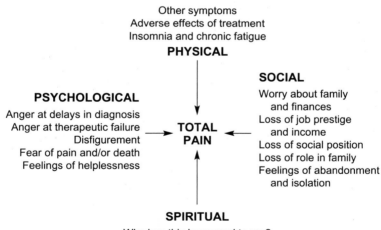

Figure 1. Factors influencing perception of pain.

right hand and she was no longer able to sculpt; this caused her suffering. Later still, she sustained a fracture of a femur caused by a secondary cancer in the bone, but this in itself did not cause her suffering. What caused her suffering was the overt disagreement between three specialists standing around her hospital bed discussing what would be the best treatment of the fracture. One could not anticipate what she would describe as suffering; she had to be asked. Some things she would call painful, upsetting, uncomfortable, or distressing, but not a cause of suffering. (Cassell, 1982)

As noted in a study in the *Journal of Palliative Care*, people commonly report suffering from pain when:

- they feel out of control
- the cause is unknown
- the pain is intractable
- the intensity of the pain is overwhelming
- the meaning of the pain for them is that the cancer is progressing inexorably and that they will soon die. (Daneault, et al., 2004)

Of course, pain is not the only distressing symptom that patients may experience. Severe breathlessness can be terrifying and can precipitate panic attacks, and it is important for doctors to recognise when this is the case.

Relief of pain and other distressing symptoms is rightly seen as the primary goal of palliative care. Where palliative care is available, competent symptom management means that patients can generally expect to be largely pain-free; and a high measure of relief can also be expected with many other symptoms (World Health Organization, 1990). However, as one hospice liaison psychiatrist wrote:

We now expect our patients to be almost pain-free, and we feel we've failed if they have to endure other symptoms like vomiting or breathlessness for any length of time. Having achieved this level of symptom control, we are faced with a new problem. No longer overwhelmed by pain and other symptoms, our patients become more aware of the emotional and spiritual distress that often accompanies dying. They are free to contemplate what they are losing and to look death in the face. Only a few can do this with equilibrium. Many defend themselves against this in a variety of ways, and some are almost overwhelmed with anguish, rage or fear about what is happening to them … Should we redefine a hospice as the place where it is safe to suffer? Perhaps our goal should be to provide an environment where people can come to terms with their own death as easily, fully, and constructively as they have it in them to do. (Stedeford, 1987)

Although "coming to terms with one's death" inevitably carries a wide range of individual meanings, it can often be associated with the work of dealing with hitherto unresolved psycho-spiritual issues. Indeed in palliative care we meet people who work through great psycho-spiritual distress and eventually achieve a remarkable measure of acceptance and peace (Byock, 1996).

Even though most palliative care services have a chaplain, I suggest that the spiritual (existential, transcendental) dimension of palliative care is generally more implicit than explicit; manifesting primarily in staff attitudes (unconditional acceptance and affirmation of each and every patient), a commitment to beauty in architecture (inpatient hospices and day centres), and the incorporation of creativity through the arts and complementary therapies (particularly in day centres).

Patient-centred, not disease focused: "Never forget the person in the patient"

Table 1 contrasts schematically the different ways in which the patient and the doctor view things. In palliative care, although the doctor still needs to maintain objectivity, he/she must also learn to look at the situation as if through the patient's eyes. In other words, it is necessary for the palliative care doctor to be a "psycho-physician".

Table 1: Different perspectives: illness versus disease (Reading, 1977).

Experienced by patient (illness)	Observed by physician (disease)
Subjective symptom	Objective signs
Unique	Replicable
Affects whole person	Affects various organs
Affects quality of life	Affects quantity of life
Cause of suffering	Possible cause of death

It follows that an essential feature of palliative care is a patient-centred approach. The focus is on "the person", writ large, who has end-stage disease, as distinct from the person with "end-stage disease", writ large. On paper this may seem a small difference but in practice the change of focus has a huge effect.

Partnership with and empowerment of the patient and family

Palliative care is a partnership between experts. In relation to the disease, the experts are the health professionals; but, in relation to the impact of the illness, the experts are the patient and family. It is crucial to recognise this because, through listening to their story and their problems, the patient and family can be helped to begin to shift from being passive victims to empowered persons. An important first step is to let the patient set the agenda, for example, by asking them what is troubling them the most, or what they hope will come out of the consultation.

In reply to this last question, I have received a wide range of replies over the years, even from patients with severe pain or other major physical distress, including "I want to be cured, of course", but also: "I want peace of mind", and "I want to be treated as a whole person". Such responses clearly represent the patient's foremost concerns, and need to be explored before moving on to what, for most doctors, is felt to be "safer ground".

Openness and honesty in communication

Skilled communication is essential for quality palliative care. Unfortunately, globally, good communication skills are still the exception rather than the norm in the medical profession. In an article entitled "Truth may hurt but deceit hurts more" (Fallowfield, et al., 2002) examples are given of deliberate attempts to withhold the truth from patients, together with cases of unintentional deception created by the use of ambiguous language. The evidence all points to the conclusion that, although truth may hurt, deceit hurts more.

It is still often said that telling patients that they are terminally ill destroys hope and leads to irreversible despair and depression. However, the opposite is more often the case; lies and evasion isolate patients behind a wall of words or silence which prevents them from sharing their fears and anxieties (De-Hennezel, 1997). As one patient put it: "Cancer is isolating, and the isolation can hurt far more than the treatment. Suddenly, you, the person with cancer, find yourself on one side of the wall, the sick side. Everyone else in your world is on the other side of that wall, the normal side".

It is impossible to offer hopeful palliative care without a prior commitment to openness and honesty. Sherwin B. Nuland, an American surgeon, has written:

> A promise we can keep and a hope we can give is the certainty that no man or woman will be left to die alone. Of the many ways to die alone, the most comfortless and solitary must surely take place when the knowledge of death's certainty is withheld ... Unless we are aware that we are dying, we cannot share any sort of final consummation with those who love us. Without this consummation, no matter their presence at the hour of passing, we will remain unattended and isolated. For it is the promise of spiritual companionship near the end that gives us hope, much more than does the mere offsetting of the fear of being physically without anyone. (Nuland, 1997)

Death-accepting, but also life-enhancing

"Add life to days when it is no longer possible to add days to life" is a central tenet of palliative care. At its best, palliative care encourages patients to be creative, even against the backdrop of progressive physical deterioration. This helps to enhance or restore self-esteem.

An emphasis on "doing" rather than "being done to" helps the patient to live and die as a whole person. In many cases, gentle and imaginative encouragement is all that is needed to entice a patient into an activity that leaves him with an increased sense of well-being. Thus, many palliative care day centres encourage creative writing and art. In the UK the overall result is that approximately fifty per cent of inpatient admissions to hospices and palliative care hospital units end with the patient returning home or to relatives. This demonstrates that the goal of palliative care, to provide a support system to help patients live as actively and creatively as possible until death, is not empty sentiment.

The concept of living with cancer until death comes is still foreign to many patients and their families, and to many doctors and nurses as well. Indeed, many terminally ill patients, although capable of a greater degree of activity and independence, may at times be unnecessarily restricted, even by well-meaning relatives.

However, cancer is a spectrum of disorders and, even when incurable, rates of progression vary. Bearing this in mind already allows us to think about the potential of each individual patient. This can be maximised only if troublesome symptoms are relieved and gentle encouragement given. Thus rehabilitation, that is, helping people achieve their maximum potential, should be seen as an integral part of palliative care.

Those visiting a hospice/palliative care unit for the first time often comment that it is not the depressing place they had imagined it would be. Instead they find a place permeated by life, and even joy. A strange discovery, but it is perhaps in this paradox that the "secret" of palliative care resides. Life and joy in the midst of death and distress can result from relatively ordinary professional activities—like nursing care, pain and symptom management, and psychological and spiritual support—when motivated by *practical human compassion*. This, in turn, is the outworking of an attitude of respect for the patient and of corporate activity in which individualism is balanced by teamwork and vice versa.

Concerned with healing, not curing

"You can't die cured but you can die healed". (Frimmer, 2000)

These words by a dying doctor sum up much of the existential dimension of palliative care. This is reflected in what a widower wrote after his wife's death:

> Of course terminal cancer is unspeakably awful. That aspect needs no emphasis. More difficult to imagine is the blessedness which is the corollary of the awfulness … I think my wife learnt more of our love during those dreadful months than she did at any other time, and we of hers … The suffering of a long and terminal illness is not all waste. Nothing that creates such tenderness can be all waste. As a destroyer, cancer is second to none. But it is also a healer, or an agent of healing.

As it has been said:

> The aim of healing is not to be cured;
> The aim of healing is not to survive;
> The aim of healing is to become whole.

Healing is about restoring right relationships—with self, with others, with the environment, and with God/Ultimate Reality. Dying healed includes being able to convey five important messages to one's nearest and dearest:

> I love you;
> Forgive me;
> I forgive you;
> Thank you;
> Goodbye. (Byock, 2004)

In practice, palliative care doctors do not often overtly witness this process of "completion". However, working within a multi-professional team, they aim to create a physically comfortable supportive environment which facilitates it.

Goal-setting and hope restoring

Hope needs an object or a goal. Without an object or goal, there can be no hope; just hopelessness which all too often leads to a vicious downward spiral of desolation and despair. Setting realistic goals jointly with a patient is a key way of restoring and maintaining hope. In one study, it was shown that doctors at two palliative care centres set, on average, twice as many goals as doctors at a district general hospital (Lunt & Neale, 1987). To be helpful, however, goals must be realistic. Thus to a patient who says to me, "I want to be cured" or to a paraplegic who says, "I want to walk again", I might initially say:

> I hear what you're saying ... that is your ultimate goal. But I think it could be helpful if we agreed on a series of intermediate mini-goals ... because reaching some of these would give everyone a sense of achievement ... How does that seem to you?

Obviously, some hopes will have to be abandoned in the light of unfolding events but, even so, goals are essential for most patients in order to maintain hope, and for doctors as well in order to optimise their input in the patient's care. It is indeed possible for hope to increase when a person is close to death, provided care and comfort remain satisfactory (Herth, 1990).

It is generally very hard to adapt to progressive physical deterioration and to the growing realisation that one's earthly future may be only months or even weeks. However, alternative hopes, based on being rather than on achieving, are important. Ultimately, when there is little else to hope for, it should still be realistic to hope for a peaceful death.

Multi-professional teamwork and community (volunteer) involvement

Total active care, encompassing attention to the soma and to the psyche of the individual, along with attention to the spiritual and social aspects of care is generally best provided by a multi-professional team. Although this will vary from centre to centre, depending on local resources, generally the "nuclear" team comprises a doctor and a nurse. To these might be added a physiotherapist, occupational therapist, social worker, chaplain, clinical psychologist, liaison psychiatrist, and even music and art therapists.

Volunteers are crucial. Their presence conveys the message that the dying patient has not been abandoned or banished to a death ghetto, but that they are still a valued member of their local community. Depending on their background and suitability, volunteers may be used for a wide range of jobs, particularly in the day centre. Typically, there is a paid voluntary service co-ordinator. Bereavement support services generally comprise a carefully selected and specifically trained group of volunteers who visit bereaved relatives identified by staff as being in need of extended support.

When all is said and done

As stated earlier, palliative care developed at least partly as a reaction to the attitude (spoken or unspoken) that, "There's nothing more we can do for you", with the inevitable consequence for the patient and family of a sense of abandonment, hopelessness, and despair. It was stressed that this was never true; there is always something that can be done. But, even so, there are times when doctors, nurses, and other health professionals feel that they have nothing more to offer:

> Slowly, I learn about the importance of powerlessness.
> I experience it in my own life and I live with it in my work.

The secret is not to be afraid of it—not to run away.
The dying know we are not God.
All they ask is that we do not desert them. (Cassidy, 1988)

When we have nothing to offer except ourselves, a belief that life to its very end has meaning and purpose is essential. However, to speak glibly about meaning and purpose to a despairing patient would be cruel. This conviction manifests more by attitudes and deeds than by words; more by how we respond to the dying and care for them than by what we say. Particularly at such times, actions speak louder than words, and the essential message to be conveyed is:

You matter because you are you.
You matter to the last moment of your life,
and we will do all we can, not only to help you die peacefully,
but to live until you die. (Cicely Saunders)

Postscript

Books on the experience of living with cancer have been increasing in number in recent years, with one of the latest to have come my way being *Gift of Time: A Family's Diary of Cancer* by Rory MacLean with Joan MacLean (Rory's mother) and Katrin MacLean (his wife) (2011).

Joan died from cancer several years ago but the three individual diaries were only integrated and published in 2011. The book covers the last six to seven months of Joan's life. Like comparable accounts, this is gold in terms of helping people to understand how awful it is having to cope with progressive irreversible physical deterioration, for the patient and, sometimes more so, for the immediate family.

I think it true to say that we doctors (and possibly nurses too) generally grossly underestimate the demands made on individuals and families by a slow terminal decline. If you have never read any books by people who are dying or by their relatives, this is a good one to start with. Maybe those working in palliative care should read one such book every few years. It helps to prevent you beginning to see everything through rose-tinted spectacles, and enhances understanding and empathy.

Acknowledgements

It is more than forty years since I began to work in palliative care and, inevitably, I have absorbed many pearls of wisdom and numerous anecdotes from colleagues, books, and articles, but whose origins are now long-lost or forgotten. For all those who see their choice of words or anecdote unacknowledged, I offer both my apologies and my deep gratitude.

References

Byock, I. (1996). The nature of suffering and the nature of opportunity at the end of life. *Clinics in Geriatric Medicine, 12*: 237–252.

Byock, I. (2004). *The Four Things That Matter Most: A Book About Living*. New York: Free Press, p. 216.

Cassell, E. J. (1982). The nature of suffering and the goals of medicine. *New England Journal of Medicine, 306(11)*: 639–645.

Cassell, E. J. (1983). The relief of suffering. *Archives of Internal Medicine, 143*: 522–523.

Cassell, E. J. (2003). *The Nature of Suffering and the Goals of Medicine* (2nd ed). Oxford: Oxford University Press.

Cassidy, S. (1988). *Sharing the Darkness*. London: Darton, Longman and Todd, pp. 61–64.

Daneault, S., et al. (2004). The nature of suffering and its relief in the terminally ill: a qualitative study. *Journal of Palliative Care, 20*: 7–11.

De-Hennezel, M. (1997). *Intimate Death*. Boston: Little Brown.

Fallowfield, L., et al. (2002). Truth may hurt but deceit hurts more: communication in palliative care. *Palliative Medicine, 16*: 297–303.

Frimmer, D. (2000). A doctor's journey to the other side. *Time Magazine*, September.

Herth, K. (1990). Fostering hope in terminally ill people. *Journal of Advanced Nursing, 15*: 1250–1259.

Lunt, B. & Neale, C. (1987). A comparison of hospice and hospital: care goals set by staff. *Palliative Medicine, 1*: 136–148.

MacLean, R., with MacLean, J. and MacLean K. (2011). *Gift of Time: A Family's Diary of Cancer*. London: Constable and Robinson.

Nuland, S. B. (1997). *How we Die*. London: Vintage.

Reading, A. (1977). Illness and disease. *Medical Clinics of North America, 61*: 703–710.

Stedeford, A. (1987). Hospice: A safe place to suffer? *Palliative Medicine, 1*: 73–74.

Twycross, R, et al. (2009). *Symptom Management in Advanced Cancer* (4th ed). palliativedrugs.com, Nottingham.

Twycross, R. & Wilcock, A. (eds). (2011). *Palliative Care Formulary* (4th ed). palliativedrugs.com, Nottingham.

World Health Organization. (1986). *Cancer Pain Relief.* Geneva: World Health Organization.

World Health Organization. (1990). *Cancer pain relief and palliative care. Technical Report Series 804.* Geneava: World Health Organisation.

World Health Organization. (2002). *National Cancer Control Programmes, Policies and managerial guidelines* (2nd ed). Geneva: World Health Organization, p. 84.

World Health Organization. (2007). *Cancer Control: Knowledge into Action. WHO Guide for Effective Programmes: Palliative Care.* Geneva: World Health Organization.

CHAPTER NINE

The nature of religious/spiritual concerns in addressing the psychological needs of people with cancer

Jonathan Wittenberg

Two encounters have stayed in my mind over many years.

The first took place in hospital. "They want to see you urgently; he's dying and they'd like you to say prayers", said the nurse quietly as she led me to the room of a couple in their late thirties whom I'd never met before. "What am I to say?" I wondered anxiously, "What are they expecting?"

The man was lying on the bed; his wife sat in an armchair next to him and they held hands. "Tell us a prayer about life's beauty, because we've loved it", he said, without any unnecessary ado. I thought for a moment and recited a sentence from the Jewish morning service: "How great are your works, O God; the whole earth is full of what is yours". The couple interrupted me: "Yes", they said. "We've always loved walking, both in the countryside and in the city". For a few minutes they reminisced together about the paths and places they'd enjoyed in each other's company. Then the man turned back to me and asked calmly, "Now say a prayer about life's ending because I know I'm soon going to die". I can't recall how I responded. He died a few days later.

Years afterwards I am still moved by the good grace of this couple, their unselfishness, gratitude, and generosity towards life. I have to imagine that they too must have passed through periods of pain, anger,

141

and resentment at being parted so young and that after his death she must have faced the long attrition of loneliness and sorrow. Moments of deep acceptance are usually the fruits of a long and complex inner voyage.

But the attitude of this couple shows that it is possible, and far from rare, for people to complete their journey through the ravages of cancer, even when it ends in death, remarkably free from rancour and with a profound awareness of a greater life into which our existence merges. It is partly this which makes me feel ambivalent about such sentences as "She lost her battle with her illness", understandable as the imagery of conflict may be. Of course it's true that striving to recover after cancer, living as fully as possible in remission, struggling with the numerous indignities which can easily undermine any returning self-confidence, including weakness, nausea, loss of hair, and anguish before the unknowable future, all require courage, persistence, fortitude, patience, and a determined spirit. We are often called upon as ministers, thera-pists, doctors, nurses, and friends to help to sustain that spirit through encouragement and love. But when, after everything a person has been through, I hear the words "He lost the fight", as I often do, I feel not only sad because of the person's death, but out of a sense that an injustice is being done. I once discussed those very words with a good friend who was dying. We acknowledged that her losses were profound, including the curtailment of her very life. But we also talked about the "victories" along the way, the months well used, the times she'd looked great, the depths of closeness and reflection into which she had drawn so many around her, reminding us all of what really mattered in life, the sense of beauty she had shared, the way she was approaching death knowing how deeply she loved and was loved, and her faith that she ultimately belonged to a greater and all-embracing whole. These were very con-siderable achievements which deserved better than to be summed up only in the words "I'm losing my battle with cancer". I sensed in them not only her own helplessness, but a feeling that she ought to have been able to do more, that in dying she was somehow letting others down. But what more could she actually have done?

I'm reminded of Rabindranath Tagore's challenging sentence that "truth comes as conqueror because we have lost the art of receiving it as guest". Though we can, and in the overwhelming majority of cir-cumstances should, struggle hard to preserve life, we cannot ultimately "defeat" death. We also need to be open to the humility and wisdom which can help us to accompany one another when the end of our individual lives becomes inevitable.

The second scene was no more, at one level, than a passing encounter in the street. I asked a man I knew only slightly which synagogue he was planning to attend over the Jewish New Year and the Day of Atonement. "I'm not going anywhere", he replied, and by his look reminded me that it was no more than a couple of years since he had lost a child. "I'm not going to add insult to injury by listening to all those prayers about our sins and God's great justice and mercy. Am I supposed to think that what happened was somehow my fault? I simply can't take it".

I've had many occasions to lay these words to my heart. Are our religions, with their fine ideas about the goodness of God and God's rewards for the righteous, simply lying? Do they, with their doctrines of sin and punishment, merely point the finger back at the person who is suffering, as if to say, as his cruel friends keep telling the hapless Job in the Bible, that God would never have let this happen to us if we didn't deserve it? Do they add to the anguish of suffering by compounding it with the burden of guilt? Or is this simply the bystander's way of deflecting the troubling thought that the illness might just as well have, or might indeed yet, descend upon him or her too, by providing a convenient, but false, rationale: these things only happen to those who've done something to merit them? Does God pass us the blame, or just let us down, by failing to fulfil those attributes of mercy and grace precisely when we need God most? I do not find it difficult to understand the person who feels betrayed by what he or she thought his religion to have promised, and resentful at being forsaken.

The hospice where I was a volunteer on the multi-faith chaplaincy team for many years invited patients to tick a box indicating whether they did, or did not, wish to receive visits from the chaplains. I often wondered what lay beneath the decision to indicate "no". Was it in order to be spared the attentions of the "God-squad", who might prove dogmatic and insensitive? Or did it indicate a measure of anger with their fate and a wish to be spared any presumed attempt to justify in the name of God something so painful and cruel as the pain and anguish of dying? I often wished for the opportunity to explore the meaning of that "no" and wondered if it mightn't have been precisely those who marked that box negatively with whom it could have been most important to spend time. I've also pondered whether those who might vent their frustrations with life to other staff to their face, often preferred to show their anger toward religion by refusing to allow members of the clergy anywhere near them. I remember how I once entered a room and before I could say a single word the patient began to struggle for the bell. "Can I help you find that bell?" I asked. "No", he said, "I'm looking for it so that I can call the nurse and get her to take you out of here". As a rule I never enter the space of a person who is ill without first enquiring if I'm disturbing them, or whether now is a good time to come in. It strikes me as a presumption to impose myself on someone who is unable to make their own getaway.

Yet I've also been witness to how people find new depths of spirit and discover profound resources of love and courage in the very midst of the most intense engagement with vulnerability and mortality. It may be precisely then that what God means to us, and what we understand by faith and prayer, become immediate and real. The inherited words and rituals of our tradition become transformed as we begin to grapple with them and give them meanings of our own. We may come to realise more deeply than ever before that they are not formulae for summoning God, but ways of reaching inwards into the resources of the spirit. They become metaphors, symbols, and structures through which, sometimes explicitly but often unconsciously, we express our hopes, our awareness, and our struggles with our faith and our fate.

What both these encounters indicate is that illness, suffering, and dying entail a profound spiritual journey. How we accompany each other through it can, like the quality of medical and psychological care, make a profound difference to how the experience feels, to the inner narrative we form about the meaning of what is happening, and to how we are ultimately able to accept our destiny. It is in this light that I want to explore some aspects of what religious and spiritual care may have to offer to people with cancer.

"Religious" and "spiritual" are not synonymous terms. A person may be religious, that is, belong to a faith community and share in some or many of its traditions and practices, without necessarily being particularly concerned about God and the soul. Alternatively, people may describe themselves as spiritual, as caring about a relationship with a deeper, transcendent sense of belonging and meaning, which they may or may not relate to God or an ultimate being, without having any connection with a formal religion. This was the outlook of the woman who told me that music was her worship and the mountains and forests her house of God. But it is often also the case that these two kinds of engagement intersect and that a person seeks through the liturgy and practices of his or her faith to deepen and explore a spiritual bond with God and all of life.

In a largely secular society, the "spiritual" is sometimes regarded as more enlightened, more inclusive, and somehow "better" than the merely "religious", which is often relegated to refer to a merely formal relationship with rituals and dogmas. But it would be wrong to underestimate what religion may have to offer a person struggling with cancer.

In the first instance, religion is generally practised in congregations, thus offering an immediate sense of community and belonging which is rare in the individualistic and often lonely environment of the big cities in which most of us in the Western world now live. This can make a huge difference to a person who is ill, as well as to his or her family on whom the immediate tasks of daily care are bound to fall. A community is able to mobilise many kinds of practical assistance for a person who has cancer. In a concerned and committed congregation this may include lifts to and from hospital appointments, doing the shopping, cooking for the family, making sure the children are taken to play with friends, walking the dog, and other such everyday matters with which people more or less manage to cope when things are fine but which become a struggle when one is feeling weak, sick, anxious, or simply overburdened. Friends may offer to sit with the patient during the long, lonely hours of intravenous chemotherapy. People mention him or her in their prayers. On many occasions I've heard it said, "I feel strengthened and encouraged by so many people praying for me. A Catholic friend told me she's thinking of me; so have my Jewish friends; and my Hindu colleague also let me know that she has me in mind every day during her morning rituals". This communal and spiritual solidarity communicates itself to the heart of a person who now feels less deeply alone and may experience renewed hope and inner strength as a result. This in turn may make a significant difference to his or her physical condition.

The importance of tradition and ritual should not be belittled either. It is possible that they may offer, albeit on an inexplicit level only rarely openly articulated, something similar to the "containment" discussed in the more therapeutically focused chapters of this book. The very existence of ancient rituals attests to the fact that religions have long experience in negotiating human anguish; they know of structures and meditations with which to mark the transitions from health to sickness and, hopefully, from sickness back to health. They are the repositories of reflections accrued from the journeys of many tens of generations. This awareness may in itself bring a feeling of being somehow "held", the reassurance that there exists a path to follow, a tradition which has meditated on these matters and has the capacity to offer comfort, support, and understanding. The vulnerability of the individual mortal life is thus embraced in a wisdom which has expressed and guided human anguish, joy, and love for millennia. Even without an explicit belief in the immortality of either body or soul, one may come to feel that one belongs to a chain of generations which transcends the isolated self. The fear of being utterly on one's own amidst mortal danger is mitigated both for the sufferer and for his or her family. It may be that one of the worst fears, together with the fear of pain, disability, and helpless dependence, is the horror of being totally alone with one's anguish, in an unreachable prison of the mind to which there is no way in. Several times I've overheard the words "The minister is here" spoken with relief when I've arrived at the house where someone is sick. Despite feeling daunted whenever I hear it, I've understood that there is nothing personal about this comment, which expresses the deep relief of being included and embraced within the compassion of an ancient faith. Or perhaps the relief belongs mainly to the family who may feel, rightly or wrongly, that there is someone here now who ought to know what to say and do.

This brings me back to the question of the inner journey of the person with cancer and the kind of help a minister of religion may be in a position to offer. Before addressing specific issues, I want to set down what is for me a general principle in such situations. When invited to meet with a person who is ill, I do not see my role as seeking affirmations of faith, promoting dogmas, asserting my own beliefs, or insisting on rites or prayers of any kind. It seems to me that this is an imposition on the other person at any time, and an especially objectionable one when he or she is in a state of extreme vulnerability. I consider myself to be there primarily to listen and to offer the companionship of quiet presence and reflection. I do of course bring my own personal beliefs with me in private; that is inevitable. Their gist is summed up in the Talmudic dictum that "the presence of God rests above the pillow of the sick". To me this means me that a person who is ill deserves deep respect and that the sanctity of his or her life invites humility and attentive concern just as if God were in that place, because God, who is within us all, is indeed here. The Talmud goes on to teach that one should not seat oneself higher than the sick person. This ancient advice about the bedside manner tells us not to stand over a patient but rather, whenever possible, to sit on the same level or lower; after all, wouldn't just about every patient love to be able to stand up too, and walk away, if only he or she could?

Often all a person wants is quiet, compassionate presence. I shall never forget sitting down next to the bed of a man whom I'd never met before. He took my hand and held it tight for many minutes. After a while I made to let go, fearing that I might be intruding and preventing the close relatives waiting outside from returning to sit with their loved one. In response he held my fingers even more firmly and I remember feeling a deep bond of vitality passing between us as if we were together touching the very spirit of life itself. I now also wonder whether my mistimed move to leave was prompted by the mistaken feeling that because we weren't speaking to each other I was somehow not "doing" anything. But, as Joan Halifax writes, "we mistakenly think that our practical caregiving skills are all we have to give. Yet our presence born of openness is often the greatest offering we can make" (Halifax, p. 20).

Frequently, however, people do want to talk. Perhaps our most important role in such situations is to be a thoughtful listening companion to the unfolding of the story a person is trying to tell himself or herself about what's happening. The conversation may sometimes remain banal, but often the great questions of "Why?" and "What does this mean?" are touched upon, sometimes directly and bluntly: "Where is God now?", "Is there any point in all those prayers?" These conversations may also take place with relatives who are equally struggling emotionally and spiritually with what this change in the life of the person they love means to him or her, and to themselves. For some, the loneliness they know they will have to face without their life's partner may feel like the harsher fate. People who are seriously ill are often troubled by the thought that they have brought pain and suffering on their family and may be burdened by guilt, as if they were somehow responsible for risking falling short of their anticipated number of years.

A spiritual carer can be a helpful witness as a narrative is formed about what illness and suffering may mean to this particular and unique person. "Narrative" is an imperfect term because it suggests a complete and coherent story. More often the reality is that the significance of becoming ill, recovering, or travelling onwards towards death changes and grows. Insights may be poignant, yet fragmentary and passing; the tone may vary between gratitude and bitterness. Understandings develop, and change. The journey may traverse landscapes of great beauty, plateaus of resignation, unforeseeable crevasses filled with fear or despair, and unexpected vistas of joy which bring a deep sense of love and gratitude. The process of seeking meaning may remain largely unarticulated. Yet somehow at least a partial sense may emerge of how it is that we, and those around us, are telling the story of all this turmoil to ourselves. In the end, a person may pass beyond that story into the vast sea of life and death.

As I listen I don't feel entitled to challenge a person's own faith and values or to assert my particular beliefs, though sometimes I may be asked about them. Often issues are explored through the texts of my own religion, Judaism. But I have also kept company with those of other faiths and listened to them interpret the symbols and parables of their traditions. Sometimes the conversation is about the spirit in general, without reference to religion at all, but focusing rather on the wonder of nature, the beauty of poetry and music, the meaning of letting go, and what, if anything, may await us in the unknowable beyond. Sometimes the words are about anger and guilt, loneliness and fear.

During such conversations I might offer a prompt— 'You seem to be thinking that …', or ask a tentative question in order to help clarify a feeling or take an inference one stage further. I would only challenge a conclusion or call an assumption into question if I felt that the way a person was telling the story of what was happening might be unhelpful, unjust, or even cruel to themselves or to others, and that there could perhaps be a more compassionate way of formulating matters which might offer an opportunity for understanding and healing.

I will devote the rest of this chapter to some examples of such interactions.

A young woman came to see me; she felt deeply disappointed because her father, to whom she was very close, had suffered an unexpectedly swift return of his cancer. They had hoped that the illness was cured, or at least that he would have many years of remission. No sooner had we sat down than she asked me straight out, "Does prayer work?" If she prayed harder and focused on following her religion and doing the right thing, would it make a difference in heaven and change God's mind? There was something deeply touching about her devoted love, her readiness to do anything for her father, and her traditional faith. But immediately behind her question lay her antici- pated disappointment—"Or does it just not work like that and none of it makes any difference whatsoever?" She had been brought up, she explained, on very conventional views of religion. But now she felt that the system was letting her down; God wasn't doing what God was sup- posed to do. She didn't say if her father shared her doubts.

The questions raised strike me as of the deepest importance. In the crisis which faced this woman and her family, was faith going to be a cause of disillusionment, leaving a sense of feeling cheated by life and God, or would it develop into a source of real inner strength? At the heart of the matter is how we understand God and prayer. Does our God, if we believe in or care about God at all, remain a kind of super- person in heaven who in some inscrutable way controls everything on earth and who says either "yes" or "no" to our prayers? To some peo- ple such a view of God can be deeply helpful, enabling them to accept what has happened with great humility as "God's will". But that was not the case for this young woman. Her questions reminded me of a brief exchange I overheard many years ago. The mother of one of my friends had made a remarkable recovery from heart disease. The father of another had recently died of cancer. "It was all because of our prayers that my mother got better", said the first. "Do you mean to say that my father died because we didn't pray hard enough?" retorted the second. But neither the impact of prayer nor the value of religion can be quanti- fied in simple outcomes. They must be understood in terms of inner, and not just outer, realities.

I tried to think together with that woman of different ways to consider God and prayer. Could we think of God not as an agency in heaven, a God above who might, or might not, be cajoled into doing what we wanted, but rather as a living presence all around us and inside us, within our heart and within all being? Then prayer would become less a means of seeking to obtain practical results and more a way of putting ourselves in touch with the deepest resources of life inside ourselves and others. Rachel Remen, affected by a lifetime of experience in work- ing with cancer patients and their carers, expresses the matter in just these terms:

> I think that prayer may be less about asking for the things we
> are attached to than it is about relinquishing our attachments in

some way. It can take us beyond fear, which is an attachment, and beyond hope, which is another form of attachment. It can help us to remember the nature of the world and the nature of life, not on an intellectual level but in a deep and experiential way. When we pray, we don't change the world, we change ourselves. We change our consciousness. We move from an individual, isolated making-things-happen kind of consciousness to a connection on the deepest level with the largest possible reality. (Remen, 1996, pp. 270–271)

In her remarkable diary of living with leukaemia, Gale Warner, a young woman who was probably not religious in any formal sense but who experienced all of existence as full of vitality and divinity, wrote of prayer as "a call to partnership, a conscious placing of our spirits and intentions in alignment with the creative spirit. This call to partnership is always noticed. It affects the whole. It can help tilt the balance, draw forth hidden resources. So prayer—humble, undemanding, simple prayer—is always worth it" (Warner & Kreger, 1998, p. 106).

Neither writer precludes the possibility that prayer may make a practical difference to our physical well-being, or that of those for and with whom we pray, through the effect it has on our spirit, feelings, and levels of energy. But this is very different to considering that its impact is dependent on how it affects the decision-making process of a person-alised God in heaven. Rather, its value lies in guiding our consciousness to feel more in touch with God's presence and part of a deeper bond with life.

I don't know the effect our talk had on the young woman whose father was so ill. I hope it may have suggested new possibilities for her within her faith, allowing her to find a way of gaining strength and hope from her religious tradition rather than feeling caught between an almost magical belief on the one hand and a concomitant sense of disappointment on the other.

Very different was the series of conversations I had with a man in his fifties which began soon after his diagnosis and continued through the many months of his illness until his death. A popular person with a large family and many devoted friends, he received a lot of support as well as much advice on how he should respond to his cancer. This was all well-meant and mostly helpful, but it also exerted an unintended pressure: "I've been given all these books I'm supposed to read", he said, pointing to a small pile of literature on his bedside table. "I've been taught how to visualise the cancer cells and how to struggle against them. I've been told that I need to keep my thoughts focussed and positive". He paused for a moment, before adding: "I'd have liked to listen to some of my favourite music and just allow it to carry my feelings wherever it leads them, but I've been counselled against this". As we talked it became clear that his spirit really craved that music. He wanted me to give him permission to listen to it, and I did.

It quickly emerged that beneath this seemingly unimportant matter lay a difficult and profound consideration. Everyone longed for him to get better; they wanted to help him harness all his activities and capacities, from what he ate to the substance of his thoughts, in the direction of recovery. But he needed to be allowed his inner freedom, including the liberty to entertain the possibility of his own death. This was expressed more as an inner prompting than as a conscious realisation: "I don't know where it is that I'll have to travel", he said, "and my soul wants to get ready". He wasn't in any way "giving up", but he felt instinctively that a journey awaited him for which he wanted to prepare. For this he needed his inner life of music, the sight of trees and birds, and time for unstructured reflection. At this point the direction of that journey, back to health but with a new and more poignant understanding of life, or towards death and whatever it was that might perhaps lie beyond it, was not clear. There was a tension between galvanising his energies around the exclusive conscious focus on recovery and allowing them also to be guided by his inner intuitions.

Within this dilemma were significant issues about hope. Hope is vitally important; in certain religious traditions it is considered paramount. Sometimes it can lead families to seek to deny all the indications that their loved one is evidently dying. They may persist in recommending and, in extreme situations, in virtually enforcing, treatments the patient himself would have preferred not to have had to endure, while talking all the time about how everything is going to be alright.

The patient may also not want to know anything more about his or her condition and may find support in such "denial", so long as it is maintained in a kind and gentle manner. Even though she may really know with a different part of the self that it isn't the reality, she may be glad to collude with it as a way of keeping unbearable feelings at bay or of trying to avoid further pain to her family. As my teacher Rabbi Hugo Gryn used to say, "You have to let the dying play it their own way".

The insistence on "the plain truth", whether or not a person wants or is ready to absorb it, while masquerading as "honesty", may amount to little more than bluntness and cruelty.

But the refusal to admit the possibility of death, and an insistence on only ever being positive, may create a dissonance between the attitude of family and friends and the true inner feelings of the patient. He or she may end up feeling surrounded by a conspiracy of conscious or unconscious suppression which it becomes virtually impossible to break through, leaving a deep inner loneliness. Important communication may be prevented and the opportunity of preparing for death in profound and helpful ways may be hindered. Death, after all, belongs to life's journey, and I don't believe that we have the right, or that it is wise, for us to stand in the way when a person is seeking to make emotional and spiritual preparations.

Such acknowledgement of the reality and possible nearness of death doesn't amount to the abandonment of hope. Hope may remain; only its focus changes. At its heart, of course, is hope for life. But hope for complete healing may, if the cancer sadly does return after treatment, become hope for lengthy remission. If the cancer worsens once again, it may become hope for freedom from further indignities, for quality time with loved ones, for the chance to see a beautiful place or special person once again, for quiet hours of companionship. It may become hope for freedom from pain, for a peaceful death close to those we love, for the welfare of our family after we are gone. It is thus possible to affirm realistic hopes at every stage. At the same time, other more fanciful yet emotionally important hopes may remain. A dying man once told me that he knew he had only a few more days to live, as was indeed the case, then said in the very next sentence how much he was looking forward to the cruise his wife had arranged for the following summer: "We're going on a cruise, you know ..." This brought to mind T. S. Eliot's observation that "human kind cannot bear very much reality" (1944). It would be a cruel person who insisted on an unyielding rejection of all dreams.

Indeed, it has sometimes struck me when listening to people close to the end of their lives that there is a strange connection between dreaming and dying. The *dramatis personae* of the whole of our life re-emerge, unaffected by distance, time, or even their own deaths years ago. People call out to family long since gone; different planes of reality intersect. One woman who was dying told me about her dream of setting forth on a voyage to a group of beautiful islands in a tropical sea. A scene which stays painfully in my mind is of a man, scarcely conscious anymore, who suddenly sat up in bed and called out for his suitcases. His carer told him firmly that he wasn't going anywhere and made sure he was safely tucked back down between the sheets. But perhaps in his spirit he was indeed embarking on a journey and needed those cases: I regret that I wasn't quick enough to ask him where it was that he was going and what he wanted for the journey.

Over the months of his illness my friend often listened to his music and frequently asked me to pray with him; we read poems and psalms together, sometimes talking about them afterwards but more often just appreciating the opportunity to share them. I regret that I was not with him when he died.

The final conversation I want to record was simple and brief; it took place in a hospice room where an elderly Irish lady was close to the end of her life. "I'm afraid I don't really believe in God", she said, giving me a kindly look. I often feel embarrassed at the thought that I might impose expectations on people by my very calling and that they should feel obliged to apologise to me as if, by their lack of commitment to a conventional form of faith, they had personally let me down. She explained that she had cancer of the liver and that, although she was fortunate that it had previously been possible to effect a measure of treatment, those options were now exhausted. She had reached the end. "I see it like this", she continued. "There's a vast world of land and sea out there, full of creatures living and then dying, while new life is constantly reborn. I shall be joining this great process". She seemed content and unafraid. Her words have stayed with me and bring me consolation to this day.

I do not want to give the impression that dying always is or can be gracious. I have also been in rooms where the dying person turns restlessly in bed, anguished by some physical or spiritual pain which seems beyond all reach, and with families where the suffering of their loved one leads them to ask me to "please say a prayer, not for him to get better, but rather to help him be at peace". In such situations I've tried to focus on being calm and quiet inside myself, on not being agitated or afraid, hoping and believing that this might assist in lessening the anxiety of those around me and in creating a shared stillness, allowing our consciousness to settle down in quietness before the mystery of life and death.

It's not rare at such times for people to ask me about what lies beyond. In the face of the attrition of illness and dying many of us instinctively seek the widest possible context for meaning. I will therefore conclude with some brief reflections, not on the theological dimensions of the subject of life after death, but on what it seems to me that such questions might mean at the time for those who asks them.

I remember a particularly painful meeting; the hospice staff had told me that there was a woman who wanted to speak with a member of the chaplaincy team because she was afraid. It emerged that she was tormented by the thought of what might await her after death. "I'm frightened God's going to punish me", she said. What was really called for was a conversation about why she felt she would be punished. This may have led to reflections on whether there was anything she could still say or do which might help to effect either an outer reconciliation with the significant others in her life or an inner process of making peace with her own self. I didn't have the opportunity to follow this through and don't know if others were in a position to do so later. What she wanted to talk about with me was God: if God was the judge before whom she would have to appear after death then surely she would be found guilty? I wondered aloud whether God could be experienced as loving as well as judging, and if it was possible that there could be understanding and forgiveness even within judgement. My guess is that how forgiving or unforgiving she imagined God to be would be premised on how loving or unloving she had experienced the key people in her life to have been, and perhaps even more on how loving and understanding of her own self she was capable of being. Theology never exists in a vacuum.

On another occasion a dying man asked for his funeral arrangements to be changed so that he could be buried in a cemetery where a relative of his already lay. "I'm frightened of the loneliness", he said. He found great consolation when his wish was accomplished. The Biblical phrase about being gathered unto one's ancestors came to mind.

I'm most often asked about the afterlife by those who have lost a loved one and want to know where he or she is now. Behind this question lie many others: Is it still possible to find a way of staying close? Will we meet again? Can we still communicate? Is the sense I have that my husband is nearby an objective spiritual reality, or is it only the effect of memory, or of my own feelings? Is there some dimension of heaven or earth concealed to mortals in which those I love will be able to find me, and I them; or is our relationship finished for all eternity? Must I accept that death really has parted us forever?

Whatever our theological beliefs, most of us seek something to mitigate the devastating totality of loss. I will never forget listening to a conversation among a circle of parents who had each lost a child. "He is in a world beyond time", said one mother, "So time can never push us further apart". Each parent in turn offered a personal view of where their child now was; what their thoughts all had in common was a sense that some domain existed in which they and their children could still encounter each other. The feeling that death has utterly and totally taken away the person we love, especially if this person is our precious child, may be more than we can bear.

But people do also ask about what may happen to themselves after death: Does the whole of me die forever, or is there some part which lives on? Does that part consist only of the memories left behind, or do I actually continue in some manner? This is not the place to discuss the respective responses of different theologies and philosophies. But I do briefly want to consider the essential implied question: What am I? What is this "I" which has somehow defined me all my life? To some, the suggestion that there is anything which transcends our consciousness and unites it with any greater being is no more than a comforting fiction at best and a cowardly form of self-deception at worst. To others it speaks as a partially intuited, or even as a deeply experienced, truth.

It is of course impossible for us, who have not yet visited "the undiscovered country, from whose bourn no traveller returns", to comment definitively on the ultimate existential realities. But the issue itself is important. In daily life we are frequently, if not constantly, occupied with ourselves, our actions, our feelings, our responsibilities, our pleasures, our aggravations, and our hopes. Illness and dying invite us to question the deepest context of our lives: what is the ultimate reality in which we exist? Part of this may derive from the fact that when we are seriously ill we are usually unable to follow our habitual routine. Even if we want to, we can no longer submit to the often comforting tyranny of our diaries and are forced to ask wider questions about the meaning and purpose of our lives. Spirituality and religion may appeal to us at such a time precisely because they have languages for addressing these issues.

Thinking about dying, most of all about our own death, may lead us to take those questions beyond our known experience to the borders of the transcendent: Do I end for ever with my death? Is my consciousness part of a greater being? Is it at some level not really "mine", but a fragment of God with whom it will be reconnected when I die? Does it bring any consolation to understand my reversion to the elements as belonging to a constant cycle of dying and rebirth, to the vast process of change and transformation of energy and matter? Pondering these issues can help us to find a humility which may make it easier to let go of our immediate attachments and lead us to comprehend our life as a portion, even if an almost infinitesimally small one, of a great journey of being which is at once chastening and inspiring.

I realise that much of my focus has been on the end of life. "From the moment of diagnosis, death becomes the bell that won't stop ringing", writes Ira Byock (Halifax, 2008, p. xi). Byock may well be correct, but I want to conclude with a reflection on the courage to live. Something I often hear people talk about when they become seriously ill is uncertainty. Illness, and perhaps especially cancer, brings a great deal of not knowing. The diagnosis may remain unclear for a long time; the prognosis will probably have to acknowledge many different variables and possibilities. After treatments, before each scan, during remission, a person has to live with the awareness that the news may be good and that things may be fine, but that one can never be sure. It is of course the case that no one ever knows what the morrow, or even the next hour, may bring. But that is no more than a truism for most of us, who live on the presumption that Tuesday will probably be very similar to Monday. It is very different when a chasm has opened up between yesterday and tomorrow, when the assumptions that make up our basic confidence in the very continuity of our own life have been shattered. Then a person really has to live in the now, to live with not knowing.

On countless occasions, in such circumstances, I've witnessed, alongside their fears and struggles, people's honesty, courage, dignity, humility, generosity of spirit, gratefulness, love, and openness to wonder.

References

Eliot, T. S. (1944). Burnt Norton. In: *Four Quartets*. London: Faber & Faber.

Halifax, J. (2008). *Being With Dying: Cultivating Compassion and Fearlessness in the Presence of Death*. Boston: Shambhala.

Remen, R. N. (1996). *Kitchen Table Wisdom: Stories that Heal*. New York: Berkley.

Warner, G. & Kreger, D. (1998). *Dancing at the Edge of Life: A Memoir*. New York: Hyperion.

PART II

CONTAINMENT AND CREATIVITY

CHAPTER TEN

Finding creative expression*

Carole Satyamurti

I would like to divide this paper into two parts. In the first, I want to think about what is involved in general in finding creative expression. What is going on when we write a poem or paint a picture, and what light does psychoanalysis shed on that? How might a poet address painful experience, such as having to confront approaching death? I will begin by looking at a couple of poems, not by me, which represent contrasting responses to this, and by considering with the reader what seems to work, and perhaps not work, in these poems.

In the second part of the paper I will speak autobiographically, and refer to some poems of mine which were a response to the experience of having cancer.

I should say that in talking about the creative process itself from a psychoanalytic point of view, I will be drawing on the chapter that I contributed to the book *Acquainted with the Night* (Canham & Satyamurti, 2003).

In thinking about what is involved in the making of a poem, I have in mind ideas derived both from the Kleinian tradition and from the

---

*This paper was first presented at the London Centre for Psychotherapy (now part of a new organisation: the British Psychotherapy Foundation) on 26 November 2011.

work of D. W. Winnicott. The two traditions clearly share a certain amount of common ground. They both see the origins of creativity—in a wide sense, as well as in a more specifically artistic sense of that word—as located in infantile experience. Both see the creative act as essentially object related; that is, as originating in an inner world constituted by relationships with others and parts of others—particularly the maternal figure. Both schools, too, see the process of maturation as having to do with the development of an authentic self, and an authentic way of being in the world which depends on the establishment of a relationship with truthfulness, centrally involving the capacity to acknowledge, and to bear, loss. This kind of relationship is also the artistic project.

I want to think briefly about the Kleinian concepts of reparation and containment as they illuminate different aspects of what it is to make a poem, and then to consider Winnicott's concept of potential space (1971) as having, I will suggest, most bearing on the writing *process*.

Adrian Stokes (1947) and Hanna Segal (1950) both highlight the ways in which reparation, the urge to repair phantasised or actual damage for which one holds oneself responsible, may lie at the heart of creative endeavour. In the work of art a whole version may be offered of the precious object—originally the breast—which has been destroyed or lost, the object being not magically restored but made real again symbolically. Here is a poem by the American poet James Merrill that makes this explicit:

The Broken Bowl
James Merrill

To say it once held daisies and bluebells
Ignores, if nothing else,
Much diehard brilliance where, crashed to the floor,
The wide bowl lies that seemed to cup the sun,
Its green leaves wilted, its loyal blaze undone,
All spilt, its glass integrity no more.
From piece to shattered piece
A fledgling rainbow struggles for release.

Did also the heart shatter when it slipped?
Shards flash, becoming script,
Imperfection's opal signature

Whose rays in disarray hallucinate
At dusk so glittering a network that
The plight of reason, ever shakier,
Is broadcast through the room
Which rocks in sympathy, a pendulum.

No lucid, self-containing artifice
At last, but fire, ice,
A world in jeopardy. What lets the bowl
Nonetheless triumph by inconsequence
And wrestle harmony from dissonance
And with the fragments build another, whole,
Inside us, which we feel
Can never break or grow less bountiful?

Love does that. Spectral through the fallen dark,
Eye-beam and ingle-spark
Refract our ruin into this new space,
Timeless and concentric, a spotlight
To whose elate arena we allot
Love's facets reassembling face by face,
Love's warbler among leaves,
Love's monuments, or tombstones, on our lives. (1996)

This is a highly wrought and complex poem and not one that we can unpack in its every aspect, but it is clearly speaking to the experience of damage, of loss and catastrophe. I want to draw attention to the way Merrill fully takes on the depressive pain of the bowl never again being able to be the perfectly beautiful object it was; the way the breaking of it does violence for a moment to the whole sense of the world as a harmonious place. We are not told who broke the bowl or how or why, and in that way we can imagine ourselves implicated. Yet "love" can build it whole again inside us, and a bowl restored symbolically like this is durable in a way the original could never be—because it is the product of the kind of dwelling in the truth of loss which is inherent in healthy mourning. It is, in a sense, earned.

The poem both describes, and is, a reparative act, an act of integration. The process of moving through shock and loss to some mode of recovery is not just *described* in the poem. The poem *embodies* that process. The word "tombstones" in the last line is a worry, though. It seems to convey an eleventh hour loss of conviction that the poem can, after all, reconstruct the bowl—since a tombstone can be seen as merely a marker rather than a symbol.

"Love" is perhaps a surprising word to use with such seriousness of a glass bowl, even one so beautiful. Merrill's use of this word is an indication that more than a shattered artefact is at stake here. The bowl is an internalised good object, a "bountiful" object that "seems to cup the sun"—and we might hear "son" as well as "sun" here.

Freud, in his 1914 essay *On Narcissism*, quotes part of a poem by Heine in which God is imagined as saying this:

> Illness was no doubt the final cause
> Of the whole urge to create.
> By creating, I could recover;
> By creating, I became healthy.

In early nineteenth-century German usage, the word "*gesund*", translated as "healthy" here and closely related to the English word "sound", would have incorporated meanings of both physical and psychological well-being. Freud quotes this passage in support of a point which at first sight looks rather different—namely that "we must begin to *love* in order not to fall ill, and we are bound to fall ill … if we are unable to love" (my italics). Freud and Merrill seem to be seeing love as central to creativity— one definition of love, perhaps, being a devoted attention to a person or object (which might include the work of art itself)—the wish for it to be as fully itself as possible.

It has been said that we are constituted by what we do about loss, and reparation is one possible response to loss which a poem might carry. Another possibility is to build a bridge, to forge some sort of connection with the lost object. In a poem that attempts this, there may be an analogy between the time it takes to move through the poem and the time needed to reach the loved object—buttressed by a stubborn belief that the poem can be strong enough to sustain the writer, and the reader, through that journey.

Linked with the idea of art as reparation is the idea of containment— the way that the infant's unbearable and chaotic feelings can, in normally good circumstances, be projected into the mother who is able to tolerate and digest the infant's distress and, through the way she talks to and touches him or her, transform the painful feelings into something manageable. Central to this idea is a process. The feelings are not just dumped or evacuated but given some sort of shape, and the infant learns from this that such feelings can be borne and can be thought about, and comes in time to be able to do this for herself or himself. In time she can internalise the good containing object, the bowl that could "cup the sun" and make it her own.

I suggest that a poem can function in this way too. Hamish Canham, my co-editor on the book *Acquainted with the Night*, who himself tragically died of cancer at the age of forty while the book was being put together, had previously written a paper about Larkin's extremely gloomy poem, "Aubade", about waking up and seeing the threat of death all around him. What Hamish suggested is that the fact itself of being able to write a poem about it, to be able to articulate and provide a shape for that terror, is itself a contribution to the reader: a containment of the dread.

Poets can be quite scornful about writing as therapy, by which they often have in mind precisely a kind of dumping, as though it were enough to get the feelings out there—feelings like fear, for instance, in the case of cancer, or grief. What an achieved poem does is more than that. Fear of death is universal, and a successful poem on this subject—and by "successful" I mean a poem that will resonate in the minds of strangers—cannot only be concerned with the unique personal experience of the poet; it has to be more. Through its choice of language it transforms the experience by giving it a shape. It does so by drawing on a repertoire of poetic resources such as form, simile, and metaphor, and poetic strategies each of which has its own effect. Subject matter which is painful may call for strict form in order to avoid a sort of splurge of emotion, and it may require that the subject be addressed obliquely, letting the subject matter emerge gradually.

The following are two poems which address the fear of death in very different ways. In the first, by Vernon Scannell, the poet confronts his own death head-on, in a poem that has a regular pattern of rhythm and rhyme (Scannell was a great formalist). In the second poem, by the American, Mark Doty, the poet comes at the subject of his partner's death indirectly, through finding a symbolic representation of the mystery that is death. The form the poem takes is free verse, somewhat corresponding to what the poem is drawing attention to.

Missing Things
Vernon Scannell

I'm very old and breathless, tired and lame,
and soon I'll be no more to anyone
than the slowly fading trochee of my name
and shadow of my presence: I'll be gone.
Already I begin to miss the things
I'll leave behind, like this calm evening sun
which seems to smile at how the blackbird sings.

There's something valedictory in the way
my books gaze down on me from where they stand
in disciplined disorder and display
the same goodwill that well-wishers on land
convey to troops who sail away to where
great danger waits. These books will miss the hand
that turned the pages with devoted care.

And there are also places that I miss:
those Paris streets and bars I can't forget,
the scent of caporal and wine and piss;
the pubs in Soho where the poets met;
the Yorkshire moors and Dorset's pebbly coast,
black Leeds, where I was taught love's alphabet,
and this small house that I shall miss the most.

I've lived here for so long it seems to be
a part of what I am, yet I'm aware
that when I've gone it won't remember me
and I, of course, will neither know nor care
since, like the stone of which the house is made,
I'll feel no more than it does light and air.
Then why so sad? And just a bit afraid? (2007)

Beach Roses
Mark Doty

What are they, the white roses,
when they are almost nothing,

only a little denser than the fog,
shadow-centered petals blurring,
towards the edges, into everything?

This morning one broken cloud
built an archipelago.
            fourteen gleaming islands
hurrying across a blank plain of sheen:
nothing, or next to nothing

—pure scattering, light on light,
fleeting.
      And now, a heap of roses
beside the sea, white rugosa
beside the foaming hem of shore:
                  brave,
waxen candles...

      And we talk
as if death were a line to be crossed.
Look at them, the white roses.
Tell me where they end. (1995)

Scannell's poem is very particular and specific. It's a touching poem, it seems to me, but Doty's poem is more memorable in my view because it has a haunting quality that gestures towards something beyond what is immediately visible. Scannell is holding on to what's in front of him even though he is explicitly saying that he won't know anything about it soon. I think this poem was written shortly before he died.

Containment and reparation can obviously be very fruitful ideas in thinking about the poem that we might be looking at, but they don't seem to me to be sufficient in thinking about the process of writing a poem; the impulse to make something doesn't just derive from a desire to repair. It also goes back to something more primary, an experience described by Winnicott: the activity of playing as an infant, which is initially just about itself, rather than about an attempt to heal anything. It's an urge to explore the world and to shape materials in new ways, as he puts it, "For the first time ever". He says the place where cultural experience is located is in the potential space between the individual and the environment. It begins with creative living first manifested in play, and we might say that play is also a prototype for having an effect on the world around us.

Given a "facilitating environment"—a maternal figure who is present but not intrusive—the baby can explore the shifting relationship between "me" and "not me". It is a profound paradox that the baby feels most wholly him or herself when the matter of what is self and what is not self is least in question; and the same is true for the artist. What Winnicott calls the "transitional object"—whether it is a toy or a piece of cloth or whatever—partakes of the qualities both of self and not-self, and is analogous to the object that the artist creates. The infant needs the object to survive her attacks, her neglect, her treating it like rubbish. The art object has to survive the process of making which is likely to involve pushing it around, changing it, cutting it down, abandoning it perhaps, and coming back to it.

What is at issue can feel, as it did for van Gogh, like a matter of life and death. The artist may feel that only by making art can he or she exist at all. To imagine a void in which there are no objects is far more terrifying even than a world of damaged objects. As Michael Parsons has said, "Art which has this at stake is not about repairing damage but about bringing something into existence and sustaining it in being" (2000).

Moving on to the more autobiographical part of my chapter, I will begin by saying that my forties were years in which a number of momentous things happened to me. I was bringing up a child on my own, and because she was disabled I was having a lot of contact with the medical profession and wrestling with sometimes difficult decisions. Then, when she was seven, I became involved with doctors on my own account when I developed Hodgkin's lymphoma and was treated with surgery and radiotherapy.

A few years later I began to write poetry. Before that I had been very preoccupied by my daughter, watching her spine become more and more distorted, as though my concentrated attention could somehow slow the process down. But after she had spinal surgery and the operation was a success, it felt as though relief created a space for me to do something new.

Never having written poetry even as a teenager, although I read a lot of poetry, I went on a creative writing week at the Arvon Foundation— with enormous trepidation, I have to say.

It was like a conversion experience. It was a real eye-opener. I was an academic, used to writing papers within certain conventions, dutifully referring to the work of others. Now I could write with no footnotes. It did feel like exploring the world of language for the first time ever.

Soon after starting to write poetry, I had a dream: I climbed onto my desk in order to reach a door I had never noticed before high up on the wall. I hauled myself through it, in a kind of reverse birth process, and found myself in a railway waiting room that looked as though it had been frozen in time. On the seats were a number of mummified old women who had died waiting for a train that never came, and dried up where they sat. Thick china cups, stuck to tea-stained saucers, stood on a pine table.

I passed through this room and into a light, large space beyond it which was empty apart from a tapestry hanging on one wall. I knew the tapestry was me in some way. It was like the painting in Dorian Gray, but also connected with a story I loved as a child but can't identify now in which a girl finds her way to an attic where she discovers a tapestry into which all her deeds, good and bad, are woven.

This tapestry represented not only me as I was, but also the colours and textures I had at my disposal from now on. (Some of this may be a lending of coherence to the dream in retrospect, but it did feel like that, I think.)

The mood of the dream was one of joy and of gratitude to these des-iccated ancestors, for I knew they were that. There was a sense that I had arrived here at the expense of the dead women who had waited and waited and never gone anywhere. The dream ended there without my doing anything either in the bright room or in the gloomy waiting room. What I could do with these spaces and their content lay beyond the boundaries of the dream.

Then I was diagnosed with breast cancer, possibly a consequence of the radiotherapy I had undergone six years earlier. That dream had seemed like a very feminist dream, a dream of empowerment convey-ing a good deal of positiveness and optimism about being able to cre-ate something good partly derived from what I had inherited from my foremothers. The experience of cancer, and in the breast, seemed like the opposite: a crucial site of femininity gone horribly wrong. Other people have talked about how a cancer diagnosis or a diagnosis of any serious illness, I think, undermines confidence in one's body, throws into question what was previously taken for granted, and makes one feel as though one is inhabiting a different terrain from that of other people, healthy people.

I didn't write poems about it immediately, but a few months after my treatment ended, I wrote a sequence of fourteen poems which charted my route through the illness and, provisionally, out the other side. In relation to the models of creativity that I talked about earlier, I think the writing of these poems, both the content and the process of writing them, can be seen as having something to do with both.

I'll end by presenting some of those poems. The title of the sequence—and the title of the book that contains it—is *Changing the Subject* (1990). That title carries more than one meaning. It refers to the milieu in which I grew up, and the way that, in that social setting, cancer was a word that was never said. It was an unmentionable word and an unmentionable phenomenon; and that gave rise for me to an intense dread of cancer and a preoccupation with it. But the phrase, "changing the subject", also refers to the way that one's subjectivity, one's sense of oneself, is changed by a serious illness.

I don't offer these poems as great poems, but simply as the best I could do at the time.

Changing the subject

The Word

It started with my grandmother
who, fading unspeakably,
lay in the blue room; disappeared
leaving a cardboard box,
coils of chalky-brown rubber tube.

I inherited her room, her key.
The walls were papered bright
but the unsayable word
seeped through; some nights
I heard it in the dripping of the tap.

I saw it in my parents' mouths,
how it twisted lips for whispers
before they changed the subject.
I saw it through fingers
screening me from news.

The word has rooted in my head
casting blue shadows.

It has put on flesh,
spawned strong and crazy children
who wake, reach out their claws.

Out-Patients

Women stripped to the waist
wrapped in blue,
we are a uniform edition
waiting to be read.

These plain covers suit us;
we're inexplicit,
it's not our style to advertise
our fearful narratives.

My turn. He reads my breasts
like Braille, finding the lump
I knew was there. This is
the episode I could see coming—

although he's reassuring,
doesn't think it's sinister
but just to be quite clear …
He's taking over,

he'll be the writer now,
the plot-master,
and I must wait
to read my next instalment.

Diagnosis

He was good at telling,
gentle and direct;
he stayed with me
while I recovered breath,
started to collect

stumbling questions. He said
cancer with a small c—

the raw stuff of routine—
yet his manner showed
he knew it couldn't be ordinary for me.

Walking down the road
I shivered like a gong
that's just been struck—
mutilation ... what have I done ...
my child ... how long ...

and noticed how
the vast possible array
of individual speech
is whittled by bad news
to what all frightened people say.

That night, the freak storm.
I listened to trees fall,
stout fences crack,
felt the house shudder as the wind
howled the truest cliché of them all.

(It was actually the night of the storm in October of 1986 that knocked
down half the trees in southern England. So—talk about an "objective
correlative" (Eliot, 1921), as T. S. Eliot called it! It felt very strange.)

The following two poems are about the experience of being an
inpatient:

How Are You?

When he asked me that
what if I'd said
rather than 'very well',
'dreadful—full of dread'?

Since I have known this,
language has cracked,
meanings have rearranged,
dream, risk and fact

changed places. Tenses tip
word-roots are suddenly
important, some grip
on the slippery.

We're on thin linguistic ice
lifelong, but I see through;
I read the sentence
we all are subject to

in the stopped mouths of those
who once were 'I',
full-fleshed, confident,
using the verb to die

of plants and pets and parents
until the immense
contingency of things
deleted sense.

They are his future
as well as mine,
but I won't make him look.
I say, 'I'm fine'.

Knowing our Place

Class is irrelevant in here.
We're part of a new scale
—mobility is all one way
and the least respected
are envied most.

First the benigns,
in for a night or two,
nervous but unappalled;
foolishly glad their bodies
don't behave like that.

Then the exploratories;
can't wait to know, but have to.
Greedy for signs, they swing
from misery to confidence,
or just endure.

The primaries are in
for surgery—what kind? What then?
Shocked, tearful perhaps;
things happening too fast.
Still can't believe it, really.

The reconstructions are survivors,
experienced, detached.
They're bent on being almost normal;
don't want to think
of other possibilities.

Secondaries (treatment)
are often angry—with doctors, fate ...
—or blame themselves.
They want to tell their stories,
not to feel so alone.

Secondaries (palliative)
are admitted swathed in pain.
They become gentle, grateful,
they've learned to live
one day at a time.

Terminals are royalty,
beyond the rest of us.
They lie in side-rooms
flanked by exhausted relatives,
sans everything.

We learn the social map
fast. Beneath the ordinary chat,
jokes, kindnesses, we're scavengers

gnawing at each other's histories
for scraps of hope.

Finally the next three poems are about the experience of being back
home again:

Outside

I've hung the washing out
and turn to see
the door slammed shut
by a capricious wind.

Locked out, face to the glass,
I see myself reflected
in the mirror opposite,
framed, slightly menacing.

No need for wuthering
to feel how it might be—
I have that sepia, far-seeing
look of long-dead people.

Perhaps I wouldn't feel dead,
just confused, lost track of time;
could it be years since I turned
with that mouthful of pegs?

And might I now beat on the glass
with jelly fists, my breath
making no cloud in this crisp air,
shout with no sound coming?

Death could seem this accidental—
the play of cells
mad as the freakishness of weather,
the arbitrary shutting out.

Might there be some self left
to look back, register

the shape of the receding house?
And would it feel this cold?

I Shall Paint My Nails Red

because a bit of colour is a public service.

because I am proud of my hands.

because it will remind me I'm a woman.

because I will look like a survivor.

because I can admire them in traffic jams.

because my daughter will say ugh.

because my lover will be surprised.

because it is quicker than dyeing my hair.

because it is a ten-minute moratorium.

because it is reversible.

Watching Swallows

In my fiftieth year,
with my folded chin
that makes my daughter call me Touché Turtle;

in my fiftieth year,
with a brood of half-tamed fears
clinging around my hem,
I sit with my green shiny notebook
and my battered red notebook
and my notebook with the marbled cover

and I want to feel
revolutions spinning me apart,
re-forming me

—as would be fitting in one's fiftieth year.

Instead, I hum a tune to my own pulse.

Instead I busy dead flies off the sill
and realign my dictionaries.

Instead, through the window,
I make a sign of solidarity
at swallows, massing along the wires.

References

Canham, H. & Satyamurti, C. (2003). *Acquainted with the Night*. London: Karnac.

Doty, M. (1995). *Atlantis: Poems by Mark Doty*. Toronto: HarperCollins.

Eliot, T. S. (1921). Hamlet and his problems. In: *Selected Essays 1917–1932*. London: Faber & Faber.

Merrill, J. (1996). *James Merrill: Selected Poems*. Manchester: Carcanet.

Parsons, M. (2000). *The Dove that Returns, the Dove that Vanishes*. London: Routledge.

Satyamurti, C. (1990). *Changing the Subject*. Oxford: Oxford University Press.

Satyamurti, C. (2005). *Stitching the Dark: New & Selected Poems*. Tarset, Northumberland: Bloodaxe.

Scannell, V. (2007). *Last Post*. Beeston, Nottingham: Shoestring.

Segal, H. (1950). Some aspects of the analysis of a schizophrenic. *International Journal of Psycho-Analysis, 31*: 268–278. In: *The Work of Hanna Segal*. London: Free Association Books, 1986.

Stokes, A. (1947). *Inside Out*. London: Faber and Faber.

Winnicott, D. W. (1971). *Playing and Reality*. London: Tavistock Publications.

CHAPTER ELEVEN

The cancer memoir: in search of a writing cure?

Anne Karpf

In 1996 the British journalist John Diamond was writing a weekly column for *The Times* in which, seizing on a personal experience, he would expatiate humorously on an aspect of modern life or mores. Diamond, a wry vivisector of his own magical thinking around illness, duly chronicled a succession of ailments, all through the microscope of his supposed hypochondria. When, after seven months, a swelling in his neck became too persistent to dismiss as glandular fever, he underwent a series of tests. On 27 March 1997 he was diagnosed with cancer.

Almost until his death in 2001 Diamond continued to report on his illness and treatment in his *Times* column (which, he later recalled, had "become a cancer column" (Diamond, 1998, p. 120)), as well as in his acclaimed book, *C: Because Cowards Get Cancer Too* (Diamond, 1998), and a BBC TV documentary (*Inside Story: Tongue Tied*, 1998). Meanwhile another British journalist Ruth Picardie was writing about being diagnosed and treated for breast cancer in five equally celebrated columns in *The Observer*, published in a book after her death in 1997 (Picardie, 1998), just as, ten years later, journalist Dina Rabinovitch's *Guardian* columns about breast cancer would be turned into book form (Rabinovitch, 2007).

Such books have been called "pathographies", "a form of autobiography or biography that describes personal experiences of illness, treatment, and sometimes death" (Hawkins, 1998, p. 1). Although not entirely new—American writer John Gunther's memoir of the death of his son, Johnny, from a brain tumour when he was seventeen was published in 1949 (Gunther, 1949)—book-length personal accounts of illness were uncommon before 1950 (Hawkins, 1998), and those about cancer rare before 1980 (Jurecic, 2012). In the years since they have proliferated: 102 cancer pathographies are listed in the Library of Congress as being published between 1988 and 1992, and 194 between 1993 and 1997 (sixty on breast cancer alone) (Hawkins, 1998). They figure routinely on best-seller lists.

This chapter examines the characteristics of the cancer memoir, and tries to account for its growth. It explores the ways in which the cancer pathography has made visible the lived experience of the person with cancer, but has also shaped it according to the demands of narrative. It argues that while the cancer memoir has played an important role in exposing and challenging norms of medical care, at the same time it is historically and culturally determined: its silences are as significant as what it articulates. The chapter ends by considering more recent mutations of the cancer memoir, such as the dissonant pathography and the cancer blog.

The meaning of illness

Kleinman crucially distinguishes between the concepts of disease and illness (Kleinman, 1988). Disease is a biomedical category and diagnostic entity, a physiological disorder for which technical solutions are sought. In this paradigm the patient becomes the case-history, the object of professional inquiry. In the biopsychosocial model, by contrast, illness is part of a symbolic network that links the body, the self, and society. Kleinman, a psychiatrist and anthropologist, argues that medical training has blinded doctors to the meaning of illness: he wants to restore "the experiential realm of suffering" (Kleinman, 1988, p. 267) to the physician's gaze, calling for them to attend to patients' own narratives. As the American memoirist Anatole Broyard asked rhetorically, "How can a doctor presume to cure a patient if he knows nothing about his soul, his personality, his character disorder?" (Broyard, 1992, pp. 23–24).

Pathographies embody the biopsychosocial model; in them meaning—the meaning that the patient attributes to his symptoms and disease—is paramount. Cancer memoirs reinstate the patient's narrative, but not as elicited by a doctor taking a medical history. In the memoir the patient constructs his own narrative, which roams far beyond the medical encounter—indeed the medical encounter itself is scrutinised by the memoirist. Here subjective experience is not some "soft", devalued aspect of psychosocial concern in contrast to the "hard", scientific management of symptoms (Kleinman, 1988): disease *becomes* meaning and subjective experience. So the cancer memoir is less about cancer per se, and more about "what it feels like to be me with cancer".

In restoring the patient's eye-view, pathographies also explicitly contrast it with the medical gaze. "The medical world may know how to kill off a tumour", writes one of the youngest recent British cancer memoirists, Lisa Lynch, "but it doesn't know how to rebuild the self-esteem that the tumour-busting treatment ruined in the process" (Lynch, 2010, p. 192). Doctors, argues Rabinovitch, "don't know ... how various procedures hurt. It gives them a detachment that is almost tangible" (Rabinovitch, 2007, p. 174). American cancer memoirist Joni Rodgers wittily translates the discourse of disease into the gestalt of illness. Of her physician, listing the side-effects of the proposed chemotherapy, she says: "She laid out the gruesome possibilities in clinical nomenclature, couching blatant realities like 'barfing' and 'agony' in palatable terms like "nausea" and "discomfort" (Rodgers, 2002, pp. 44–45). Janice Day even interweaves her own account of the treatment with extracts from her clinical records, and letters between the doctors treating her (Day, 2009). The contrast, in language alone, is eloquent.

The cancer memoir usually begins with the author, in apparent health, going about their daily business, oblivious of the life-change that lies in wait. The authors describe their symptoms and blithe attempts to dismiss or deny them. Most memoirists linger on this stage of their pre-cancer life, as if they cannot bear to leave it, or might somehow resurrect it through memory alone. Then comes diagnosis, usually still accompanied by optimism and hope, until these give way, in most cases, to profound fear and apprehension. Sometimes there are decisions about treatment to be made: exercising choice in this context can feel burdensome, as can living with the resulting uncertainty. In an early breast cancer memoir the American poet, Audrey Lorde, wrote, "I weighed my options. There were malignant cells in my right breast encased in a fatty cyst, and if I did not do something about that I would die of cancer in fairly short order. Whatever I did might or might not reverse that process and I would not know with any certainty for a very long time" (Lorde, 1980, p. 32). This is a long way from the randomised controlled trial's assessment of risk or the study coolly written up in the medical journal: these are lay people's medical decisions—situated, contingent, potentially life-threatening and very frightening. Lorde decided on a mastectomy.

Pathographies demonstrate the extent to which cancer becomes a family condition, shared by relatives and friends. "I realised for the first time that it wasn't just me who'd had this diagnosis", writes Lynch, "it was *us*: Me *and* P" (Lynch, 2010, p. 35). Most memoirs recount the difficulties of disclosing the illness to family members, but spouses and partners, parents and friends also often emerge as heroes, accompanying the person with cancer to check-ups and hospital, nursing them, passing the bedpan and buoying up their morale. Cody reproduces what he calls a "touching page" from one of his mother's notebooks, detailing "the constant errand-running, the housekeeping the caretaker of the ill must sustain" (Cody, 2011, p. 98). Picardie's book includes her email exchanges with a wide circle of intensely engaged friends, all touched by her illness (Picardie, 1998). Inevitably, some fall short of the idealised supportive spouse or relative: cancer can reveal the fault-lines in a relationship (Day, 2009), or expose intra-family dynamics. Diamond has to confront his father with the fact that his denial is making the cancer harder for Diamond himself to bear (Diamond, 1998). While the biomedical disease model situates illness in an individual, the cancer memoir embeds the person with cancer in a web of significant, often sustaining relationships (Bregman & Thiermann, 1995).

Cancer treatment demands of patients resilience and a strong stomach; so too does reading about it. Memoirists are unsparing in their accounts of the gruesomeness of treatment and its side-effects. They document forensically the experience of mutilation—mastectomy (Day, 2009; Lorde, 1980; Lynch, 2010; Murray, 2008; Rabinovitch, 2007; Rollin, 1976), amputation of the leg and part of the buttock (Want, 2011), the removal of part of the tongue (Diamond, 1998), as well as colostomy (Rose, 1995). They share stories of hallucinating (Cody, 2011), diarrhoea (Lynch, 2010) and livid rashes (Hitchens, 2012). Numbness, weight loss, fatigue, a "hellish tide of pain" (Hitchens, 2012, p. 67), not to mention surging nausea and waves of depression—the cancer memoirist knows what it is like to feel abject and urgently needs to communicate it. Indeed one of the rationales of the pathography is to bear witness to the depredations wrought by treatment, in some cases so savage that the author needs to record them so as to convince their post-cancer self that they really took place (Bregman & Thiermann, 1995).

By situating treatment in the patient's own world, the pathographer also draws attention to other, sometimes non-medical, aspects of medical advice and treatment. "There is a gap in understanding between these doctors and the actuality of my daily life", Rabinovitch contends. "Just how do you refuse to cuddle a small child after a whole day at school?" (Rabinovitch, 2007, p. 184). To read the cancer memoir is to become aware of the significance that can be assumed by logistical problems surrounding treatment—say, the problem of parking near the hospital when going in for treatment—or the setting in which it takes place (for instance the layout and décor of the waiting-room), as much as the actual treatment regime.

Having broken the taboos against describing intimate bodily processes (after her colostomy, Rose ruminates candidly about excrement (Rose, 1995)), many cancer memoirists have no compunction about recounting the effects of their illness and treatment on their sexual relations: they have already bared all and so take us (without apparent embarrassment) further, into the marital bed itself. Much more troubling to them is taking on the identity of cancer patient, an identity which does not necessarily arrive immediately with diagnosis, indeed rarely seems to. Most memoirists resist it, at least until they are no longer able to. Picardie, for example, whose cancer columns span only two months, actively disidentifies with other sick people, "wanting to stay as far as away from them as possible" (Picardie, 1998, p. 72). Lynch has what she calls a tantrum when the pyjamas her mother has bought her to wear in hospital "made me 'look like an ill person'" (Lynch, 2010, p. 20). Their sense of themselves as cancer patients emerges through a slow process of attrition—perhaps by greeting and being greeted by medical staff in a familiar way; or realising that they know something about the hospital routine that they would not have known before. For the memoirist, this first recognition of her metamorphosis into cancer patient is shocking. Rabinovitch's rite of passage occurs when she first gives herself an injection to boost her white blood cells. "This one feat, more than any other, is a sign of how far removed I now am from my former pre-cancer self" (Rabinovitch, 2007, p. 143). When Diamond goes into hospital for a biopsy, he notes how "depressingly familiar" it now seems, down to its most mundane workings, such as the coins that the car park ticket machine will accept. It is around this time that he acknowledges that "I was beginning to look, and, more importantly, *sound* like a patient of some sort" (Diamond, 1998, p. 56).

The experience of serious illness constitutes "biographical disruption" (Bury, 1982, 1991), and language and narrative help "in the repair and restoring of meanings when they are threatened" (Bury, 2001, p. 264). Cancer memoirs movingly show how the writer's former psycho-social identity frays and then tears; they mark the different stages in the course of which the author-patient reluctantly lets go of his old, pre-cancer self, and develops a new one. The night before surgery to remove part of Diamond's tongue, he wrote: "we lay together in our bed for what was to be the last time as the couple we had been for eight years. Tomorrow I would become somebody else" (Diamond, 1998, p. 144). Later on, when he could no longer broadcast, he caught a vaguely familiar voice on a repeat of a BBC radio programme. Realising that it was his own, he likened it to "seeing the twin brother I'd forgotten I'd had" (Diamond, 1998, p. 209). The American TV reporter, Betty Rollin, in one of the earliest breast cancer pathographies, *First, You Cry*, described going outside soon after her mastectomy: "I felt as if I were already dead, come back like a ghost" (Rollin, 1976, p. 97). When later she began to bathe her chest wound for the first time, she tried out another identity: "I pretended I was a nurse and that the body I was washing was someone else's" (Rollin, 1976, p. 122).

What these new identities also reveal, along with the loss of a taken-for-granted self, is the induction of the person with cancer into another new role: that of expert. Close proximity with doctors and treatment regimes inevitably provides patients with medical knowledge. In addition they must manage their own medication, and become authorities on their own reactions to it. At one stage Diamond devotes three pages to listing, under their generic as well as brand names, all the medication he has been prescribed so far, along with its purpose (Diamond, 1998).

As they venture into this new world, they leave some of their former friends and intimates behind. A prominent theme of the pathography is other people's unhelpful reactions: these become a useful dartboard for the cancer memoirist's rage. Susan Sontag famously anatomised the metaphors used to describe cancer—the language of attack, invasion, and battle—and pleaded for its de-mythicising (Sontag, 1978). While few cancer memoirists explicitly reference her, again and again they challenge the discourse of bravery through which many friends and colleagues try to address them. Their supposed "bravery" seems to be a way for others not to engage with the much more tumultuous feelings commonly felt by the person with cancer: parcelled up as "brave", the cancerous can be kept apart from the non-cancerous.

In place of courage, what the most compelling cancer memoirs play out is the process of mourning. Interestingly, very few cancer memoir-ists go into therapy (the act of writing, I suggest below, is often made to function therapeutically instead), but their pathographies trace the tra-jectory of grief—the loss of the healthy self—and constitute an attempt to work through it. As Picardie put it, "What hurts most is losing the future" (Picardie, 1998, p. 58). Most remarkably certain authors begin to be able to contemplate their own death with composure, acceptance, and even curiosity—cancer has inspired some brilliant, powerful, and vital writing. Anatole Broyard, in a memoir aptly entitled *Intoxicated By My Illness,* discovers a "brand new infatuation" for his body and his life at the point that it is threatened by extinction (Broyard, 1992). Christopher Hitchens's polemical verve doesn't falter in "this year of living dyingly", in a memoir he calls *Mortality* (Hitchens, 2012, p. 54). Philip Gould becomes a crusader—a little messianic and hubristic, to be sure—for the idea that accepting death offers an opportunity to complete relationships. No natural writer, he nevertheless declares winningly that "I am enjoying my death" (Gould, 2012, p. 128). Art critic Tom Lubbock, in *Until Further Notice, I Am Alive,* painstakingly unpicks, with an astounding matter-of-factness, what is to be feared and not feared about dying. As he moves into his transitional state between living and dying, his "going towards dying", "his full stop-ping" (Lubbock, 2012, pp. 38–46), at times he seems like a disinterested observer of his own mortality. This is ontological probing of the high-est order, describing "holding your allegiance to the world, even while accepting your links to it are very weak" (Lubbock, 2012, p. 40) and, as the end nears, "I feel now that I am becoming dead" (Lubbock, 2012, p. 133). He includes letters he has written to his young son; similarly Picardie's book reproduces the scrawled letters she leaves behind for her small children. Poignant in the extreme, these are an acknowledgement not only that the children's lives will continue after the parent-author's has ended, but that these young children will go through childhood without one parent. At points like this, reading the cancer memoir is a painful reminder of the inexorability of the human condition.

The birth of the patient

I have argued elsewhere that the 1970s and 1980s saw a paradigm shift in the reporting of health and medicine, away from a medical model and towards a consumer approach (Karpf, 1988). The consumer approach, I suggested, identified the issue of power in the doctor-patient relationship and proposed that there was a conflict of interest, the doctor exercising power, the patient struggling to empower herself. Some of the earliest cancer memoirs explicitly sing to this tune. Rose Kushner's *Why Me?*, for example, subtitled her experience of treatment for breast cancer: *What Every Woman Needs to Know about Breast Cancer to Save Her Life* (Kushner, 1977). (A few decades earlier and it would have been assumed that it was the doctor, or the prescribed medical treatment, that would save her life.) Pathographies like this marked a cultural change in which trust in doctors and an uncritical acceptance of medical routines shifted from the norm to the exception (Hawkins, 1998).

Of course there have always been mavericks critiquing biomedicine. Simone de Beauvoir, for instance, challenged the doctors about why, despite her mother's advanced malignant tumour, they repeatedly brought her back from her impending death (de Beauvoir, 1965). Yet it is hard to imagine it being possible much earlier than the mid-1990s, for Janice Day to have coolly quizzed her consultant about the percentage improvement in survival which chemotherapy after surgery was likely to bring her (Day, 2009). The explosion of medical information on the internet meant that doctors could no longer act as sentinels of medical knowledge, controlling access to it: the cancer memoir has proliferated alongside the web. AIDS brought forth a cohort of educated, active campaigners, so fundamentally changing the relationship between patients and medicine (Mukherjee, 2011). AIDS activists played their part in helping to destigmatise cancer, in a sense preparing the ground for the cancer memoirist with a destigmatising mission. Jenni Murray, presenter of BBC Radio 4's *Woman's Hour* programme, decided to "go public" with her own breast cancer, first on air, and later in a cancer memoir, because "I am old enough to remember the days when cancer was so feared it was barely breathed about and only ever referred to as the C-word" (Murray, 2008, p. 159). In 1975, Rollin recalled in 2000, obituaries never mentioned the word: the phrase they used instead was that s/he died "after a long illness" (Rollin, 2000). The cancer memoir helped make the disease less shameful and propelled it onto the public agenda.

It also shone a beam onto the medical consultation, often to baleful effect. The pathography brought us doctors not in clinical isolation but as seen by their patients. It gave a graphic sense of how depersonalising the medical encounter could be (a key aspect of the consumer critique, and one also noted in Dr. Twycross's chapter on palliative care)—the displays of coldness where kindness was craved, of inhumanity at a time where a thoughtful gesture could reassure. "A new registrar arrives", notes Lubbock, "arrogant, inattentive, supercilious" ... "What disgusts me is his smug indifference, his total lack of professional concern for the patients in his care" (Lubbock, 2012, pp. 106, 111). Broyard instinctively takes against one of his doctors: "I see no reason why he has to stop being a doctor and become an amateur human being" (Broyard, 1992, p. 44). But the cancer memoirist's isn't a generic but rather a particularised view: it's not so much a case of doctor-bashing but identifying those individual members of the medical team who make the treatment regime even tougher.

The pathography exposed differences between medical staff not only in personality and behaviour but also in diagnosis, so fissuring any notion of medical orthodoxy: the doctors in cancer memoirs often disagree. Rose is faced with such wildly discrepant opinion between two of hers, who refuse to talk to each other, one of them declaring "This is my cancer" (Rose, 1995, p. 101), that she is reduced to pleading, cajoling, and flattering in order to try and get them back into communication. Sometimes these divergences of opinion can prove fatal. Gould chooses the more conservative treatment plan of prestigious private American physicians over the more radical proposal of the British NHS, only to conclude later, after hearing an admission of error from the American doctor, that his decision had been wrong (Gould, 2012). In these cases medical unanimity goes out through the window.

The cancer memoir, though, is also a vehicle through which to draw attention to medical negligence, as in the cases of Betty Rollin and Fran Drescher. In 1974 the lump that NBC news reporter Rollin found in her breast was dismissed by both her internist and mammographer, but a year later it was diagnosed as a malignant tumour, necessitating a mastectomy (Rollin, 2000). Drescher's experience was even worse. In

1997 the writer, director, and star of the TV drama series *The Nanny* experienced cramps and bleeding in the middle of her menstrual cycle. She recounts how, over a period of more than two-and-a-half years, she saw a succession of eight different doctors—she numbers them Doctor #1 to Doctor #8—who responded with a series of improbable, sometimes outlandish, diagnoses for her increasingly debilitating symptoms. Finally Doctor #8 ordered a D&C and discovered uterine cancer. A hysterectomy and an appendectomy were required, along with the removal of forty lymph glands—"What a high price I paid for other people's negligence" (Drescher, 2002, p. 122). The experience turned Drescher into a cancer activist, exhorting women to educate themselves and insist on treatment. This is the cancer memoirist as crusader ("Somone gimme a podium!" (Drescher, 2002, p. xiv)), enlisted in the "battle" against cancer (Mukherjee, 2011). Neither woman names the miscreant doctors, presumably because in a country as litigious as America it is either sue or be sued, but also because they are intent on drawing attention to the more structural reasons, beyond the fallibilities of individual doctors, that women's intuitive reactions to symptoms are ignored.

But it would be wrong to polarise the consumer model and the medical one, or position the cancer memoir as necessarily oppositional. Not only because most memoirists are sensitive to the differences between medical staff, and hymn those who make their life easier, but also because the consumer approach or the lay account of illness is often saturated with medical thinking. The birth of the patient does not necessarily signal a critique of the biomedical knowledge base, which in Western cultures remains the dominant paradigm through which to think about health and illness. Almost all the memoirists cited here, for example, are not just uninterested in but actively hostile to alternative medical therapies (Picardie dubs the practitioner she visits briefly "Dr. Charlatan" (Picardie, 1998)), and view them through the lens of allopathic medicine. Indeed, what these writers want is not less medicine but better. Again and again they describe their anxiety when a treatment regime ends. Discharged from hospital, where they feel cared for, lacking the sense of containment that comes from regular scans, blood tests and medication, some (e.g., Diamond, 1998, Rabinovitch, 2007) go into a freefall of anxiety—how quickly institutionalisation mutates from anathema to comfort.

The most gendered of all illness narratives is the breast cancer memoir, because it describes a condition and treatment that are experienced as damaging women's sexuality and sense of femininity. The women's movement, it has been argued, "transformed breast cancer from a private, even shameful ordeal into a publicly narratable personal crisis" (Couser, 1997, p. 39). Certainly the breast cancer memoir is permeated with feminist ideas, whether explicitly (as in the case of Lorde) or implicity (Day, 2009; Rollin, 1976; Drescher, 2002); these pathographies brim with the tender feelings that the authors have for their breasts, and the terrible grief of losing them. Lorde's memoir famously challenged the pressure exerted on post-mastectomy women to wear a prosthesis. She would feel so much better with it on, insisted the nurse at her doctor's surgery. But equally important, not wearing it is "bad for the morale of the office" (Lorde, 1980, p. 59)—the "morale" of medical staff and other patients evidently more important than Lorde's own. This she saw as an act of collective denial, one which also denied women the space to mourn the change in her body. Was the Israeli politician Moshe Dayan, she asks, ever exhorted to get himself a glass eye? Lorde rejects the "empty comfort" of "nobody will know the difference"—it's the very difference that she wants to affirm, her aim to come to love herself "one-breasted". Few subsequent cancer memoirists have emulated her stance: in the three decades since her book was published, on the contrary, they have produced humorous but impassioned riffs on the verisimilitude of prostheses, or the effects of reconstructive surgery, and the search for authentic-looking synthetic nipples. This is less, perhaps, an example of "post-feminist" thinking than testimony to the fact that women's appearance has become culturally more important than ever, and breasts have become fetishised once again to an extent that would have been hard to predict in 1980.

But if prostheses have become unproblematic, the cancer memoir positively throbs with vexed struggles over hair: anguish over its loss as a result of chemotherapy is a central trope. These authors do not seem excessively vain: the loss of their hair is seen as the stigmata of cancer treatment, a metaphor for a body turned fugitive, wayward, beyond the cancer memoirist's control. This doesn't stop them telling droll stories about wig-buying expeditions: it's as if the loss of hair is a synecdoche for the many other larger losses, and can be mourned more easily than the loss of health.

Narratives

While it is tempting to see the cancer memoir as an authentic facsimile of the patient's experience, it is important to recognise that "there is no such thing psychologically as 'life itself'" (Bruner, 1987, p. 693). Jerome Bruner, in his influential paper "Life as narrative", draws attention not only to the limitations of memory, but also to the fact that "recounting one's life is an interpretive feat" (Bruner, 1987, p. 693). Narratives, Bruner suggests, help structure our perceptual experience and memory, even the very events of a life, and in turn are structured by culturally shaped processes: "a life is not 'how it was' but how it is interpreted and reinterpreted, told and retold: Freud's *psychic reality*" (Bruner, 1987, p. 708). Narratives thus play an ontological role: Anthony Giddens argues that "A person's identity is not to be found in his behaviour, nor—important though this is—in the reactions of others, but in the capacity to *keep a particular narrative going*" (Giddens, 1991, p. 54). Giddens also suggests that the body has become part of the reflexivity of modernity, subject to continuous attention and monitoring. In this context, it is perhaps unsurprising that narratives about the body became such a prominent feature of late twentieth century and early twenty-first century writing. Or as Broyard put it, "Once we had a narrative of heaven or hell, but now we make our own narratives" (Broyard, 1992, p. 42). Examining the narrative construction of the cancer memoir is not therefore a means to undermine or discredit it (Jurecic, 2012)—Hawkins reminds us that "these books are of value to us not because they record 'what happened' … but precisely because they are interpretations of experience" (Hawkins, 1998, p. 25)—but rather to help plumb its implicit beliefs and covert assumptions.

In the first place, the cancer memoir embodies a particular view of the world because it is not given to everybody to write one. While, as I argue below, the cancer blog has helped to democratise cancer discourse, the authors of cancer memoirs turn out to belong to a relatively select and homogenous group. They are all writers; hence the genre is produced by those with the ability to convert experience into text (Bregman & Thiermann, 1995) and the contacts to get it published (Couser, 1997). This, therefore, is not so much cancer as writer's cancer. Indeed, as Bregman and Thiermann point out, writing is one of the few occupations where life-threatening illness may not hamper a person but instead provide them with material. The cancer memoirist is also likely to be white middle-class or upper-middle-class (Couser, 1997). This inevitably shapes their experience of treatment. Almost all the British cancer memoirists, for example, make use of private medicine and consider this normal. They also bypass certain aspects of treatment, such as long journeys by public transport; these pathographers can drive themselves or be driven, or take a cab to hospital. Some, because of their high profile (such as Rollin) are recognised by medical staff; others may get preferential treatment because their cancer columns are published in a prominent newspaper. They may even become "celebrity cancer survivor of the year" (Drescher, 2002, p. 235).

Crucially, as Hawkins reminds us,

> [t]he narrative description of illness is both less and more than the actual experience: less, in that remembering and writing are selective processes—certain factors are dropped because they are forgotten or because they do not fit the author's narrative design; and more, in that the act of committing experience to narrative form inevitably confers upon it a particular sequence of events and endows it with a significance that was probably only latent in the original experience. Narrative form alters experience … organising events into a beginning, a middle and an end, and adding drama— heightening feelings and seeing the individuals involved as characters in a therapeutic plot. Writing about experience … inevitably changes it. (Hawkins, 1998, pp. 14–15)

Indeed most memoirs belong to the genre of creative nonfiction, which applies the narrative devices of fiction (characters, scenes, plot, and dialogue) to nonfiction, thus enhancing their dramatic momentum. Conversations have to be not only remembered but also recreated, according to narrative conventions. Discrete incidents need to be picked out, longueurs eliminated. Experience must be transformed into a story. Most cancer memoirists are only too aware of the narrative conventions of the genre. Hitchens recalls reading Diamond's column (cancer memoirs are awash with intertextuality) and admits to certain narrative expectations: "Diamond had to die; and he duly, correctly (in narrative terms) did" (Hitchens, 2012, p. 89).

Many cancer memoirs originated as weekly newspaper or magazine columns. This produces imperatives of its own. In a column a certain levity of tone has to be developed and sustained, and depression modified by humour. A column needs to end with a punchy, ringing line. As Diamond wrote in one of his columns, "there's no guarantee that I'll be able to keep up the jauntiness" (Diamond, 1998, p. 60), and later he found that he could not. What does it do to a person to undergo treatment and, almost simultaneously, write about it? A weekly column eventually leads a writer to see the world through the prism of "columnability": there's pressure to cannibalise experience, ransack it for "copy". At the very least, cancer treatments and weekly columns do not share the same periodicity or temporal rhythm. Little might change in cancer in seven days but the weekly column demands something new, a fresh dispatch from the front line. (The cancer blog, by contrast, can follow the ebbs and flows of the treatment cycle more easily, since it is up to the blogger when and how often they post.) On the other hand, faced with a new symptom, Diamond admitted that his thoughts were not of how it would affect his life or family but how best to share it with his readers. Similarly, when his pre-surgery consultation was being filmed for a BBC documentary he felt inhibited from asking questions that would divulge the extent of his fear, asking stoical ones instead. Cancer comes to be experienced through the prism of the writing. Eventually Diamond came to rue the surge of "confessional" writing about cancer that he had helped launch, a field now so large that a decade later Rabinovitch received a letter from a publisher rejecting her book proposal on the grounds that the breast cancer memoir was a crowded market (Rabinovitch, 2007), a cruel reminder that the genre—its topic notwithstanding—was subject to normal commercial considerations. (That he thought of other cancer memoirists as rivals was honestly acknowledged by Diamond when, riled by Picardie's column, he found himself thinking that he was the journalist with cancer "for God's sake" (Diamond, 1998, p. 172)).

The cancer memoir must tread carefully. As part of the trend for confessional columns and blogs, which also produced the "misery memoir", it requires a good deal of self-exposure—the boundary of where public ends and private begins has radically altered, making voyeurs of us all. And yet when Diamond recounts the detail of how he removes debris and mucus from his mouth after surgery, he feels compelled to apologise and make a joke about it being gross, but what did the reader expect when they bought a book about cancer? A *Guardian* editor gently urges Rabinovitch to write less about breasts (Rabinovitch, 2007), while Drescher's editor wonders if she really needs to spell out the changes in her stool (Drescher, 2002). That the memoirists include these communications suggests not only that they themselves realise that narrative imperatives weigh as heavily on their accounts as verisimilitude but also that they want us, the readers, to understand this too.

It has been argued that writing about illness or trauma can be therapeutic (Pennebaker, 1997). The reality, especially in published writing as opposed to private accounts, is more complex. For writers who draw on their personal life for material, not writing about their cancer is inconceivable. It is also felt to be a way of maintaining their prior sense of self, of remaining the person they were, or integrating the person and the disease. "Writing is a counterpoint to my illness", says Broyard. "It forces the cancer to go through my character before it can get to me" (Broyard, 1992, pp. 23–24).

Yet the process of writing can function as a defence against cancer as much as a way of making sense of it. Lynch deems her cancer blog a way of distracting herself from cancer, and uses it as a method of communicating her experience to family and friends (Lynch, 2010). Broyard admits that his first instinct, on learning his diagnosis, was to try and "bring it under control by turning it into a narrative … We describe what is happening, as if to confine the catastrophe … Stories are antibodies against illness and pain" (Broyard, 1992, pp. 19, 20). Even BBC radio presenter Nick Clarke, who recorded a graphic audio diary about his cancer treatment, used it, according to his widow, "as a way for him to avoid looking too deeply at the awfulness of what was happening to him" (Want, 2011, p. 132). Diamond confessed candidly that turning his cancer into an "objective spectacle" was an attempt to distance himself from it. He was reflexive about his column, in his column. "What I was doing … was looking for a way to make my cancer acceptable … a form of very public denial therapy … trying to change the problem from one of pain and physical constraint and possibly impending death into one of best journalistic practice" (Diamond, 1998, p. 127). Bion argued that the infant, when faced with overwhelming bad feelings, projects them into a containing mother, who then transforms them, allowing the infant to introject the feelings back but now in tolerable form (Bion, 1962). Cancer memoirists strive to turn their narratives into a container for unbearable feelings, transformed (they hope) by the very process of writing. But narrative cannot sustain this burden: it is not up to the task. After his death Diamond's wife acknowledged the extent of his anger, depression, and the suicidal impulses that never made it into his column. "You can do an awful lot of that [being droll] in 800 words a week. But doing it in your life is another matter" (Farndale, 2001).

The cancer memoirists, I want to suggest, not only narrate their disease but also narrativise it; these authors attempt in some sense to become authors of their own illness, to become its subject and not its object. The cancer memoir marks the point at which affluent Westerners have to engage with their bodies beyond trying to perfect them; the pathography articulates this shocked moment of involuntary embodiment, when they come up against the limits of their ability to control. Cancer robs them of a taken-for-granted confidence in the body. "My body's turned on me", declares Drescher (Drescher, 2002, p. 2). Lorde recognises that "I had grown angry at my right breast because I felt as if it had in some unexpected way betrayed me" (Lorde, 1980, p. 33). Lubbock, by contrast, recognises all too easily when the game is up: "We know the deal. We're bodies. We are not in our own hands" (Lubbock, 2012, p. 13).

One way of dealing with the sense of affront caused by a loss of control is humour: most cancer memoirs are funny. There is a flippancy of tone, a self-deprecating wry mordancy to these texts; in Picardie's case one that her husband attributed to bravado—"a means of both acknowledging the inevitable and denying it" (Picardie, 1998, p. 99). Freud argued that jokes could lift suppressions and repressions (Freud, 1905, p. 188). The cancer memoirists' humour allows them to talk about the gross (in Diamond's terms), as well as about aspects of treatment that might otherwise have been transgressive or intolerable, yet many of them are aware that it also plays a defensive role and at times constitutes a mask. Their comic names for their tumours (Lynch calls hers The Bullshit (Lynch, 2010)) or medical staff (Rollin dubs one nurse Saltimbocca (Rollin, 1976)) are similarly attempts to tame their illness, to become its redactor and not its victim. Some memoirists seem to want to share their cancer so that they feel less alone with it: they remind the reader how common it is and that s/he, too, is at risk at some stage of joining the club. Sontag famously argued that "everyone who is born holds dual citizenship, in the kingdom of the well and in the kingdom of the sick" (Sontag, 1978, p. 3) but that most of us preferred to use only "the good passport". The pathographer, you could say, tries (and not always altruistically) to ready readers to use the other one.

The cancer memoir is shaped by culture, which makes certain ideas thinkable and occludes others. So pathographies enshrine a Western view of the body, in which sickness is deviant (because the default body is healthy) and is experienced as an attack on an individual subjectivity. Stoller, an anthropologist diagnosed with lymphoma, makes this explicit by comparing it with the beliefs of the Songhay in West Africa where he trained as a sorcerer. In traditional cultures such as the Songhay's, illness is ever-present, greeted with fatalism rather than surprise. It is conceptualised less as a marauding outsider than as something to be respected: the sick must learn to live with illness, and incorporate it into their lives. Comfort is provided by healing rituals and incantations, which help foster patience and strength, as well as by traditional remedies (Stoller, 2004).

Most cancer memoirists seem strangely incurious about their disease's origins. Outside the crusading pathgraphy campaigning against carcinogens, such as Lorde's, few ponder what may have made them sick. There are other silences too. Rabinovitch first presents to the doctor three years after finding a lump in her breast. Apart from a single comment to him ("'I should have come earlier, shouldn't I?' childlike, seeking dispensation" (Rabinovitch, 2007, p. 2)) and the fleeting suggestion that GPs' tendency to make mothers feel stupid was a factor in her delay, there is not another reference to the subject in the entire book. While female readers will readily identify with the fears that might have held Rabinovitch back from visiting her doctor, she is conspicuously mute in an otherwise fearlessly frank memoir about an issue that presumably occupied at least some of her thinking, almost as if she had made the decision to skirt round it in both column and book. Or else that her feelings on the subject were so unmanageable that she concluded, probably correctly, that her narrative could not contain them. (So touching, that one word "dispensation".) The cancer memoir has emerged as part of a culture of disclosure, but books such as Rabinovitch's are a reminder that there is always a performative element to disclosure; it is selective in what it chooses to divulge in public.

Various typologies of illness narrative have been proposed (Bregman & Thiermann, 1995; Bury, 2001; Hawkins, 1998). The most useful is probably Frank's (Frank, 1995), where he identifies the restitution narrative, the chaos narrative, and the quest narrative. The plotline of the restitution narrative is essentially "Yesterday I was healthy, today I'm sick, but tomorrow I'll be healthy again" (Frank, 1995, p. 77). The restitution narrative's body is split from the self—no ontological crisis here. On the other hand there is no happy ending to the chaos narrative, no neat arc of resolution to keep chaos at bay. The quest narrative, meanwhile, transforms illness into a journey, one which brings the traveller benefits as well as pain. The published cancer memoirs analysed here are mostly hybrids, drawing on elements from all of Frank's types: they often start out as restitution narratives but then, when the prospect of a cure becomes unsustainable, metamorphose into a chaos narrative, before a quest narrative imposes itself at the end.

The quest narrative, I want to suggest, has created a genre of its own—cancer-as-transformative. The subtitle of Day's memoir sums it up: *How I Lost My Breast and Found Myself* (Day, 2009). In this genre the losses suffered by the person with cancer end up by being offset by the gains. Nowhere is this truer than in Gould, who believes that through cancer he has discovered the purpose of his life—to campaign for an acceptance of death—and that this has made him a different and better person, as well as affording him the opportunity to make reparation to his family (Gould, 2012).

Even a memoirist like Lynch, who explicitly rejects the notion that cancer can make you a better person or give you a new appreciation of life (a formulation she satirises as "Zen and the Art of Cancer" (Lynch, 2010, p. 236)), ends up acknowledging that some good changes have come about as a consequence of her cancer. The cancer memoir struggles to produce a happy ending: remission, as Stoller points out, does not entail a fully fledged return to "the village of the healthy"—instead the person with cancer has to learn to live with uncertainty and anxiety (Stoller, 2004). Perhaps cancer-as-transformative provides an alternative happy ending.

And then there is what I think of as "cancer-as-memoir". In this, illness is a vantage point from which all other events are viewed and connected (Hydén, 1997). Far from lacking a sense of causality, this perspective conscripts numerous different aspects of the writer's earlier life and reconfigures them to make it seem as though they have led inexorably to the present moment. You could argue that this is simply a function of writing about cancer: the disease is bound to figure prominently in an illness narrative. But "cancer-as-memoir" does more than this: it is written as if the cancer were somehow hovering in the writer's early life. In this formulation the writer was only ever pre-cancerous, never entirely non-cancerous. Day, for example, marshals together discrete events from diverse stages of her life, as though cancer has supplied her with a lens through which they could all be understood or made sense of (Day, 2009).

"Cancer-as-memoir" is also "memoir-as-cancer". In the most poignant examples, cancer is seen as attacking a core element of self, some central identity without which the writer will lose any sense of ontological worth. With Diamond, Clarke, and Hitchens it was their voice. Diamond believed that his personality resided almost entirely in what he said and the way he said it and that that was what made him lovable: "The fact is that I *am* talking" (Diamond, 1998, p. 169). Similarly Hitchens, who developed cancer of the oesophagus, declared, "To a great degree, in public and private, I 'was' my voice" (Hitchens, 2012, p. 48), and felt his "personality and identity dissolving" as he contemplated being unable to write (Hitchens, 2012, p. 71). For Rabinovitch, it was her identity as breast-feeding mother that was under assault from breast cancer, and her memoir recounts her (unsuccessful) struggle to continue breast-feeding through her treatment, and her (successful) attempt to keep her large and complex household going through sheer determination and drive. Lubbock, for whom lucidity and the capacity to analyse were core, identifies loss of coherence with loss of mind. He used his formidable linguistic skills to record the rupture between thinking and writing, and ultimately, in the poignantly fragmented ending of his memoir, the dissolution of language itself (Lubbock, 2012). In cancer-as-memoir the disease is possessed of the power to eviscerate not just the body but also the self.

Dissonant voices

Segal has argued that personal breast cancer stories are a means of maintaining ignorance about breast cancer and, because of the values they embody—humour is good, despair is bad, surviving is noble, dying is not—require a counter-discourse (Segal, 2007). Tilting at the same kind of metaphor that Sontag found so objectionable, she took aim at the concept of the "embattled survivor", and the obligation to react positively to cancer—indeed to the whole "cancer-as-transformative" discourse. Two years later, American author and columnist Barbara Ehrenreich duly provided this counter-discourse (Ehrenreich, 2009). The infantilising cornucopia of pink-ribbon-themed breast cancer products, the lack of outrage over the environmental causes of the disease, the stigmatising of those whose cancers had metastasised—Ehrenreich lobbed her grenades at them all, along with the whole redemptive discourse. She insisted on her right to be angry, and, as a former immunologist, dismantled cell by cell the argument that negative feelings could impact upon the course of the disease. Ehrenreich's is, if you like, the anti-cancer memoir, documenting the personal costs of extirpating anger and fear from the genre. The inheritor of Lorde's mantle, she suggested that her own cancer might have been caused by the hormone replacement therapy that she had been taking for eight years. Breast cancer, she concluded, had not made her prettier, stronger, or more spiritual. All it did was expose her to a powerful ideology, especially prevalent in the United States—the tyranny of positive thinking.

It takes courage to challenge a dominant discourse as, in her own way, Barbara Want did. Want's belongs to a subsection of cancer memoir—that written by the relatives of the sick person. Commonly these form a preface or appendix to the book of a memoirist who has died, and act as a tribute to the dead author. Want, the widow of broadcaster Nick Clarke, however, chose to talk about herself, and foreground the very difficult task of supporting a person with cancer moving towards their death. Unabashedly self-preoccupied, she is unflinching in her descriptions of her own dissonant emotions: her struggle to accept her husband's new physical state, her tirades and tears, self-loathing and self-pity. Fiercely honest, at times downright unlikeable, she knows that she does not possess the personal qualities that would enable her to nurse her husband (Want, 2011).

More disquieting is the memoir by Susan Sontag's son, David Rieff, supposedly a meditation about whether he was right to collude with her doctors as they concealed from her the inevitability and imminence of her death from cancer. But this pathography is worlds away from de Beauvoir's and, one cannot help feeling, a gross invasion of privacy. Sontag—shockingly for an author who spoke out so eloquently against lying to patients, metaphorising cancer, the denial of death (Sontag, 1978)—turns out to have been terrified of death, willing to endure the most radical, mutilating treatments to stave it off, with a naive faith in the possibility of cure, and ever ready to attribute her own survival after earlier bouts of the disease to her own fighting instincts. Rieff paints a grotesque picture of her final state covered in sores, incontinent and half delirious, and yet requiring of him that he tell her how much better she looks (Rieff, 2009). Rieff's is an angry memoir, a posthumous attack on a parent but also on a public intellectual, showing her succumbing to all the pathetic strategies she had denounced so eloquently in *Illness as Metaphor*. One can only guess at the causes of his rage.

The newest forms of pathography are to be found online, in an explosion of cancer blogs. Most of them, inevitably, are written by young people, for whom blogging is now a natural means of expression. Their style is at once demotic, intimate, and humorous, accompanied by the gallery of photographs that Facebook has normalised. The growth of the cancer blog, like other online writing, has extended the number of writers able to write about their experience far beyond the relatively small pool with access to traditional media—the cancer blog therefore democratises the cancer memoir. They also demonstrate that it is not only professional authors who want to write about their cancer. Here cancer is embedded in daily life because it is written about (sometimes) every day. On the other hand, disappointingly, many cancer blogs call on the same limited range of tropes as the cancer memoir. They have names such as "Fighting Breast Cancer" (http://fighting-breast-cancer.com/) or subtitles like "Exploring the Intersection of Cancer and Crea-tivity" (http://jaynesbreastcancerblog.com/2010/02/in-media-res/), and their comic tone rarely falters. They depict cancer treatment as experienced by young people, and often make agonising reading, their gusts of hope suddenly ceasing (author presumed dead), or replaced by an obituary. Lynch, who included extracts from her blog in her memoir, continues the story online and it is desperately sad, after the relatively buoyant, feisty ending of her book, to learn in her latest post of new tumours in her brain (http://alrighttit.blogspot.co.uk/), and see the struggle to maintain the breezy blog-voice.

Confessional writing about cancer has spread to the stand-up routine (Tig Notaro improvises around the subject of her advanced breast can-cer; she has now been commissioned to write a memoir (Holland, 2012)), as well as to cartoons and comics (http://www.graphicmedicine.org/, established in 2007, is a site for comics about healthcare, and reviews graphic memoirs such as *Cancer Made Me A Shallower Person* (Engelberg, 2006) and *Cancer Vixen* (Marchetto, 2007)). People with cancer are no longer mute: they use any and every art form, fictional or nonfictional, to communicate the experience.

And so to the readers

Memoirists and cancer columnists report themselves inundated by letters and emails from readers—a spontaneous outpouring of reader empathy. Some simply wish them well, willing them to pull through. Others share their own experience of the illness, needing the column-ist to "receive" and not only "transmit" the cancer story (and occa-sionally even expressing resentment of the "cancer celebrity"). Still others (and these are generally less welcome) recommend esoteric alternative treatments. There is clearly a great public appetite for the pathography.

But equally, the cancer memoir can create a disturbing dynamic in the reader: we know that this is a book about cancer, even though the author qua protagonist does not, but then again (unless we are reading this as a "real time" newspaper column rather than a book, which is always, necessarily, written retrospectively) the author qua author does. Watching their denial unravel is painful, but—if my own reading is any guide—many other emotions are also activated. Frank argues that "the listener must be present as a potentially suffering body to receive the testimony that is the suffering body of the teller" (Frank, 1995, p. 144). Most cancer memoirists assume, and attract, a sympathetic reader, one whom themselves may have been diagnosed with cancer, or is supporting a friend or relative through treatment. They may be reading for information, or to feel comforted that others have been through the same experience and survived. They might be part of what has come to be called the "worried well", who are symptomless but anxious about contracting the disease. Indeed the proliferation of cancer memoirs may have helped expand this group, by propelling the disease onto the radar of more people than ever. Yet since it has been estimated that more than one in three people will develop some form of cancer during their lifetime (Sasieni, Shelton, Ormiston-Smith, Thomson, & Silcocks, 2011), it could be argued that the number of cancer memoirs is proportionate, even if they may play a part in skewing funding priorities away from other conditions such as heart disease and stroke, or diabetes.

At the same time readers do not always identify with the cancer memoirist. Instead, they may feel triumphant: theirs is a vicarious carcinoma, cancer by proxy, as though the author has got the cancer so that the reader does not have to. In this form of magical thinking the pathography can act as an amulet, a counter-phobic charm, a prophylactic against cancer.

In the middle of reading these memoirs, one of my closest friends was diagnosed with the disease. With what heavy heart I returned to them; I did not want to read them anymore. I had clearly been harbouring the phantasy that they might provide a surrogate form of cancer—a vaccination, if you like, against the real thing. Once cancer penetrated my inner circle, this could no longer be sustained.

At other times I had the bizarre feeling that I might somehow catch cancer from these books, that they were dismantling all my defences against the disease, especially since the memoirists invariably had believed that they could never get it either.

Reading the cancer memoir can be a challenging act of dramatic irony: we the readers may be burdened by more a priori knowledge than we can bear, especially if we know that the author has since died. Every expression of hope can feel like a portent or the mockery of fate, each proposed invasive treatment makes you want to shout "no! you won't survive it! just accept it and live your remaining days as best you can!" You begin to feel like the audience in a pantomime, crying out "he's behind you!" You are rewriting the book even as you are reading it, from the perspective of its known conclusion, even while you magically hope that somehow it might end differently.

Indeed we read the cancer memoir not for one reason but a whole cocktail—genuine interest, empathy, curiosity, *schadenfreude*, prurience, and even envy.

Finally, especially if the book includes its own sad afterword, you the reader have to retrieve some of the hopes that you invested in the memoir and memoirist and recognise that, however eloquently and beautifully they have written it, the life of a person with cancer remains ultimately elusive and, like that of us all, finite.

Acknowledgement

I am grateful to Bianca Karpf and Jennifer Silverstone for their valuable suggestions of books for this chapter.

References

Bion, W. R. (1962). *Learning from Experience*. London: Heinemann. (Reprinted London: Karnac, 1983.)

Bregman, L. & Thiermann, S. (1995). *First Person Mortal: Personal Narratives of Dying, Death, and Grief*. New York: Paragon House.

Broyard, A. (1992). *Intoxicated By My Illness: And Other Writings on Life and Death*. New York: Fawcett Columbine.

Bruner, J. (1987). Life as narrative. *Social Research, 54(1)*: 11–32.

Bury, M. (1982). Chronic illness as biographical disruption. *Sociology of Health and Illness, 4(2)*: 167–82.

Bury, M. (1991). The sociology of chronic illness: a review of research and prospects. *Sociology of Health and Illness, 13*(4): 451–68.

Bury, M. (2001). Illness narratives: fact or fiction? *Sociology of Health and Illness, 23*(3): 263–285.

Cody, J. (2011). *[sic]: a memoir* London: Bloomsbury.

Couser, G. (1997). *Recovering Bodies: Illness, Disability and Life-Writing.* Madison, WI: University of Wisconsin Press.

Day, J. (2009). *Getting It Off My Chest: How I Lost My Breast and Found Myself.* London: Old Street Publishing.

de Beauvoir, S. (trans. O'Brian, P.) (1965). *A Very Easy Death.* New York: Pantheon.

Diamond, J. (1998). *C: Because Cowards Get Cancer Too...* London: Vermillion.

Drescher, F. (2002). *Cancer Schmancer.* New York: Warner.

Ehrenreich, B. (2009). *Smile or Die: How Positive Thinking Fooled America and the World.* London: Granta.

Engelberg, M. (2006). *Cancer Made Me A Shallower Person: A Memoir In Comics.* New York: Harper Collins.

Farndale, N. (2001). A woman of extremes. *Daily Telegraph,* 14.05.01

Frank, A. (1995). *The Wounded Storyteller: Body, Illness, and Ethics.* Chicago: University of Chicago Press, 1997.

Freud, S. (1905). *Jokes and their Relation to the Unconscious. S. E., 8.* London: Hogarth.

Giddens, A. (1991). *Modernity and Self-Identity.* Cambridge: Polity.

Gould, P. (2012). *When I Die: Lessons from the Death Zone* (K. Blackmore, Ed.). London: Little, Brown.

Gunther, J. (1949). *Death Be Not Proud.* Hampton, NH: Curley.

Hawkins, A. H. (1998). *Reconstructing Illness: Studies in Pathography.* West Lafayette, IN: Purdue University.

Hitchens, C. (2012). *Mortality.* London: Atantic.

Holland, J. (2012). The half-hour performance that turned four months of tragedy into comic gold. *The Observer,* 21: 10.12.

Hydén, L. -C. (1997). Illness and narrative. *Sociology of Health and Illness, 19*(1): 48–69. *Inside Story: Tongue Tied.* BBC One, tx 15.06.98.

Jurecic, A. (2012). *Illness as Narrative.* Pittsburgh, PA: University of Pittsburgh Press.

Karpf, A. (1988). *Doctoring the Media: the Reporting of Health and Medicine.* London: Routledge.

Kleinman, A. (1988). *The Illness Narratives: Suffering, Healing and the Human Condition.* New York: Basic.

Kushner, R. (1977). *Why Me?: What Every Woman Needs to Know about Breast Cancer to Save Her Life.* Philadelphia, PA: The Saunders Press.

Lorde, A. (1980). *The Cancer Journals*. San Francisco: Aunt Lute.

Lynch, L. (2010). *The C-Word*. London: Arrow.

Lubbock, T. (2012). *Until Further Notice, I Am Alive*. London: Granta.

Marchetto, M. (2007). *Cancer Vixen: A True Story*. London: Fourth Estate.

Mukherjee, S. (2011). *The Emperor of all Maladies: A Biography of Cancer*. London: Fourth Estate.

Murray, J. (2008). *Memoirs of a Not So Dutiful Daughter*. London: Black Swan.

Pennebaker, J. (1997). Writing about emotional experiences as a therapeutic process. *Psychological Science, 8(3)*: 162–166.

Picardie, R. (1998). *Before I Say Goodbye*. Penguin: London.

Rabinovitch, D. (2007). *Take Off Your Party Dress: When Life's Too Busy for Breast Cancer*. London: Simon and Schuster.

Rieff, D. (2009). *Swimming in a Sea of Death: A Son's Memoir*. London: Granta.

Rodgers, J. (2002). *Bald in the land of Big Hair: True Confessions of a Woman with Cancer*. London: Review.

Rollin, B. (2000). *First, You Cry* (reprint edition). New York: HarperCollins.

Rose, G. (1995). *Love's Work*. New York: New York Review of Books.

Sasieni, P. D., Shelton, J., Ormiston-Smith, N., Thomson, C. S., & Silcocks, P. B. (2011). *What is the lifetime risk of developing cancer?: The effect of adjusting for multiple primaries*. British Journal of Cancer, 105(3): 460–5.

Segal, J. (2007). Breast cancer narratives as public rhetoric: genre itself and the maintenance of ignorance. *Linguistics and the Human Sciences, 3(1)*: 158–163.

Sontag, S. (1978). *Illness as Metaphor*. London: Penguin.

Stoller, P. (2004). *Stranger in the Village of the Sick: A Memoir of Cancer, Sorcery, and Healing*. Boston, MA: Beacon.

Want, B. (2011). *Why Not Me?: A Story of Love and Loss*. London: Phoenix.

http://fighting-breast-cancer.com/; accessed 26.10.12.

http://jaynesbreastcancerblog.com/2010/02/in-media-res/; accessed 26.10.12.

http://alrighttit.blogspot.co.uk/; accessed 26.10.12.

http://www.graphicmedicine.org/; accessed 29.10.12.

INDEX